THE STORY OF
THE SEVENTH BATTALION
THE SOMERSET LIGHT INFANTRY
(PRINCE ALBERT'S)

The Story of

THE SEVENTH BATTALION
THE SOMERSET LIGHT INFANTRY

(PRINCE ALBERT'S)

COLLECTED AND TOLD BY

CAPTAIN J. L. J. MEREDITH

DESIGNS AND ILLUSTRATIONS BY

L. R. STOKES

ISBN: 1-845743-45-8

Printed and bound by Antony Rowe Ltd, Eastbourne

DEDICATION

THIS book is dedicated to "Joe Soap"—the man whose name you will not find on any page, of whom there is no mention in the Awards and Decorations, whose work was never noticed but whose job was always done.

To his wife, his family, and his friends who waited anxiously for his letters, and to the people of France, Belgium, and Holland who welcomed him, and cheered him on his way.

LIST OF CHAPTERS

APPENDICES

D I A R Y   O F   T H E   C A M P A I G N

NORMANDY

June	23-24	Infantry landings COURSEULLES sur MER
June	25	Vehicles joined concentration NE of BAYEUX
June	27-28	CHEUX. HILL 100
June	29	Astride TOURVILLE—VERSON road west of CAEN
July	9	FONTAINE ETOUPEFOUR. Cross R. ODON. CHATEAU de FONTAINE
July	17	HILL 112
July	26	To rest area CONDE sur SEULLES
July	31	CAUMONT
Aug	1-2	CAHAGNES to ST. PIERRE DU FRESNE
Aug	7	MT. PINCON
Aug	9	LES HAMEAUX. LE SAUSSAY
Aug	12	CAUVILLE
Aug	15-16	Crossing of the NOIREAU
Aug	17	LE CANET. LE HAMEL
Aug	27-28	Crossing of the SEINE
Sept	1-14	VERNON sur SEINE and FORET DE VERNON

BELGIUM AND HOLLAND

Sept	14	Drive into BELGIUM
Sept	15	DIEST
Sept	20	EINDHOVEN
Sept	21	NIJMEGEN BRIDGE
Sept	22	OOSTERHOUT
Sept	23	ELST (opposite ARNHEM)
Sept	26-27	RANDWIJK and ZETTEN
Oct 9-Nov 10		MOOK. DE HORST

THE WINTER WAR

Nov	10	SCHINNEN
Nov	18-23	NIEDERHEIDE—HOCHEID Woods
Nov	23	GEILENKIRCHEN
Nov	25	NIERSTRASS and TEVEREN
Nov	28	GILLRATH
Dec	3	RISCHDEN woods
Dec	6	TEVEREN again
Dec	16	MEERSEN
Dec	19	BILSEN (in reserve for Ardennes counter attack)

Dec	25	Christmas Day (by permission of the General Staff)
Dec	26-31	Still in reserve for counter attack
Jan	1-2	Recces of BRUNSSUM and EYNATTEN
Jan	7	MOORVELD
Jan	11-27	GEILENKIRCHEN
Jan	27-30	SCHIMMERT
Jan	31	WORTEL
Feb	5	GELDROP

TURNING THE SIEGFRIED

Feb	8	NIJMEGEN (assembly area)
Feb	10	KRANENBURG—REICHSWALD FOREST
Feb	12	HAU (S. of CLEVE)
Feb	13-16	Towards GOCH
Feb	17	GOCH escarpment
Feb	24	To rest area CLEVE
Feb	27	NEU LOUISENDORF
March	1	RHINE sighted
March	3	KEHRUM
March	5	MARIENBAUM
March	9	XANTEN. Watch on the Rhine

FROM THE RHINE
TO THE ELBE

March	13-25	AFFERDEN rest area
March	26-27	RHINE crossing
March	27-28	VEHLINGEN autobahn
April	1	Drive through N. HOLLAND
April	5	NORDHORN
April	8	BAWINKEL
April	8-9	JELLALABAD Bridge—HASELÜNNE
April	14	FORST CLOPPENBURG
April	17-18	AHLHORN cross-roads
April	19-21	VISBEK
April	23-24	LANGWEDEL (BREMEN—HAMBURG autobahn)
April	29	QUELKHORN—WORPSWEDE
May	2	Concentrated at OSTERTIMKE
May	4	Surrender of all the German Armies in NW Europe
May	8	To the ELBE in the Province of HANOVER

F O R E W O R D

(From Brigadier H. Essame, D.S.O., M.C.)

The Seventh Somerset Light Infantry have done me the honour of asking me to write a foreword to their History.

Now that the War is over, I am under no necessity to draw a veil over the fact that I was present at the Somme, Ypres, Passchendaele and the battles of 1918 as well as in the Campaign so ably described in this book. Perhaps, therefore, my opinion that no finer soldiers than the 7th Somerset Light Infantry ever left England and fought their way across the continent to final victory, may be of some weight.

They won their battles because at every level they were better men than the finest troops of the German Army, because they had greater courage and greater skill. There was no danger which they would not face, no hardship which they would not endure, no risk they would not take.

May those who stayed at home and those who come after them be worthy of their sacrifice.

H. ESSAME, Brigadier
Commander 214 Infantry Brigade
September 1942 — June 1945

NORMANDY · *June 23rd–24th* · *Infantry landings COURSEULLES sur MER: June 27th–28th* · *CHEUX, HILL 100:* *June 29th* · *Astride TOURVILLE-VERSON road west of CAEN: July 9th* · *CHATEAU de FONTAINE: July 17th* · *HILL 112:* *August 1st–2nd* · *CAHAGNES to ST. PIERRE DU FRESNE: August 7th* · *MT. PINCON: August 9th* · *LES HAMEAUX,* *LE SAUSSAY: August 12th* · *CAUVILLE: August 15th–16th* · *Crossing of the NOIREAU: August 27th–28th* · *Crossing* *of the SEINE:* **BELGIUM AND HOLLAND** · *September 21st* · *NIJMEGEN BRIDGE: September 22nd* · *OOSTERHOUT:* *September 23rd* · *ELST (opposite ARNHEM): September 26th–27th* · *RANDWIJK and ZETTEN: October 9th to* *November 10th* · *GROESBEEK, MOOK, DE HORST:* **THE WINTER WAR** · *November 18th–23rd* · *NIEDERHEIDE-HOCHEID*

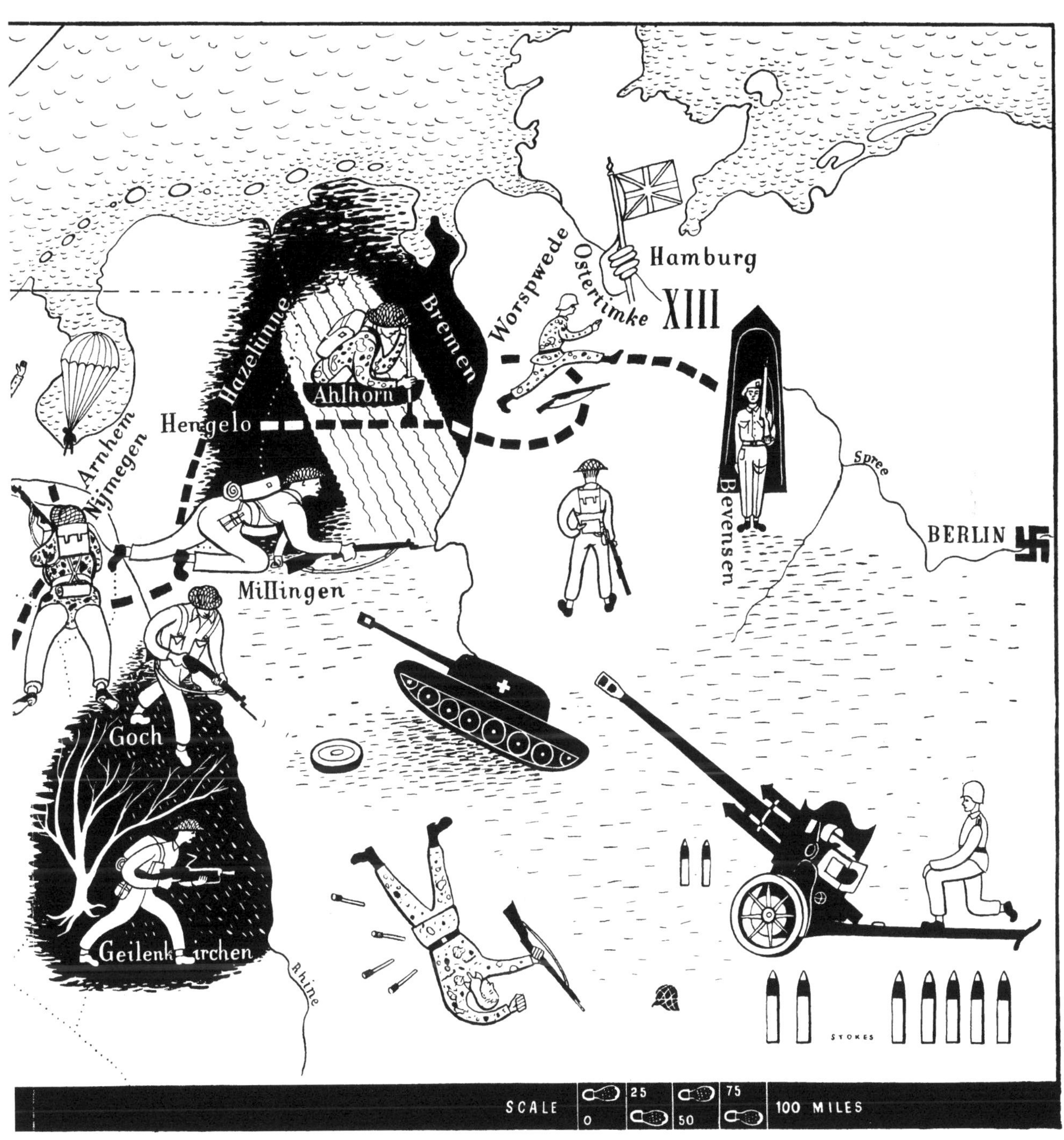

WOODS: November 23rd · GEILENKIRCHEN: December 3rd · RISCHDEN WOODS: December 19th · BILZEN: **1945** *January 11th–27th · GEILENKIRCHEN:* **TURNING THE SIEGFRIED** *· February 10th · KRANENBURG-REICHSWALD FOREST: February 12th · HAU: February 17th · GOCH escarpment: March 5th · MARIENBAUM: March 9th · XANTEN:* **FROM THE RHINE TO THE ELBE** *· March 26th–27th · RHINE crossing. March 27th–28th · VEHLINGEN autobahn: April 1st · Drive through N. HOLLAND: April 8th–9th · JELLALABAD Bridge, HASELÜNNE: April 14th FORST CLOPPENBURG: April 17th–18th · AHLHORN cross roads: April 23rd–24th · LANGWEDEL (BREMEN– HAMBURG autobahn): April 29th · QUELKHORN–WORPSWEDE: May 8th · To the ELBE in the Province of HANOVER*

STATEMENT

This is the story of an episode—a true story and an episode eleven months long, a chapter in the life of a County Regiment from Wessex.

It is not a history, though it is woven of the true fabric from which History is made. People who seek history in catalogue form will find it in the War Diary records of the War Office—this book is not for them.

For those who were there, and for those who tried to follow them across France, Belgium, Holland and Germany through the fog of war and the veil of censorship it may serve as a more intimate record of those moments, sometimes stark, sometimes comic, more often stern, and always vital which, even now, are growing dim in memory and will soon pass into History as the campaign of the British Liberation Army in North West Europe.

Battle is a very local experience; for the strategist it is the movement of flags—men, guns and supplies—on a map; for the commander in a battalion it is the launching into battle, at the correct moment and place, of a group of men trained, armed, and equipped to the best of his resources—a group whom he must know intimately, but of whom he dare not think personally in the moment of decision; for the fighting soldier it is a series of vivid experiences, each seldom the same as the last, and each seeming at the time to be the most important thing which could be happening anywhere.

Because this tale is collected from the experiences of eight hundred such men of the Seventh Battalion The Somerset Light Infantry it is hoped that the impressions may prove more than local, but for the same reason it is, of necessity, impossible that every experience and every gallant action shall be told. It is inevitable that slight differences should occur in an account of events seen by many people from as many angles. My aim has been to produce the truth, both of atmosphere and of fact, of these momentous days.

My thanks are due to the Commanding Officer for making both the time and the material available at an early date after the battle, and to the many officers, men, and friends of the Battalion who have helped to blend my notes into a coherent story.

John Meredith

7th Battalion. The Somerset Light Infantry
Province of Hanover
July 1945

Normandy

Chapter I

PREPARATIONS AND LANDING

*L*ONDON River is not easily ruffled. Down its long history ships of all nations and craft of every type have always moved about their business of trading across the oceans. Changes have come, many changes, but they have always been gradual, and London has made them part of herself.

In June 1944 this was no longer so—every dock and jetty from Tower Bridge to Southend was seething with strange urgent craft. Not tall graceful liners, not fat cargo ships, not dirty tramps with their cockney assurance—all these London was accustomed to see every day—but new squat barges, dazzle painted or grey, with tanks in their bellies, and tight-packed rows of motor lorries, barges full of guns and petrol and shells, transports quickly filling with columns of steel helmeted troops grumbling in the summer's heat. These were the mechanics, the drivers, the service units stowing into their Tank Landing Craft, Motor Transport ships, and Motor Landing craft the supply columns of an Army—setting out to make a rendezvous with their battalions on the beaches and fields of Normandy.

Day after day down the wide concrete road from London's East End to Southend at the river's mouth, branching south to London Docks, to Dagenham, to Purfleet and Tilbury rolled the endless columns of lorries, each waterproofed, weighed and indexed for its exact place on the waiting ships.

Far back around the north of London routes were signed for Trucks coming from all the stations of the Home Command, signs to marshalling area R, or S, or T where drivers would get a last chance to check up, and fitters to make the final adjustments necessary for a jeep or a tank that might have to spend several days at sea and then plunge from the ship through a hundred or more yards of salt water, and up an unknown enemy beach.

Farther away still were the Regiments themselves, scaled down to the bare necessities of equipment and rations for the landing phase, waiting at camps near the south coast beaches and channel ports for their turn to embark.

Down this road from London (had you been watching on an evening around June 14th) came a column of trucks bearing on one mudguard a Wyvern, or heraldic golden dragon of Wessex, and on the other the number 67. This—but, of course, even those who knew wouldn't tell you—was the transport of the Seventh Battalion The Somerset Light Infantry of the 43rd (Wessex) Division, and those trucks were destined before another June to be running on the roads of Hanover, three-quarters of the way to Berlin.

They were running smoothly now, well loaded, well oiled, freshly painted, packed with the best equipment an army had ever taken overseas; stores, rations, spare parts, ammunition—each in the right place on the right truck, and each with a ship space waiting. Many weeks of work were behind this orderly progress.

Mid April had seen the Seventh battalion in Kent. Talk of the invasion of Europe had been a general topic in England and in Germany since the New Year—the only question was when and where it would be launched. As part of a well laid cover plan large forces of British and Canadian troops had for some time been making their presence obvious in South Eastern England with the idea of tying up large forces of Germans in Belgium and the Pas-de-Calais area.

Already the Pas-de-Calais was the target for crushing air attacks from daily fleets of British and American bombers, and there were rumours of strange installations on that coast which were being strafed by our fighter-bombers; but there was to be a period of two months yet before that spluttering invention of the devil—the flying bomb—should turn Southern England once more into a battlefield, and give this waiting Army one more reason, if one were needed, why the rule of force must be removed for ever from civilised Europe.

*   *   *

The final seven weeks had been spent under canvas in a camp near Battle, Sussex, during which a decreasing degree of freedom of movement was allowed as secrecy, and the need to be on hand for any unforeseen developments became more important. Hard work was put in on the waterproofing of vehicles to enable them to run ashore through water three or four times deeper than a motor vehicle could normally operate. Loading exercises were carried out to decide on the best stowage for the dozens of items of kit, ammunition, and supplies which an Infantry battalion carries to war. A large number of new trucks and carriers arrived from Ordnance Depots, so that all transport should be completely reliable; while Field Service rations, and overseas methods of accounting had been in use for several months to ensure the smoothness of Administrative work.

214 Brigade organised a sports meeting; and an influx of Canadian Officers attached to battalions caused a wave of enthusiasm for soft ball, games of which could be seen all over the place in offduty moments; a type of grown-up "Puss-in-the-corner" developed which caused the camp to resound to the kicking of tin cans. The game consisted of one man guarding a tin can in any small clearing while a number of others scattered stealthily into the

bushes. The object was for a stalker to kick the tin before the guard could strike it with his stick—this gave the guard great scope for pantomime and undoubtedly the star player was Company Sergeant Major (Tommy) Trinder. The game was a great success and had the advantage that tin cans were both more plentiful, and more durable than N.A.A.F.I. footballs!

*   *   *

It was very fitting that a Brigade wearing the Wyvern emblem should assemble at Battle, for here nine hundred years ago it had been carried by the men of Wessex against the Conqueror from Normandy. Now from these same shores it was to share in the re-conquest of that friendly Allied province.

All over Southern England in the early hours of 6th June there was no longer any doubt that Invasion Day had come. Great as had been the air activity for many weeks across this coast, there was no mistaking the meaning of the massive ceaseless traffic of aircraft which had been going out from sunset to dawn. At eight a.m. the German radio announced that an airborne landing had taken place near Caen—at ten o'clock the Supreme Commander told the World that the Allied assault divisions had been landing since daybreak.

Eight more days were spent by the Seventh battalion at Battle; days of anxious waiting for the word to embark, of lovely summer weather, of final adjustments to preparations, of rest, and sport and recreation. There was no sign of enemy activity or counter-plan. Then on 14th June the marching troops moved to a marshalling camp in the beautiful park at Glyndebourne in preparation for the move on to the ships.

The stay would have been a very short one had not a great storm which lashed the Channel held up all shipping for two days. It is now known that this storm was without equal in the records for June, and that the damage it did to landing craft and beach equipment was very serious. Because of it two more days were spent amid scenes of poignant beauty. Below the tree covered hillocks were the tents in the park tucked beneath the great oaks and elms, their tops roaring in the wind. In the shelter of the valley, meadows of deep clover and hay stretched towards the curving slopes of the South Downs, over the crest of which fleecy clouds raced before the storm.

Games of soft-ball, hand-ball and football were played among the trees. A flying bomb came roaring over the Downs leaving a trail of flame and looking like a flying dagger as it tore between the clouds. It caused great interest, but was generally regarded as a freak.

Convoys of trucks now arrived (16th June) and Companies were embussed by craft loads to drive in a high wind over the downs to Newhaven. In the villages people gathered to wave good-bye and the troops unloaded their pennies on the eager children. One small boy (who must have a great future in the Exchequer) was seen with a pile of four or five hundred coins. The battalion went aboard four American L.C.I's (Landing Craft Infantry), one Company to each with Headquarter Company spread over the four. Padre Richards (Rev. I.J. Richards, C.F.) embarked with "B" Company. Everyone had to climb down the long iron ladders from the quayside. They were very well received by the American crews and fed on American rations, but the delay continued and the craft did not leave harbour.

The whole Brigade was now in the harbour. It consisted of 7th Bn. The Somerset Light Infantry, 1st Bn. The Worcestershire Regiment, and the 5th Bn. The Duke of Cornwall's Light Infantry. The Brigade Commander, Brigadier H. Essame, D.S.O., M.C., under whom it had trained since its days as an Independent Brigade on the Isle of Wight in 1942, meanwhile embarked with his Headquarters Staff, and their command vehicles, on the M.T. Convoy at London Docks.

*   *   *

During the day the whole group went ashore again to march to a nearby camp to have a wash. On arrival it turned out that the water was not running so no washing could take place, but everyone was given a mug of tea. Back at the harbour again it became known that the L.C.I's were required for other duties. The whole battalion plus two companies of the Duke of Cornwall's Light Infantry embarked on a dirty channel boat—the S.S. Biarritz. Here the battalion sustained its first casualty, oddly enough among the Quartermaster's staff, when Lance-corporal Meads slipped and fell from the companion ladder, fracturing an elbow.

S.S. Biarritz will chiefly be remembered for its crowded, stuffy 'tween decks, for the endless cups of 'Compo' tea brewed on Tommy cookers, and for the thick rich smell of countless tins of self heating ('jet-propelled') soup being brewed up in the crowded gangways.

The ship weighed anchor in the night, but lay to for another day outside the breakwater. Many more flying bombs came over, and many were shot down to the delight of the spectators. It was weeks before the troops in Normandy realised what a great deal of destruction these 'spectacular toys' were doing around London.

In the late afternoon the ships put back into harbour to take on fresh water, and almost at once slipped out again into the evening sun, running close in shore in a dead calm sea, past the white cliffs, past the long sandy beaches of Shoreham, and into the sunset at the crowded approaches to Spithead.

Excitement ran high among the troops at the tremendous activity in Spithead, and spirits were at their peak that at last the great adventure was on. The ship sailed again at midnight in a convoy of six transports in line ahead.

The Seine bay next morning looked like a fleet visit to an Eastern port. Battleships and cruisers were dotted about, with balloon barrage boats, transports, and supply ships. Landing craft and 'Ducks' plied between the ships and the beaches in a ceaseless wash of importance.

S.S. Biarritz lay off shore all day and the time was spent in sunbathing on the decks and waiting. In the evening there was a short air raid on the bay.

Assault landing craft, their crews dead beat from days of work, came alongside at 2 a.m. and the business of going oversides occupied the remainder of the night. "C" Company, in particular, who were all equipped with bicycles, had a struggle with the gangways. The majority of the battalion went ashore at dead low water which meant a long wade chest deep through the shallows, and assembled on the beach above the lines of broken boats tossed up to the high water mark by the storm. It was a cold grey morning and the beach was strangely quiet. There was no reception from the Beach Group so Companies assembled individually to move off to an assembly area on the Bayeux road. The beach was Courseulles-sur-Mer, the date 0700 hours on 22nd of June.

The Motor Transport had embarked on 17th/18th June at London and Tilbury Docks—all battalion transport with Brigade H.Q vehicles being together (with five hundred men) in the U.S. 10,000-ton Liberty ship "Will Rogers". After a twenty-four hour wait at the river mouth while a convoy assembled, they rounded the North Foreland and ran close under the Dover cliffs where one ship was set on fire by shells from Cap Gris Nez. They then followed the coast to Spithead and crossed the same day to Courseulles (20th June); here they lay off shore for four days—on the first two catching the tail end of the storm.

All Companies were assembled by the 23rd in the beautiful orchard country little damaged by the first assault. The special twenty-four hour assault landing rations were used for the first day, and most people found them very good. No civilians were to be seen, and there was no sound of firing. Company Commanders waited eagerly for the first arrivals from the M.T. ships and the precious battalion transport.

During 24th June all the vehicles were trans-shipped in the open sea to Tank Landing Ships, being swung over-sides on derricks and dropped with neat precision into the swaying ferries. The last were on the beach by early on 25th, and had got ashore without a single loss or non-starter. They moved off to the assembly area in groups as soon as they were ready.

With their arrival many of the hardships of the past ten days were dispelled. Kit packs were handed out containing a change of laundry and many other little personal comforts which their owners had managed to squeeze in, such as writing paper and envelopes for a letter to England. Blanket bundles were unrolled, and comfortable 'beds' were made down under the apple trees, beneath the stars of a perfect midsummer night. It was good to be able to stretch, and be still, and breathe clean cool air.

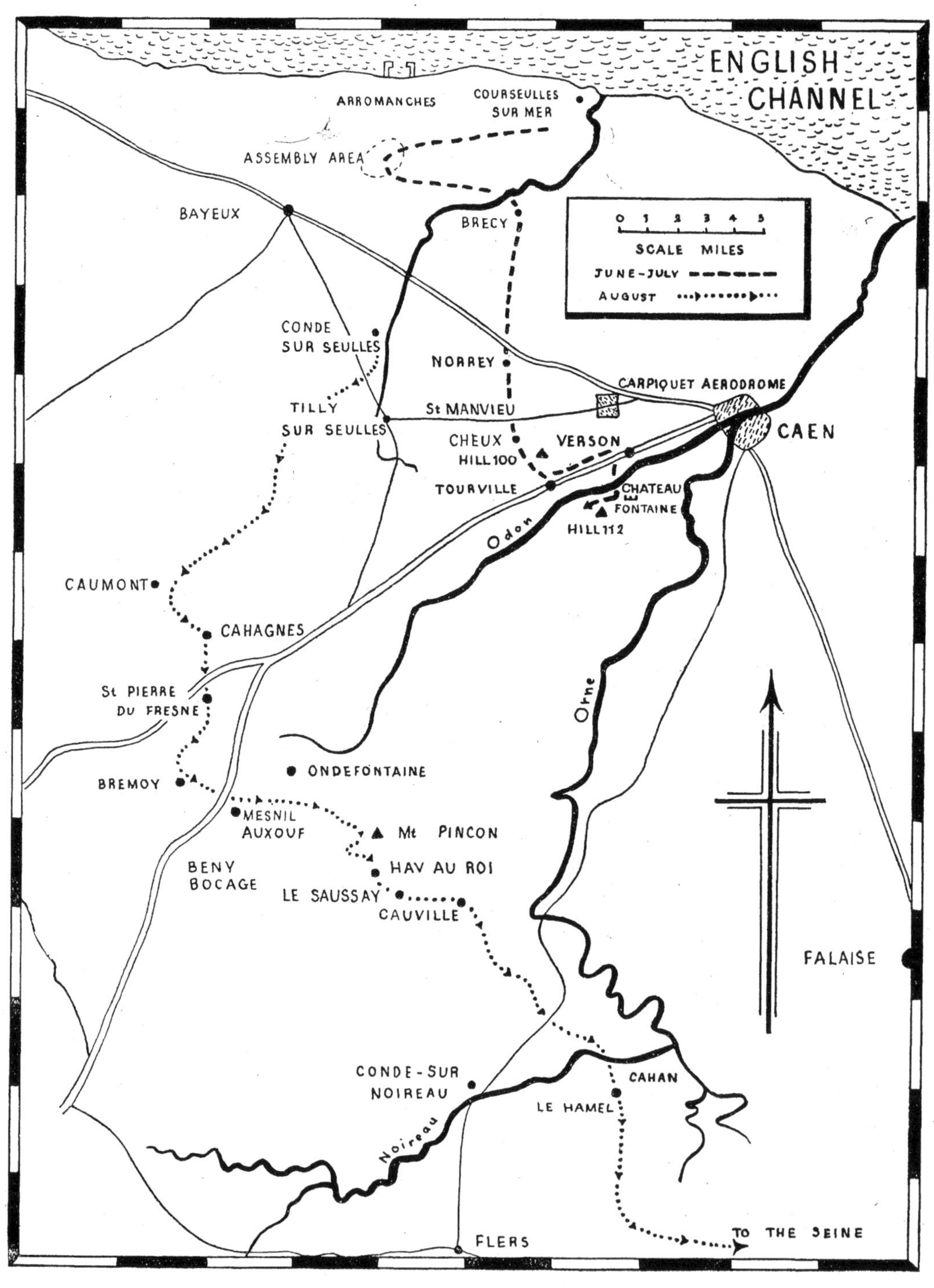

ENGLISH CHANNEL
ARROMANCHES
COURSEULLES SUR MER
ASSEMBLY AREA
BAYEUX
BRECY
SCALE MILES
0 1 2 3 4 5
JUNE-JULY
AUGUST
CONDE SUR SEULLES
NORREY
CARPIQUET AERODROME
TILLY SUR SEULLES
St MANVIEU
CAEN
CHEUX HILL 100
VERSON
TOURVILLE
CHATEAU FONTAINE
HILL 112
Odon
CAUMONT
CAHAGNES
Orne
St PIERRE DU FRESNE
ONDEFONTAINE
BREMOY
MESNIL AUXOUF
Mt PINCON
BENY BOCAGE
HAV AU ROI
LE SAUSSAY
CAUVILLE
FALAISE
CONDE-SUR NOIREAU
CAHAN
LE HAMEL
Noireau
FLERS
TO THE SEINE

Chapter II

HILL 100 · CHEUX · VERSON

*B*Y the morning of 25th June the assembly was complete and at 11.15 a.m., Lieutenant-Colonel R. G. P. Besley T.D., held the battalion's first operational Order Group. In burning sunshine at mid-day they set out to march to the villages of Brecy and Rucqueville five miles to the South East (towards Caen).

It was a tiring march along very limited roads which had been much battered by the traffic of the past three weeks, through clouds of the swirling dust which was to become such an unforgettable feature of Normandy, and through air sickly with the vapour of petrol and hot rubber from the passing lorries. Several men passed-out on the march either from the heat, or the crude Norman cider pressed on them by well meaning villagers. A letter written home that day mentions the lovely countryside and "the comments of the troops as we pass young French girls, mostly on bicycles, using exquisite perfume—cheering them on their weary march up the dusty lanes—"

The night was spent in and around the farm buildings of Rucqueville. Spirits were high everywhere since this was still an undamaged area, and everyone was pleasantly surprised at the absence of shelling and gunfire.

Next morning reconnaissance parties left amid thunder showers for Norrey-en-Bessin and St. Mauvieu. The sudden entry into the battle area came as a shock even to those who had trained for it and knew what to expect. The lovely farms and orchards were scarred with shellfire; the shattered and burned buildings; groups of 'brewed up' Sherman tanks; mine-fields littered with dead bodies and abandoned vehicles; dead cows and horses with gas-distended bellies and legs stretched stiffly in the air, were to be the unchanging landscape of the next six weeks.

At St. Mauvieu they came upon an amazing sight. Here there were four or five hundred British tanks packed side-by-side with trucks of all descriptions waiting, with a brigade of infantry, under the shelter of a reverse slope for the attack on Cheux. To get a good look at the ground or a clear indication of the future battalion plan was almost impossible. Recce parties with their Company Sergeant Majors were ordered to remain in the forward area.

The Seventh battalion moved up by march route during the night (the War Diary only states that it was 'raining like Hell'), and waited just behind Cheux throughout most of the day to take over a low feature half a mile south known as Hill 100.

Here for the first time we saw something which will live in our memories for ever—a small neat mound of earth, a simple cross, and a steel helmet; a soldier's wayside grave. Often in the months to come one passed graves, hundreds of them, but the man does not exist who, when seeing one for the first time, did not pause to wonder who this might be that gave his life on the dusty road of a foreign land, who did not think "how easily that could have been me, how easily it could be me before the sun goes down today."

No training, or exercise in England had ever led them into a situation quite like this. Never before had they seen such a mass of men and war material in such a small space.

On training, too, the artillery was just something one heard about, and knew would be supporting the infantry from somewhere far behind the lines. If it fired, its salvos had been represented by a token number of blank rounds, and its shells by a similar small number of slabs of gun-cotton thrown on the ground. Even in the big livefiring exercises the guns had been well back, and the concentrations carefully staged.

Now they saw whole Regiments going into action right alongside them, guns deployed among the lorries and tanks of the reserve battalions, muzzles spouting flame, and filling the air with smoke and fumes, rending the air with a continuous volume of rolling thunder. Sometimes it would die to a desultory barking of single guns, then the wireless sets would call from the forward troops, loud speakers would shout the range, and angles, gunners would double to their stations, the voices of the gun layers could be heard relaying the orders—"Zero line———Four, five hundred———One seven O degrees three O minutes ———Fire." An instant's pause, and the air would be torn with noise and flame. The guns would shudder and recoil, the breech would fly open, and another shell case be added to the pile of cases and boxes mounting beside the gun. Before the smoke cleared another batch of shells was screaming on its way, and another, and another—from whole batteries and regiments concentrating on a single target in support of some hard pressed Company beyond Cheux.

During this time a counter attack was launched against the 5th D.C.L.I. in Cheux who beat it off after a fierce battle in which they destroyed a number of heavy German tanks.

On Hill 100 we dug in under shellfire among former German positions strewn with German dead. These were in trampled corn fields where in places the corn was three-feet high, and to get a field of fire from the trenches was very difficult. The constant shelling made it necessary to keep in or near the slits always, we learned to recognise the sobbing scream of multi-barrel "Moaning Minnies", and the correct moment at which to bite the dust as they approached.

Lieutenant E. F. Larret (Canadian Officer attached) led three patrols within twenty four hours to Colville and Mouen, which were still occupied by S.S. Panzer troops of the first quality. He passed in behind the enemy lines and contacted French civilians. The second patrol had to fight its way out, but Lieutenant Larret went in a third time, gaining information of vital importance for the Brigadier's plan.

As a result the Worcestershires attacked through the battalion lines, through deep corn, to capture Mouen. Somerset patrols penetrated to the main road on reconnaissance.

In the evening of 28th June a battalion of Welsh Guards arrived to take over the positions, but the Somersets were not due to advance until nightfall. Consequently, for the Guards were both numerous and large, the trenches were dreadfully overcrowded during the evening shelling. The combined battalion headquarters was hit. A mortar bombardment at 10.30 p.m. took a sad toll of HQ Specialists—the battalion suffered twenty one casualties of whom eighteen were specialists—among them the Intelligence Officer, Lieutenant G. Macey, and the 'I' Sergeant, Sgt Long, were killed. The Welsh Guards lost their Commanding Officer and Second-in-Command.

In the early hours of the morning the move started in darkness across the open ground below Carpiquet Aerodrome, and in the half light of dawn Companies deployed astride the main Caen road at Mondrainville and Tourville. Deserted trenches and scattered equipment made up the desolate scene. Some of our own tanks withdrawing from Mondrainville caused a momentary panic as a rumour passed that they were falling back before an enemy counter attack. The rumour spread swiftly as rumours do when real information is scarce, but it quickly dispelled as daylight and confidence returned. Nor was the rumour quite unfounded—during 28th/29th June Field-Marshal Rommel was throwing against the British lines every tank and gun he could lay hands on. It is thought that between seven and nine Panzer divisions were being employed to break the left of the Allied line, which hinged on Caen.

Towards noon a further move was made to Haut de Mouen slightly to the East where the battalion dug in covering the main road, along which they could see straight down the six miles stretch to Caen. Patrols were sent out through Verson which was found to be a sort of no-man's-land visited in turn by patrols from both sides. In fact it was later admitted that Private W. Napper had been with Captain W. H. Goudie (O.C. Anti-Tank platoon) into Verson during the morning, and had been greeted with cherry brandy by the civilians.

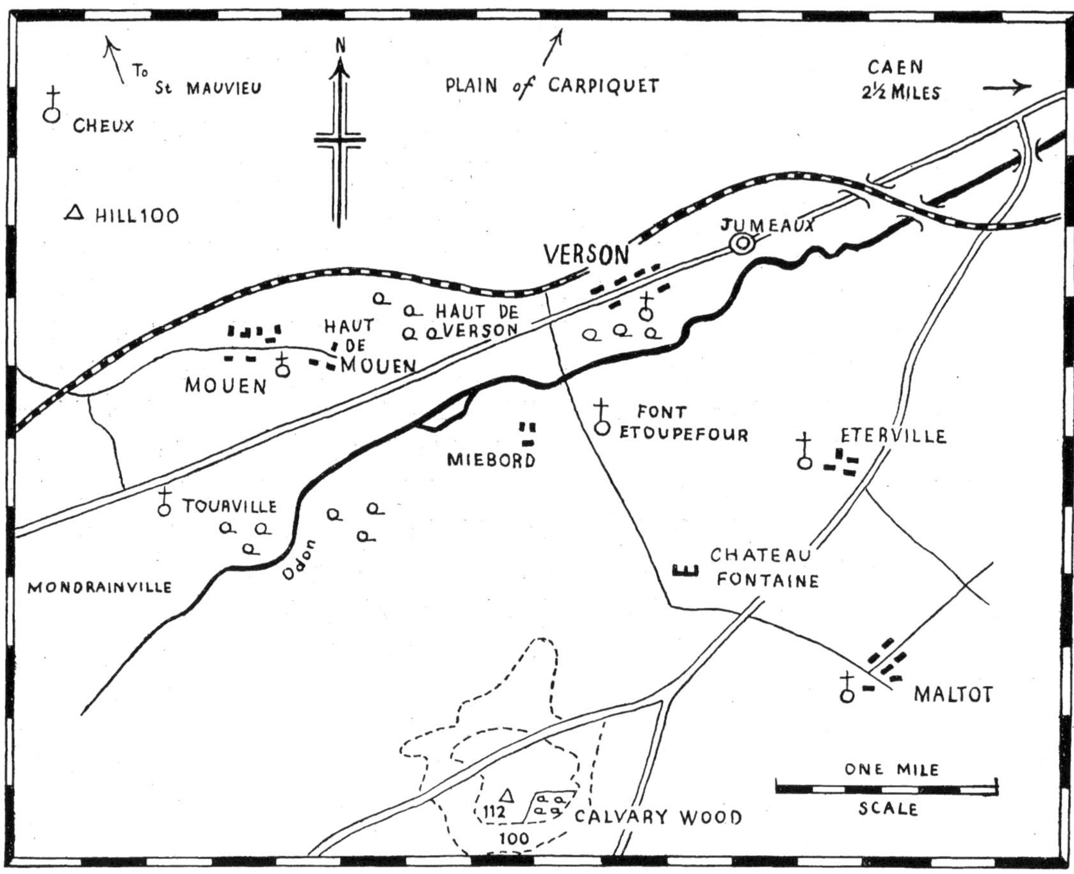

LEGEND *1. The valley of the ODON is steep and wooded.*

2. The high ground at Carpiquet, Jumeaux, Eterville, Hill 112 and Haut de Mouen overlooks the saddle formed along the road from Haut de Verson to Verson.

It must not be imagined that because this book is concerned mainly with the doings of the Seventh battalion that they were ever alone in these crowded battlefields of Normandy. Normally there were troops of many formations overlapping in every village; there were always tanks, and gunners, engineers, signal parties and ambulances which could be relied on to render assistance, or cause confusion as the situation dictated.

It was a matter of pride that every casualty, whether wounded or killed, should be treated with the speediest help that those present could give. Frequently men risked their lives to bring back the body of a comrade from no-mans-land so that he should be given proper burial. This was done unquestioningly, without sentiment but with a quiet determination that every soldier, whether friend or unknown, should have an honoured grave.

As the transport halted at Haut de Mouen, a carrier in which Captain W. H. Goudie was standing was, for a moment, alone on a stretch of the road; in it were also Private Napper and the driver, Pte Mitchell. Captain W. D. Hedges was standing in the road talking to them. A heavy mortar bomb fell by the side of the carrier, and the carrier and road were smothered in a cloud of smoke and dust. It must have been some minutes before anyone from the battalion reached the carrier where they found Captain Goudie and the crew unhurt, but dazed and semi-conscious. The body of Captain Hedges could not be found. Time was precious and the battalion continued the occupation of its new position. Private Heard (Captain Hedges' batman) made several searches of the area, and made enquiries with the Regimental Aid Post and the Field Ambulance unit without success.

Two days later Captain Goudie was sufficiently recovered to remember the details of his escape—he remembered that he had been talking to Captain Hedges. On the third day a small party of friends together with Private Heard decided to make a further search which resulted in the discovery of part of a leg which was identified from the boot, and a damaged revolver. Private Heard said that he had no doubt about the boot as he had been cleaning it for three years, the revolver had been hit by three separate lumps of shrapnel and was twisted in knots. No further trace could be found and Padre Richards held a short burial service.

Back at Battalion HQ a few days later a letter arrived. Bob Hedges was back in England and was safe in hospital. His wife wrote that he had lost a leg and had been picked up by a passing ambulance from another unit. He had been taken to an airstrip, and flown the same evening to England. Some time later he wrote "Thanks for the memorial service—the rest of the body is doing very nicely."

*   *   *

One of the tragic sights to which even those who knew the grimness of the battlefield could not get accustomed was the little groups of refugees. This afternoon from Verson came a thin stream of people, very young, or very old and feeble, their meagre possessions strapped to their backs in blanket rolls or heaped on to wheelbarrows. They had been shelled by the British and by the Germans, and their houses had been searched and ransacked night after night by German patrols, but they had not dared to go, and there was no-one to tell them in which direction safety lay. Now they had decided to evacuate themselves. Their weary gratitude was touching when they reached the battalion lines, and they were anxious to tell all they knew about the Boche.

The night of 30th June/1st July was spent at action stations as the enemy were counter attacking over the river Odon slightly to the West. During the day "C" Company had a patrol down to the river bank, and occupied a platoon position near the water mill. For the first time houses were found in which some accommodation and freedom of movement could be enjoyed.

Moaning Minnies (Nebelwerfer) and shelling kept up a harrassing fire especially at dusk. Very little sleep was possible—experiments were made and overhead cover of planks, logs and earth was introduced for slit trenches—this had a good morale effect and considerably reduced danger from shrapnel and splinters.

One redeeming feature was that there were chickens, eggs, fruit and lettuces to be had, and this improvement to the rations cheered everyone.

On three consecutive nights the Pioneer platoon were called on to work all night, laying protective minefields on either side of the road to Verson—the only unmined sector was the road which was covered by Anti-Tank guns from all angles.

Owing to the long hours of daylight it was not possible to start work much before midnight, and they had to be away again at four o'clock. All mines and stores were man-handled into position in complete silence on ten-cwt trailers, and before light each morning all mines were dug in, and all crates, and other tell-tale rubbish, removed.

At one period the field was subjected to heavy mortar fire, and the platoon had to carry on with little, or no, cover. This was their first practical operation, and it was considered that they carried it out with the same precision as they had often done on exercises.

The frequent patrols into Verson and Carpiquet, though necessary, were tiring and costly in officers and men.

On July 2nd Major S. C. W. Young led a Company patrol with a section of carriers, mortars, and anti-tank guns through Verson. The Company advanced along the line of the railway and the tracked vehicles were called up by wireless after the station had been occupied. A protective screen of anti-tank guns and carriers was formed while the village was searched. It was found to be occupied only by snipers and occasional patrols—they bombarded some snipers in the church tower with their P.I.A.Ts.

Major Young then ordered one platoon with the carrier section forward to the cross roads at Jumeaux. A glance at the map shows that they reconnoitred a deep salient between the enemy positions at Carpiquet and those South of the Odon.

During the patrol this leading platoon got into difficulties and Major Young with Lieutenant P. A. Eves, the Platoon Commander, extricated it in the face of heavy machine gun fire. He made a quick plan with Sergeant Newhouse (carriers) and called for smoke from the mortars, but they were not quite in position so Sergeant Newhouse fired a smoke screen from his carrier, and held the high ground with his Bren gun and crew while the rifle platoon carried out a quick withdrawal, Lieutenant Eves thinning out his sections one at a time, on the other two carriers and the mortar carriers. One of the carriers shed a track, while turning round under fire, and had to be abandoned.

The remainder of the Company were now well clear of the danger zone, and the whole patrol made its way back to the main positions.

The patrol lost one man killed (Private Baker), three wounded, one motor cycle smashed, and the mortar carrier (which was recovered a week later undamaged).

Valuable information was gained about enemy activity and dispositions. Major Young and Lieutenant Eves received the Military Cross, Private Carpenter and Private Gant (Bren Gunners) the Military Medal.

The heavy mortar and artillery bombardment of the main positions continued throughout the 2nd July and on the morning of the 3rd Lieutenant-Colonel R. G. P. Besley T.D., who had brought the battalion over from England, was wounded and had to be evacuated. His batman, Private Chapman, was killed.

Major Young assumed temporary command, sharing that duty with command of his own Company. He was relieved later in the day by Major E. J. Bruford T.D., previously the Second-in-Command.

Major Young was now ordered to take his complete Company Group with carriers, mortars, anti-tank guns, and gunner O.O. to occupy Verson, and form a defensive position to protect the left flank from the main road down to the steep valley of the Odon. Intense artillery cover was used for the move forward. Prisoners were taken including a Sergeant of the Adolf Hitler Regiment, and many snipers were killed or taken prisoner. The advance was under fire from enemy tanks and 88 mm guns, dug-in and concreted around the aerodrome. The mortars with "D" Company were able to engage the enemy seen moving in Carpiquet.

"D" Company pushed patrols forward again to Jumeaux three and a half miles from Caen. A bombardment and counter bombardment set in between the guns which lasted until four in the morning. "D" Company dug themselves in in the orchards and wrecked houses—their company headquarters was in a house containing a record number of fleas and other pests dislodged by the shelling.

Lieutenant-Colonel G. C. P. Lance, D.S.O., arrived to take command of the battalion on 4th July. He very soon ordered the remaining Companies to move up to Haut de Verson behind "D" Company. The move was carried out by night—it was only half a mile—and by dawn all positions were dug and camouflaged. The position was excellent as it was now on a reverse slope instead of a forward one, and the platoons had practically disappeared by morning. The new area was never spotted by the enemy, and there was a big drop in periodic shellfire.

Parties were able to go down through the woods to bathe in the river and letters to England contained many references to little services held in the orchards by Padre Richards in the early days of July.

July Fourth, Fifth and Sixth were days of constant and exhausting patrols—to Carpiquet Aerodrome (Lieutenant Tharp, Lieutenant Jones and Lieutenant Mercier, Canadian Officers attached), through Verson again to Jumeaux, and to Etoupefour across the Odon. Tiger tanks were confirmed to be dug in in concrete emplacements at the aerodrome, and at Eterville.

The reward for this position was a grand stand view of the giant air raid on the enemy at Caen, covering the Canadian attack. All enemy fire ceased at the Somersets who climbed out of their trenches to watch this terrifying display of air power. The whole countryside was obliterated in clouds of dust rising to several thousand feet, and after dark they could clearly see the silhouette of the Cathedral out-lined against the mounting flames.

Our mortars were used very thoroughly on a Brigaded plan. It was after one of their shoots that Lieutenant A. C. A. White was sent out with a small patrol to observe the results of the mortar fire at Jumeaux cross roads; he took with him Private R. W. Homer and Private Mann and penetrated into the main enemy position at Fontaine Etoupefour. Crossing a road Lieutenant White fell, mortally wounded by spandau fire which the two soldiers returned with their rifles from the ditch nearby. Pte. Homer showed complete disregard for his own safety and dashed into the road. With the help of Private Mann he lifted Lieutenant White and made off, carrying him to the outskirts of Verson.

Lieutenant White, though very weak, repeatedly asked them to leave him and get back with their information. At Verson he died, and Private Homer concealed his body before returning to the battalion.

After giving his report Private Homer went out again four times before he finally recovered the body and brought it back for burial. He received the Military Medal for his gallant action.

*   *   *

The following account is representative of many experiences in the Verson patrols. It is told by Private J. Lace, the only original member of the battalion snipers to come right through the campaign—

"We knew that the enemy were in the habit of patrolling Verson by day, when we were ordered one morning at seven o'clock to move up and watch over the village all day. The patrol was made up of Sergeant Colquhoun, myself and five other snipers. We found the village completely empty, so we made our way three-quarters of the way along the village street and barricaded ourselves in what was left of a tall building. We had a good view of the village approaches and of hundreds of Germans walking about nearer Carpiquet.

No-one came within range of us and we started to withdraw at about 7 p.m.

As we left our hide-out a stray civilian warned us that a German patrol with a machine gun (he said about ten men) had got in behind us down the street—we went cautiously, but had often found these reports unreliable. I was the rear man in the patrol when a sudden burst of M.G fire passed between me and the man in front. We all dived for cover in the doorways of shelled houses, but a second burst caught Sergeant Colquhoun, and a bullet hit him in the cheek and jaw. We put up covering rifle fire, and were able to get away through backyards and orchards; the Sergeant was able to carry on unaided.

Private Lay, before he escaped, heard more firing, and returned to see if he could help. He found that another patrol led by Lieutenant Mercier had bumped into the same Germans withdrawing. Lieutenant Mercier had been cornered by a German Officer and two men in a dug-out, and was wounded in the thigh. His batman, Private T. Evers of "B" Company shot two Germans, chased the third who threw away his rifle, and carried his officer back towards his own lines for a considerable distance. Meanwhile Private Lay went back to a telephone which was still connected at the O.P., and 'phoned for an ambulance to come up the road to meet them. The rest of the sniper patrol rallied at the outskirts of Verson, and returned to report at Battalion HQ."*

On July Eighth the whole battalion moved up and dug in around Verson, entering the desolate rubble strewn street during the night, and making "an awful clatter over the piles of broken slates". It was not a popular move since it placed them in the narrow salient between Carpiquet and the high ground South of the river Odon, which was under fire from both sides, but it was necessary in that it rendered the enemy positions on the aerodrome untenable, secured the right flank for the famous Canadian attack on Caen, and opened the way for 43rd Division to drive across the Odon towards Hill 112.

For two nights at Verson very heavy casualties were sustained under a withering shellfire, until the battalion was relieved late on July Ninth by a unit of 15th (Scottish) Division.

* Private Evers was Mentioned in Despatches. It is sad to have to record that, as happened so often after brave actions, he was killed in Verson only three days later by a salvo of "moaning minnies"

Chapter III

CHATEAU DE FONTAINE
AND HILL 112

JULY was a month of giving and receiving hard knocks, attacking, advancing a little, holding on, patrolling, beating off a counter attack, attacking, and then repeating the same sequence all over again. Rommel was doing his damnedest to make good his promise to the German people that he would drive the Allied Armies back into the sea.

The battalion was withdrawn from Verson on the night of 9th July, and at 8.20 a.m. the following morning it crossed the narrow humped-back stone bridge over the Odon in reserve and under command of 130 Brigade. The road was under constant shellfire and there was great congestion on the bridge as ambulances and supply lorries returning from the forward battalions met the oncoming transport of follow-up units.

The Medical Officer (Capt. Marshall) writes—

"The period from 10—13 July was the worst period of the campaign for the R.A.P. We left Verson on the morning of 10 July, in our usual position at the tail of the battalion column. The whole of 'S' Coy's transport had to come in ahead of us, and we were held up just before crossing the bridge over the Odon. At that point a salvo of shells dropped, aimed at the bridge. When we arrived we found one D.R. on the road—killed outright—so we laid him in a barn just off the road. Next our attention was drawn to the river itself where we found two R.E. officers thrown into the river, each with a badly broken leg. We got them out, getting rather wet in the process (it reminded me of battle courses) and we sent them away in my ambulance. Then we found another ambulance just by the bridge, badly damaged and splintered and without its driver. One of the casualties inside had been very badly hit, the others shaken, but not more than that. My ambulance had gone so I sent a D.R. back for another and we heard later that they got these casualties safely away.

Meanwhile I moved on with the R.A.P., slowly. At the top of the next hill we had an uncomfortable few minutes in ditches and slits while three or four Messerschmidts wandered around but they did not attack us."

D.Rs of battalion HQ were killed and many other casualties were suffered; there was a further hold up where the road reached the high ground.

They reached the farm buildings around Chateau de Fontaine and deployed to dig in immediately, selecting positions in the meadow land, where some sort of view could be got between the hedges of 30-ft high bushy trees—the main rifle company positions were just north of the road on the reverse side of the ridge above Maltot.

Mortar and shellfire was devastating. Colonel Lance was killed by a shell from an 88, while sitting in his jeep, the Gunner Battery Commander, Major Mapp, was killed, the Adjutant, Capt. A. Scannell, was wounded and evacuated; a steady stream of wounded was arriving at the Regimental Aid Post. Major Young and Major Chalmers shared command of the battalion with that of their own companies. Snipers were at their worst. Shortly after Colonel Lance was killed Major Young's company was clearing some farm buildings at Chateau Fontaine. A shot whistled unpleasantly close and the Major turned to Pte. Lace (battalion sniper) who was with him "That's the fifth shot that basket has fired at me, we must get him." They found him hidden in a junk heap in the middle of a duck pond. They found another, he could not have been more than seventeen years old, who had buried himself in the mud of a wet ditch—only his head, arms and rifle were free and even these he had covered with slime and weeds. Another was burned out from a hayrick set on fire by a German shell. Several days after the occupation of Chateau Fontaine snipers were still being found. One was barricading himself in a room on the first floor of a barn of which a platoon of "D" Company occupied the ground floor. They got him with a burst from a Bren gun fired through the closed door, when he refused to come out. Enemy trenches in the area were full of German dead passed over by the leading troops, the usual scene of mutilated farm animals was all around. The air was rancid with the smell of dead animals and flies.

Two attempts by the Dorsets and Hampshires to take Maltot were met by intense gun fire and massed tanks, and failed with very heavy casualties. They then had to pull back behind the ridge and dig in alongside our own positions. The battalion was losing men at a higher rate than at any time during the campaign that day and for nearly a week to come.

This long spur of ground between the Odon and the Orne ran right into Caen and was vitally important to the Germans. Along its crest ran the road through Esquay to Eterville and between them lay the hill which became known as "The Hill called Calvary"—officially it was Hill 112.

On the night of 10th/11th July the 5th Duke of Cornwall's Light Infantry took Hill 112 and the small rectangular wood just to the South. They were immediately counter attacked by large forces of Tiger tanks which drove round and round the outside of the wood, raking it with their guns. It was a night of very heavy losses for the D.C.L.I. but they managed to break out and, by morning, had rallied their sadly depleted numbers and were established again on the right of the Somersets. The Canadians also had cleared most of Caen, and had come up to Eterville on our immediate left.

Mortaring increased still more on the eleventh and the Brigade Commander visited the battalion with orders that should the counter attack develop against them, which seemed imminent, the Somersets would stand fast at all costs. The day passed much as the previous one and between the eleventh and thirteenth the enemy were seen several times to form up on the battalion front with tanks and infantry for a counter attack—each time they were broken up with terrific losses by artillery and mortar concentrations, and steady execution was done by the 17-pounders of our Anti-tank Regiment. Major Young wrote "We sit like a colony of rabbits around our trenches, not daring to venture far away in the evening sunshine."

But, though men were forbidden to move about, and all cooking and washing had to be done in the slits, the casualty rate remained high. Captain Howarth (O. C. Carrier Platoon) had changed trenches with his batman in order to be near the telephone, when he was killed by a direct hit on his trench on the night of 12th/13th. Officers, N.C.Os, runners and snipers, whose business it was to move around the positions, suffered heavily.

Again the Medical Officer writes:—
"After three days the Padre and I were the only original officers left in battalion HQ, and we never had a period of more than two hours, day or night, without a casualty. Two R.A.M.C. men working with me were killed and my truck and ambulance were put out of action.

During this time, and in all the fighting, Padre Richards was more help and comfort to me, and to all of us, than I can say. He was always to be seen visiting the Companies calmly and coolly. It must have been a great strain on him because he knew the men intimately, and many of the casualties were his friends.

He had many burials to perform and many graves to dig, and he never flinched from this distressing duty. Often he dug a whole grave himself when he was unable to get help — on one occasion while he was working in his cemetery, a shower of mortar bombs fell, scattering the crosses: without any fuss he re-arranged the crosses on their graves and carried on. He never spared himself danger or strain in his task of comforting and encouraging the wounded, and the frightened."

An unlucky shell on the 13th pierced the roof of a farm building at the Chateau, killing the Acting Commanding Officer, Major E. J. Bruford T.D., and the Commanding Officer and Second-in-Command of the 7th Hampshires who were with him in conference. It also killed Sergeant Barnes (Provost Sgt) and "HQ" Company clerk, Lance-corporal Mitchell: the Intelligence officer and his whole 'I' Section were wounded.

It is a miracle that under such losses a battalion can carry on, but they did. The rifle companies stuck it out in their trenches, the mortars gave bomb for bomb and added a few for luck, the gunners answered every salvo with four of their own. On this occasion Captain W. H. Goudie (now Adjutant), who was the only officer left in "HQ", assumed command and with coolness and efficiency effected the relief which the Commanding Officer and C.O., 7th Hampshires had been planning.

On the late evening of the same day, after four days spent almost without sleep and in a state of constant alertness, the battalion was called back to Miebord, a mile behind the ridge.

Captain R. P. Townshend, who was in charge of the reconnaissance party consisting of Sgt. Williams, Pte. Duckham, Pte. Hillier, Pte. Parsons and Pte. Scott, had been in the village since afternoon. Sgt. Williams was wounded and evacuated during the reconnaissance. When everything was ready to receive the battalion the guides set out to meet them: on the way up to the dispersal point they were caught in a mortar 'stonk' and Pte. Duckham was killed, Pte. Hillier seriously wounded (and later died of wounds), Pte. Parsons wounded in the shoulder and Pte. Scott was sent off as escort to the R.A.P. with the wounded on a jeep. This left Captain Townshend alone to sort out the companies to their correct areas in the dark.

At Miebord the shelling was more spasmodic, and a little rest was possible. However the gun lines just across the river received a fair share of attention which frequently spread itself over the Somersets' position. Lieutenant-Colonel J. W. Nicol arrived to take command during the next day. Small bathing parties were able to slip down into the valley and refresh themselves in the soothing water of the pebble-bottomed stream.

During the next night the German Air Force carried out a raid on the gun lines dropping cascades of small anti-personnel bombs. One of these set a mortar carrier on fire, which blew up, and "A" Company suffered rather a lot of casualties. Nevertheless it was a slightly safer piece of country.

July 15th saw the launching of another attack by the Canadians—it was the beginning of the push towards Falaise. Artillery fire increased on both sides, and the battalion was confined to trenches after rehearsing a counter attack role on Eterville. The 15th (Scottish) Division moved up to the right, through our lines, with large forces of tanks. After two days of fierce fighting the enemy had again halted all attacks, but slight bulges had been pushed forward at both ends of the ridge.

The battalion then went forward to the back slopes of Hill 112 (17th July) and held on till 22nd, when it again became reserve. There was very little difference between the forward and reserve positions except for the degree of alertness for section posts. It was impossible to leave the slits by day and all cooking and washing had to be done in trenches—water was very limited and no supplies could come up except at night. The days were unbearably hot, interspersed with thunderstorms and morning mist. Flies and mosquitos bred in thousands.

One strange reminiscence from Hill 112 is of a queer little, undersized, half starved black goat which lived among the shell scarred fields. It seemed to lead a charmed life as it trotted contentedly around the slit trenches uttering idiotic little bleats. It survived the whole battle and was always a welcome visitor at the trenches where it was fed small pieces of tinned plum pudding. It showed us that, with faith, life itself was still a frolic.

A large batch of reinforcements arrived on the 19th from the 9th Battalion. Headed by Major (then Captain) D. B. M. Durie and Major (then Lieutenant) E. R. H. Harvey, it comprised officers, Sergeant-Major, NCOs and men of approximate strength of a complete company.

The enemy took to firing oil and phosphorous bombs and their tanks fired solid shot. Our own mortar platoon was plastering away with 1,000 rounds a day—and despite this tremendous volume of fire were very pleased to report that for six days their own positions were never mortared or shelled at all.

Counter attack plans were again rehearsed from the reserve area on the 22nd: it was much quieter here, and the rate of fire and casualties began to decrease.

At midnight on 25th July, after four weeks and two days in the line, we started to withdraw to a rest area. A halt was made till dawn at Mouen, and then the march continued back over our former battlefield, the plain of Carpiquet.

It was a hot and dusty march, and everyone was too glad to be away from the guns and too keen to get back to a good wash to do much romancing over the familiar scene of the battalion's first battles. The Divisional Commander took the salute on the line of march, and we reached our first rest area at Conde-sur-Seulles, south east of Bayeux.

The rest amounted only to a two-day break, but it was very much needed and was taken in lovely weather. Rest and recreation were the chief needs: the Divisional Commander visited and addressed the battalion on its achievements and future plans.

The rest was interrupted at one time when a Company, carrying out experiments with 2-inch mortar smoke bombs, landed one among the wreckage of a crashed bomber in a neighbouring field. This caught fire and a dozen 250-lb bombs, which were still in the fuselage, blew up. No-one was hurt.

French refugees helped the troops with their mending and sewing.

Chapter IV

ST. PIERRE DU FRESNE

A long dusty march brought the Battalion to an assembly area just north of Caumont, where the day was spent in studying air photographs of the next objective. Here the 4th/7th Dragoon Guards reported as the first tanks to come directly under command of the Battalion.

The operation began in the early evening 31st July, with the Infantry riding on tanks past Caumont as far as Cahagnes where they reached the forward positions held by the Worcestershires. The route forward will be chiefly remembered for the thick coating of fine white dust which covered the road like a soft carpet and smothered the vehicles and the riding troops.

Cahagnes itself was in flames, and here the Companies de-bussed and forked right towards St. Pierre, across country heavily pockmarked by bomb craters.

"B" Company as vanguard to the Battalion had under command a section of our own pioneers under Lieutenant D. Bean and Lance-corporal Brister, an Engineer reconnaissance party and a Troop of tanks. Dusk was already falling when they moved off on foot at about 10.30 p.m. Progress astride the road was slow as all buildings had to be searched, and a small number of prisoners was taken.

Shortly after the start enemy tracked vehicles were heard approaching. The Company dispersed and a half-track troop carrier drove right into their midst. It was heavily engaged from all sides and those bullets which did not hit the half-track gave attackers on the other side of the road the impression that they were having a hell of a battle: however it was successfully set on fire by a P.I.A.T. bomb fired by Private Jones. A second armoured vehicle managed to get away.

The advance now continued in total night, but well lit by a half moon. The country was enclosed, suitable for ambush, and dotted with buildings which had to be searched. Through skilful leadership and personal example, and with eager support from his Company, Major K. J. Whitehead led his Group until the cross-roads at Les Haies. Here two enemy cyclists, from the 21st Panzer Division, rode into our column and were shot—one dead, one wounded and died shortly afterwards.

Ten platoon took up a firm base on the main cross roads while Eleven platoon went forward to the right and Twelve platoon to the left, but progress was again slow while farms and cottages were searched.

The Company pushed forward until it was disposed around the small village of St. Pierre du Fresne on either side of a road leading down to the bridge over a small stream. Positions were found in the moonlight almost exactly as they had been selected from the air photographs. The village comprised a small stone church and some immensely strong farm buildings. The forward platoons linked at the sunken road with section posts in hedges of close clipped yew, and among the orchards.

By 2 a.m. all platoons were digging in, the two forward ones observing into the valley: P.I.A.T.s were placed to cover the road, and a necklace of 75 (anti-tank) grenades was made to form a road block. Considerable tank movement was heard on the other side of the valley during what was left of the night.

At 8 a.m. a patrol with Sergeant Palmer and Private Neath pushed forward to have a look at the stream. One Tiger tank was reported about 300-yards forward on the road. Major Whitehead decided to destroy the tank and sent two P.I.A.T.s up covered by three-inch and two-inch mortars, he himself, with Lieutenant Pizzey, Private Johnson, and a Bren gun team, got to within 50-yards.

From here it was possible, in a lifting mist, to see large numbers of enemy infantry coming down the far hillside, who had not been visible from the main positions. The Company Commander withdrew to call down artillery fire on the infantry while Lieutenant Pizzey concentrated on the Tiger. The tank was hit but not knocked out, and returned fire, killing the Bren gunner and wounding another member of the patrol. The remainder withdrew safely.

After an anxious wait of some minutes while Gunner Observation Posts called up their batteries, our shells began to arrive, and though they were very close to our lines (since the enemy were 150 yards away) no-one worried very much. Very soon three Gunner regiments were firing and the chance of an organised infantry attack was reduced.

However, two tanks, both of them monster Ferdinand S.P. guns had managed to get up along the sunken road, supported by small numbers of crawling infantry,—the leading one got right up alongside Twelve platoon's forward section. Private Johnson now showed his mettle and put four P.I.A.T. bombs into its rear from close range, stalking it from behind walls and hedges in order to do so—Private Jones hit it twice more from Eleven platoon side.

Enemy infantry were now discovered in Eleven platoon's forward post. There was heavy and close fighting in which Corporal Burge and three men were wounded, two more were killed, and the remaining two had to withdraw. In consequence the 75 Grenade tank trap was never closed.

Confused fighting then ensued along the banks of the road with Twelve platoon grenading their infiltrating enemy and Eleven platoon firing two inch mortar H.E. at low angles. It was extremely difficult to bring effective small arms fire to bear on the road owing to the deep banks and thick hedges. Several enemy were eliminated and their officer was killed by a 77 phosphorus grenade thrown by Corporal McClernon (formerly of the Middlesex Regiment)—the remainder of this group withdrew.

Captain Pinn with Company Headquarters took on some more enemy on the left with their two-inch mortar, and the Gunner officer directed this fire as well as the artillery. They all enjoyed this shoot and several enemy were dislodged from the banks and ditches.

The first tank, covered by the second, was by now right in the middle of the Company and approaching "C" Company. Its guns were firing viciously at the buildings, but fortunately "B" Company's positions were all in the gardens. Suddenly, no-one quite knows when, the crew abandoned the tank unobserved and left it grinding forward still in gear. The second tank, blinded by phosphorus grenades bouncing on its roof, withdrew. Corporal McClernon played merry hell with his grenades—throwing them about like tennis balls, and at the same time leading his own section and another which had lost its N.C.O.

Soon after this the action died down, not too soon for the Company who had, by now, exhausted their whole stock of grenades and mortar bombs. The crewless tank was finally brought to a halt by "C" Company in their area.

Consequently, on the advance of the Wiltshires, thirty prisoners were brought in who had been pinned down in odd places of cover by the artillery, two-inch mortar, and L.M.G fire.

About twenty enemy dead were discovered in front of the positions, mostly killed by gunner fire.

Casualties in this action were one officer (Lieutenant Greenwood of Twelve platoon) wounded by the M.G fire, five other ranks killed by the enemy mortar or tank H. E. fire, five other ranks wounded.

The main attack appears to have been from two directions, for "D" Company, who were on the left rear of the battalion position with the tanks of 4th/7th Dragoon Guards in support, made this report on the same action:—

"At about 0930 hrs on 1st August information came over the air that a strong enemy force was attacking "B" Company, and that some infiltration had taken place. I ordered my Company to stand to and went myself to the left flank where one of my platoons was just about to dig in. They had hardly started when the Bren gun sentry gave the alarm that a section of enemy was advancing across a field on the opposite side of the valley. We waited until they were in open country, when the order to fire was given, and at the same time a troop of our tanks arrived in the platoon area and opened up with their Besas. The tank men saw about thirty enemy further down the valley. All were successfully pinned to the ground, engaged, or scattered.

The enemy fired Verey lights and put down smoke. We called on our own three-inch mortars and they undoubtedly caught the retreating Hun. At this point the Artillery joined in. The field was covered by what appeared to be dead Boche, and I ordered a patrol to be taken out by Lieutenant Tharp to investigate whether a house and orchard, for which the enemy made a dash, were occupied, and to obtain information about the "dead" enemy.

We noticed, after the patrol had left, that some of the "dead" were wounded, and moved slightly. When the patrol eventually reached them I was amazed to see five Germans stand up—three from a large shell hole and two "dead".

There were three wounded brought in on my jeep by the Company Stretcher Bearers, who said the men were very happy to be collected.

There had been a M.M.G. team, upon which Sergeant Williams, the Platoon Sergeant, took pains to direct his fire. They were all killed, and we found that our two inch mortar shooting had accounted for two of the wounded".

This was primarily a "B" Company battle, and the securing of St. Pierre du Fresne and the valley paved the way for an attack by the Wiltshires towards Jurques. For his leadership and tenacity in seizing and holding the Battalion objective Major Whitehead received the Military Cross. Corporal McClernon was awarded the Military Medal, and Private Johnson a Mention in Despatches.

*   *   *

Later in the morning two prisoners rode into Headquarters to surrender; they stated that there was a report among the Germans that Rommel was dead, and also that our shellfire had that morning killed their Commanding Officer and a Company Commander. They said that their losses had been severe and that many more were anxious to surrender.

Two days were spent at St. Pierre during which a battle was fought at Jurques by 5th D.C.L.I., while the Wiltshires and 1st Worcestershires leap-frogged through each other on the right to take an important piece of hilly country known as the Bois du Homme.

Captain E. A. A. Warner, the Mortar Officer, had a lucky escape when a shell scored a direct hit on his slit trench while he was away getting orders at Headquarters.

August 3rd and 4th saw the battalion advancing cross-country on a long 'right hook'. The transport was unable to follow and was taken round still further to the right by Captain J. W. Baden. The marching troops halted and bivouaced one night on the railway line at the foot of Bois du Homme, and next day, once again in blazing heat, wound their way up the heather covered slopes, through the battalions on the hill, and on to Bremoy which was found abandoned, and heavily bombed and shelled. From here, and Montamy on the main road, they were given a great welcome by the first really resident French civilians that they had met.

Positions were occupied, with minor opposition, with Companies at Montamy and Mesnil Auzouf. Headquarters was in a magnificent chateau. After so long among blackened ruins and heaps of broken tiles it was strange to move through drawing rooms furnished with chairs with fine tapestry coverings and presided over by a Grande Dame, said to be a cousin of a premier Scottish Duke.

As usual the Germans had taken all the silver, cutlery and food, and had shot all the farm animals on the estate.

Chapter V

MONT PINCON

THE break-out of the American Army on the Western flank, with its armoured drive which swept along the boundary of Brittany, through Tours, and East again along the valley of the Loire towards Paris, was the beginning of the terrible Falaise pocket which became the graveyard of the German Seventh and Fifteenth Armies. At Caen the Canadian, British and Polish forces broke the hinge of the German line and started to close the open end to cut the lines of retreat and supply. In the centre British pressure was closing the 'sack' and squeezing the enemy back on themselves, and ever closer into a target for the Allied air forces.

In the closing ring Mont Pincon was the dominating feature—a steep, heather covered hill, one thousand two hundred feet high, from which the country could be seen for many miles on every side. The following account of the action of 43rd Division in reaching the summit is told by a military press correspondent, and is reprinted by permission of the Western Gazette (September 22nd 1944).

VICTORY ON MONT PINCON

"A glorious page in the war history of the 43rd (Wessex) Division was the assault on the one thousand two hundred foot Mont Pincon, highest point in Normandy's 'Little Switzerland,' which was triumphantly stormed by troops of this Division.

It is a story of West country infantrymen, including battalions of the Somersets and Wiltshires, pinned to the ground for six and seven hours on end by vicious machine gun fire, of a battalion commander who, swinging a walking-stick, and with a red rose in his battle-dress lapel, went forward across a bridge through withering cross fire and gave his life in an attempt to hearten his troops, of a gallant rally which gained the vital objective when the whole assault seemed broken, of a troop of tanks which charged and gained the summit alone and of desperately weary infantry who, having reached the hill-top, dropped over their spades and fell in sleep as they attempted to dig their slit trenches.

Mont Pincon stood athwart several roads vital to the advance on the British sector south of Villers Bocage. With the hilltop in their hands, the Germans could paralyse any movement of ours for several miles in almost any direction.

Possession of the feature was the key to the communications of a wide area on this sector of the Allied front. The assault in which the 43rd Division took part met with the fiercest German resistance. Men of the Pioneer Platoon of one battalion removed the mines and built a tank crossing in thirty-five minutes from the rubble of the demolished bridge, working under enemy fire. The Germans shelled and mortared our infantry. Intense shelling greeted our troops each time they changed location. Where the infantry advanced they did so in twos and threes only, by short dashes, separated by long periods during which they were pinned tight to the ground. One company only had got across the stream towards La Varmiere before nightfall. And these men, after hanging on grimly through the night, were forced early next day to pull back across the stream again by intense machine gun fire from the woods.

A new attack was launched on one of the hottest days of the campaign, with the artillery putting down a heavy barrage and smoke to neutralise the dangerously exposed south flank.

Two battalions stormed the stream, crossing under the western crest of Mont Pincon. Men tried individually, and in small groups, to rush the bridge crossing. They nearly all fell as they ran. The bridge was completely enfiladed by many German machine guns. Yet this vicious defence had to be broken.

The Battalion Commander, a regular soldier of the South Lancashire Regiment—wearing a red rose—the battle tradition of his old regiment—and with a walking-stick in his hand, strode coolly down the middle of the road and across the bridge, determined to steady his men and carry them forward through the wall of fierce resistance. A little beyond the bridge this gallant Colonel fell, mortally wounded.

Immediately, his Adjutant took command. Over the radio he received orders from his Brigade Commander that the La Varmiere crossroads, eight hundred yards ahead—key point of the entire assault—must be taken at all costs. A quick, simple plan was evolved. They plunged forward under the one remaining Company Commander, and with close tank support, beat the Germans down. The vital crossroads was theirs. Within the space of some twenty minutes the Adjutant and his resolute Westcountrymen had turned a near defeat into a splendid victory.

The Adjutant was still confident that the hilltop itself could be reached and planned to push on. One of the first shells wounded the Adjutant badly and he had to be evacuated. Shortly after, the new Battalion Commander had arrived and took control. It was decided to pass the reserve battalion through the La Varmiere position with the hilltop as its objective, leaving the battalion which had captured the crossroads to hold on there. At 7 o'clock (approximately) the reserve battalion passed through La Varmiere and proceeded up the slopes. The men were heavily laden and very tired after more than twenty-four hours of battle, but the final, evening attack, in the words of the Battalion Commander, was 'a walk up the hill in single file.' Many of them dropped over their spades, falling asleep from sheer exhaustion as they dug themselves in.

At the time the dramatic change came over the attack at La Varmiere, a fourth battalion was pushing down from the north on Roucamps, a village north-east of Mont Pincon, in a separate attack. In diverting the enemy's attention this attack contributed greatly to the success of the assault on Mont Pincon itself. But the battalion thrusting through La Roguerie was still pinned. Late in the afternoon another reconnaissance was made in an attempt to get tanks across the stream. It was then decided that it was just possible, at great difficulty, to get the tanks over the obstacle and through any likely minefield. One tank crossed just before nightfall to give direct support to the infantry, but still got no further than one hundred yards beyond. At that time one troop of our tanks was seen by the infantry to be milling around on the crest of Mont Pincon. With great pluck these tanks had gone right forward, unsupported, to gain the summit by another route. The effect of this sight on the men still pinned below was most heartening. They determined to get up there to support the tank crews. The assault went in under a combination of smoke laid by the artillery, dust, mist, and fast failing light. Visibility was soon reduced to nothing. As it later turned out, the final assault had infiltrated right through a German company position without either side being aware of it.

The battalion which had come up through La Roguerie had previously been given the far eastern spur of the hill as its final objective. Contact was quickly made with the tanks which had harboured amongst the infantry for the night, and the attack on the spur planned. The tanks reported a considerable number of Germans dug in there. With a tank squadron in support, the infantry moved forward and quickly crushed the final German resistance on Mont Pincon. The whole of the hill area was in our hands after a three-day operation".

*   *   *

It was the Fourth battalion of the Regiment, in 129 Brigade, who finally reached the hill-top. The Seventh Somersets, who had not been engaged at the approaches, came forward on August 7th (August Bank Holiday), along roads powdered to a heavy red dust, ready to carry the assault over the crest: They moved up close behind the Fourth.

An under-strength platoon of "C" Company lost the way in the morning mist at the foot of Mont Pincon, and continued straight east towards Le Plessis Grimoult. They bumped into the enemy and got away in the confusion, taking fifteen prisoners. Later on it was discovered that there were enemy positions of a strength of about two battalions on this road, but that our route to the hill-top had by-passed them in the haze.

The weather was the hottest of the summer—the sultry air, thick with dust and flies, and the acrid smell of bursting shells.

The enemy now abandoned the whole position, and the Seventh took over the hill, expanding to the south and east ridges with 'B', 'C' and 'A' Companies forward. The summit, a curved plateau dropping steeply to the north and south, and more gently towards the east, was quite easily observed by the enemy gunners and, though the shelling was no heavier than had been experienced in July, it was both concentrated and accurate.

There was a steep climb for the supporting vehicles up a winding sandy track to the crest, and, once there, it was impossible to move without being sky-lined for the enemy. So accurate was their gunfire that, as the Anti-Tank guns pulled into position, the Boche were able to leave them alone while they were moving and shell them as soon as they stopped. In this way the Anti-Tank HQ carrier was knocked about and the batman (Private Scott) had his leg broken.

Once again the Company jeeps did splendid work as stretcher carriers. Their drivers were in constant demand throughout the campaign, running over open ground to all points of the battlefield, and they always worked extremely long hours on this very exacting work. It was true that, when engaged as stretcher carriers, they were permitted to fly a Red Cross flag, but this was small protection against shells and mortar bombs.

On their way back to the R.A.P. they had to negotiate the winding sandy track, and the carriage of stretchers always required the most considerate driving. Just at the foot of the hill there were three Sherman tanks on fire where the jeeps had to make their way past them, through burning petrol and exploding ammunition.

Among those wounded on Mont Pincon were Major K. J. Whitehead M.C. (Commanding "B" Company), and Captain F. J. Pinn ("B" Company Second-in-Command). The Mortar Platoon HQ driver, Lance-corporal Reilly, and the Rangetaker, Private Oldfield, were killed by the same shell. Captain Pinn's wound was slight, and he was returning to his Company after having it dressed, when he was hit again, this time severely. Casualties in "A" Company, who were on the forward slopes, were heavy.

We were now well used to digging in, and everyone disappeared into slit trenches in a cloud of dust and gravel, and was below ground in record time.

There was no attempt to counter-attack Mont Pincon, and the night was only memorable for the unpleasantly accurate enemy fire.

* * *

Next morning an officer (who perhaps would like to remain nameless) was standing on the hilltop watching a column of tanks slowly crawling its way forward round the foot of the hill. He heard a voice behind him say, "Have you seen the Corps Commander?" "The Corps Commander," he replied without looking round, "Good God, you don't expect to find him this far forward, do you?" He then turned to find, to his embarrassment, that he was talking to a Major-General.

But the Corps Commander was on Mont Pincon; in fact he had just passed Private Pursey (Anti-Tank platoon) who saw only a tall officer striding along the ridge, and unpardonably failed to notice the General's badges or his red cap band, so he called, "Got any 'Gen' Sir?"

Yes, Lieutenant-General B. G. Horrocks, C.B., D.S.O., M.C., Commander of 30 Corps from El Alamein to Tunis, and from the beaches to Bremerhaven, did have some "Gen". He proceeded to tell the Corps lay-out, and his plan, to a small group which quickly gathered.

General Horrocks then walked on to "C" Company, where he talked of recent events, and his plans for rolling up the Boche, pointing out features on the Company Commander's map—which is still proudly preserved.

* * *

The view from the hill was striking. In some directions it was possible to see forty or fifty miles over hills and fields, heather and pine woods, but no great detail could be picked out owing to the close nature of the country. Here and there it was possible to see a chateau or part of a village peeping out among the trees, or the bend of a dusty road winding its way among the hills and valleys of this charming contryside.

Accuracy was not a peculiar privilege of the enemy, and excellent results were obtained by our own mortars and gunners on concentrations of enemy picked out by our Observation Posts on Mont Pincon.

It was not intended to hold the hill longer than was necessary to secure the movement of other units moving round its flanks, and we spent only two days there. During this time maps were studied carefully in order to learn the lie of the land with a view to future plans, particularly the village of Le Plessis Grimoult, just below the hill, and the road running away south east, with the small villages of Les Hameaux and Le Saussay on the right, and Cauville on the left.

Slowly a tremendous feeling of confidence began to grow. Perhaps it was the effect of standing on dominating ground, or of seeing our own columns moving up around the lower slopes, perhaps too it was the great news that was coming in from the American right flank. One could sense now that the Germans were no longer fighting on ground of their own choosing, but were making defensive stands where they could. There was a feeling that the slogging-match which had been measured yard by yard for two months was ended, and that a great strategic victory was not very far away.

Chapter VI

LES HAMEAUX

SHELLING again dominated all movement on Mont Pincon when the Battalion moved off on the morning of 9th August. Somewhere on the roads of Normandy we used to see a sign, put up by the Traffic Control police, "Your dust means our ashes": never was it more true than that morning!

The route was back over the north shoulder, and in this phase the Carrier platoon provided valuable help by forming an armoured screen behind which the infantry moved away, and remaining as a covering force for some time. Once the protection of the hill was gained, the route lay around the western spur—past the cross roads up which the attack had moved—and later along the foot of Mont Pincon towards Le Plessis Grimoult.

The task for the battalion was an attack on Les Hameaux, Hameau au Roi and Le Saussay—three hamlets forming a triangle of which Les Hameaux was the apex and the nearest to Mont Pincon. They had already been well studied from the hilltop but, in the closely wooded and very beautiful country, it had not been possible to pick out any outstanding landmarks. The thick hedgerows concealed the roads and the sunken farm tracks which linked the many mellow old stone-built farms.

At an early morning "O" group at Brigade HQ, the Commanding Officer had already been told that the main attack of the day was to be launched further east by 50th (Northumbrian) Division and that the 1st Worcestershires were attacking on our front at 9.30 a.m. to secure the Somersets start line. Le Plessis Grimoult itself was taken in a fine action by the 5th D.C.L.I.

Lieutenant-Colonel Nicol rejoined the battalion at his Command Post at ten o'clock and quickly gave his orders to the "O" group as it assembled—first to the Commanders of "A" and "D" Companies and the Mortar Officer, who were close at hand. During this time the battalion was moving down from the hill to an assembly area at the western end. The gist of his orders was as follows:—

"The Seventh Somersets with their supporting tanks ('A' Squadron 4th/7th Royal Dragoon Guards) will seize and hold the villages of Les Hameaux and Le Haussay and will exploit as far as Hameau au Roi and Le Saussay.

Method will be—Right, 'D' Company with the objective of Le Haussay, Left 'A' Company, objective Les Hameaux. The task of 'C' and 'B' Companies will be to follow up on the right and left, at a distance of six hundred yards and mop up the areas before exploiting forward." The Carrier platoon was given orders for right flank protection, and a smoke screen was to be held, on call, from the Mortar platoon—again to cover the open right flank.

The start line was four or five hundred yards south of the Le Plessis Grimoult road and the attack was across country, including many sunken tracks and minor track junctions. To each forward Company was allotted a troop of tanks, and an assault section of our own Pioneers.

As soon as the battalion was started on its approach march Colonel Nicol went forward, in his carrier, to HQ 1st Worcestershires to meet his Tank Commander. It soon became apparent that neither the tanks, nor the infantry, would be ready at the original H hour (11.15 a.m.) and H hour was postponed to noon. The Intelligence Officer was sent back to the battalion to announce the changed time and to tell our Gunners to alter their timed fireplan accordingly. Meanwhile the Worcestershires were meeting stiff opposition on our start line and their Company had suffered several casualties. Their Commanding Officer dispatched one of his reserve platoons, on carriers, to speed up the clearing of the area.

The Somerset Companies came under a variety of enemy fire in their approach march and the Carrier platoon was used to form a physical moving screen along the open flank. The Anti-tank platoon, too, fired H.E. shells at located enemy positions.

By 1230 a. m. "A" and "D" Companies were ready in their forming-up area and the order was given to advance. Just in time the Gunner battery commander announced that he had been able to re-adjust the artillery timings. On this start-line "C" Company lost many casualties while waiting for their turn to follow up. Their headquarters was wiped out complete, with the exception of the Company Commander, Company Sergeant-Major Evans, and one signaller, and the weakened platoons started forward without knowing of this loss.

Immediately they crossed the start-line the supporting tanks with the leading Companies got into difficulties, for the thick hedges, interspersed with sizeable trees, were tank obstacles and the tracks were heavily mined. The Pioneer platoon was ordered up to clear the mines and prepare a safe lane up the axis of advance. Likewise the Carrier screen which was moving out on the right ran into a mine belt and lost a carrier. They were later recalled to escort the fighting-echelon transport forward, but this was much later as they had to pick their way back cautiously through the minefield.

Two tanks managed to get through with "D" Company, but the Company ammunition carrier was blown up. Major Young pushed on and his Company reached the edge of Les Hameaux (about one thousand two hundred yards) meeting only scattered opposition. Here they "lost" their barrage and the Commanding Officer had to call for an artillery concentration on the village. This came down just as "D" were entering, but it was quickly stopped before any damage was done. "D" Company over-ran both Les Hameaux and Le Haussay and reported their objectives taken at 3.20 p.m.

In spite of their difficulties the tanks found a way up and arrived on the objectives with the leading troops, one tank kept with "D" Company throughout the afternoon.

"A" Company made slower progress and it was hedgerow fighting all the way. It was a question of short bounds of fire and movement across the small luxuriant meadows, and sharp assaults against the enemy machine guns dug into the strong hedges. Under these conditions they experienced great difficulty in keeping direction; they were also heavily engaged by Machine Gun fire from the left flank which caused them a number of casualties. Soon after the start the Company wireless communication to Battalion HQ had broken down with the result that Colonel Nicol had no news of their progress. He therefore sent "C" Company to pass through "D" and take the "A" Company objective from the west side. "C" were, however, in contact with "A", and they found Major Baker and his Company firmly established.

The attack had now been proceeding for just over three hours and had yielded between forty and fifty prisoners.

Early in the second phase Captain V. S. Baily and Lieutenant E. F. Larret came back wounded to Headquarters. Colonel Nicol found time to smile at them and say, "What, you too Larret?" "Yes, sir, I'm sorry, sir." Later Colonel Nicol wrote—"The conduct of the battalion was, as always, superb. I remember Baily and Larret coming in wounded and apologising as if it was their fault." On the right flank, too, Captain J. W. Baden lost one of his carrier crews near a small bridge. The ground was swept by Machine Gun fire but Captain Baden badgered the Colonel for permission to go out to rescue the crew of two, 'til, at last, it was given. He was allowed to make the attempt only on the understanding that, if enemy were located, he would at once withdraw. He was able to get near enough to see that one of the crew was dead and that the other was no longer there, but there were enemy about and he had to return as ordered.

As soon as the first objectives were secure Captain Baden and Lieutenant D. Bean with some Pioneers started to recce a route back, by road, through Le Plessis Grimoult to fetch the fighting transport. A German prisoner volunteered to show them where the mines were and helped to lift them. The Adjutant was contacted, so that before dark the vehicles were able to join their Companies.

The reserve Companies moved up to pass through at 5.30 p.m. and it was as "C" passed through "D" that their Company Commander, Captain V. S. Baily, was wounded. Major Young after settling-in his own men went forward with "C" Company to help Lieutenant Wreford, who was the only surviving officer of that Company, in any way he could.

They forged ahead in great style in spite of the confused nature of the country and secured the second bound at Hameau au Roi. It was a hurriedly staged advance and called for initiative and determination on the part of each small sub-unit. The whole was very ably co-ordinated by Major Young, and a very large number of prisoners were taken.

The final bound for "B" Company was Le Saussay which lay away to the south-east at a distance of nine hundred yards. It led them through a tangle of hedgerows, old farms, and enemy strong points. The Company was organised into two parties each slightly below a normal platoon strength. Both met stiff opposition and on the right 2nd/Lieutenant E. A. Murcott led his party straight through our own artillery barrage onto his objective. This resulted in the enemy being caught cowering in his slit trenches, dug-outs and farms. Complete surprise was achieved and a very large haul of prisoners was taken. One enemy post held out and caused a number of casualties before it was crushed. 2nd/Lieutenant Murcott was, himself, slightly wounded and went back in the evening for treatment. The battalion did not see him again.

Private Richard Lancaster is mentioned in the battalion records of this "B" Company battle, for sticking to his Bren when four men around him had been killed, and for continuing to give covering fire until his ammunition was exhausted. So, too, is Corporal David Yorke whose section was following up against this Boche machine gun nest—there was a danger that the momentum of the attack would be lost. With great courage Corporal Yorke placed his Bren gunner and silenced the Machine Gun. He then led his section forward over open ground to storm a farm. Though grenades were thrown at them, they took the farm with a large number of prisoners. Corporal Yorke was awarded the Croix de Guerre.

A strange coincidence here, this very successful combination of two such British names as Yorke and Lancaster.

Corporal R. Love received the Military Medal in the attack of his Company on Hameau au Roi. His section was leading the platoon when it came under concentrated fire; the platoon commander was wounded and Corporal Love attended to his wounds and arranged for supporting fire from a tank. Then, under cover of this fire, he led his section up a hedgerow in which the enemy had strong positions.

In the "C" Company action at Hameau au Roi Sergeant T. Richardson took command of his platoon when Lieutenant Larret was wounded in a concentration of shells which injured many members of the Company. Under his leadership this under-strength platoon took forty-five prisoners on the final objective. Lance-corporal W. H. Hewitt with Private Robinson were commended for their gallantry in rescuing a wounded man from a cornfield outside the same village while it was still swept by Spandau fire.

The enemy reaction throughout the day was most stubborn. First he shelled Mont Pincon viciously in the morning—but mainly after the battalion had moved. Then he shelled and mortared the forming-up area and the start-line, and, finally, each stage of the advance. It was an exacting and confused day, for at no time could it be said that there was any clearly recognisable dividing line between Companies or objectives.

The battalion suffered seventy nine casualties, including seven officers. By 6.30 p.m. all objectives were securely held and three tactically important villages had been taken on the flank of the main road leading down the west side of the Falaise pocket.

Prisoners for the day numbered two hundred and forty-two, including twenty-four passed back through medical channels.

*　　*　　*

A Company of the D.C.L.I. was sent forward early in the night to strengthen the position, and the short hours of darkness were alive with patrols though it soon became evident that the enemy had pulled right back. Extracts from the Intelligence Log make interesting reading here:—

1615 hours	Pioneers complete mine lifting down centre track.
1617 hours	"D" Company report fire has ceased from the right.
1700 hours	Battalion HQ moves up to Les Hameaux.
1720 hours	Enemy aircraft "strafe" our area.
1730 hours	Carriers report fired on from building marked as hospital. ? Violation Geneva convention.
1830 hours	"B" and "C" Companies report consolidation complete.
1930 hours	One hundred and four prisoners evacuated by march-route.
2130 hours	One Company D.C.L.I. placed under command. To dig in between "C" and "B" Companies.
2130 hours	Search of captured documents has produced maps and traces including one code marked MOST SECRET (sent to Brigade).

2250 hours   Order from Brigade—Pay particular attention to right flank, enemy believed in Lenault.

2255 hours   "D" Company report—no enemy in immediate area.

0200 hours   From 214 Brigade—send patrol to point... to contact patrol which is going out from 151 Brigade.

0220 hours   Company of 5th D.C.L.I. now in position.

0230 hours   Runner from "A" Company reports all quiet on their front.

0300 hours   From 214 Brigade—Patrol from 1st Worcestershires will be in area... at 0500 hours.

0340 hours   Seventh Somersets to 214 Brigade—Patrols report no enemy found in farm..., track at..., or cross roads...

and so on, with an entry every twenty minutes until dawn when a further collection of miserable prisoners was waiting to be sent back to the prison cages.

Early on the tenth Colonel Nicol put the gunners on to a selection of probable enemy assembly and forming up areas in case they should be contemplating a counter attack. We later found that the Boche were in the process of withdrawing and some groups of them were well plastered.

Corporal McClernon led a recce patrol due south from Hau au Roi with a gunner observation officer. He left his patrol on some high ground and went on by himself—the F.O.O. following at a discreet distance. On a stretch of road he met a small bunch of enemy and they saw each other simultaneously. It was Corporal McClernon who came back!

Contact patrols pushed out south east towards the main road and no enemy were found. At the same time a Carrier section found Lenault unoccupied and held it until "A" Company group was sent to maintain contact with the enemy there—Major Baker was in command. They entered the village, but came under fire beyond the southern end. There was considerable enemy fire and his orders were to avoid casualties, so the Company contented itself with some aggressive patrols. The same evening Major Baker was wounded by mortar fire. The Company collected a number of prisoners and gained useful information about the flanks, but they were not happy in this position, being too far removed from the main body of the battalion. They were later relieved by armoured cars of the Recce Regiment.

Prisoners taken on the eleventh August admitted that they had only just been brought down from the Pas de Calais and Ostend beaches where they had been waiting for the "second Allied landing".

The battalion drove cross country to Cauville the same night and while it was digging in not far from the River Orne, came in for some heavy shelling. Brigadier Essame was visiting the Command Post at the time and he appreciated the hospitality of our half-dug trenches.

Another south-eastwards move was made in the afternoon, towards Mont Gaultier—a prominent spur on the banks of the Orne. The D.C.L.I. made an independent attack on our left.

Major Harvey led the battalion down from Cauville and the information was that Mont Gaultier was clear of enemy. "B" Company was to take up a position to the right of the track over the crest facing south. The rest of the battalion was to mop up.

The battalion advanced crocodile fashion along the track on the southern slope, Twelve platoon, led by Corporal McClernon, in the lead.

"B" Company had reached the "clear" position, when Corporal Baker saw enemy in the hedgerow between his platoon and the remainder of the Company, and opened fire. A general battle ensued in which Corporal McClernon was killed, and Private Foster and Lance-corporal Moody were taken prisoner (later making their escape by knocking their captor unconscious).

It was a very uncomfortable moment. The Company found themselves virtually in the middle of an enemy defensive position, and under fire from all three sides, with little or no cover other than the banks of the track and some ferns. One Machine Gun in particular was firing at point blank range only fifteen or 20 yards away. Major Harvey himself dashed forward and flung a grenade which, however, rebounded off the parapet of the position. Whereupon he kicked it, causing it to roll right into the trench where it exploded—killing the occupants.

At this stage Major Young, observing the leading Company's plight, called down artillery fire which came down level and just right of "B" Company (rather uncomfortably close, but it succeeded in silencing the opposition on the right flank). He further directed the tanks to a more favourable position to support the leading Company, and as the battle progressed organised fighting groups to ferret out isolated pockets of enemy—who were well down in the valley and giving trouble by sniping. A considerable number of them were taken prisoner.

The approach road was heavily mortared and among the casualties in the follow-up Companies were Captain B. Pearse (killed) and Lieutenant D. Bean (seriously wounded).

Lieutenant Bean had been ordered to follow the leading Company with his Pioneer platoon to clear the road of mines for the transport. This task was most efficiently carried out under mortar fire, and it is not possible to take cover when using Polish mine detectors. Later when "D" Company were held up Lieutenant Bean went on to help in any way he could as an infantry officer. When a combined infantry and tank attack was put in, he led his men forward with a Bren gun and they chased the enemy who started to run. After the attack he was on his way back to headquarters when he came across a wounded man in the ditch and he was attending to this man when another mortar concentration came down. He made no attempt to take care for his own safety but shielded the man from shrapnel with his own body and was badly wounded. It was his own Sergeant, Sergeant Martin who found him while going forward in a jeep to bring in "B" Company casualties. Lieutenant Bean was awarded the Military Cross, and for some time we heard news from England that he was slowly recovering, and then, on 30th October, he died. His loss was felt keenly in the battalion and he had served them well in many actions.

Of Corporal McClernon Colonel Nicol wrote—"He was the best type of soldier and a very gallant man. His conduct in battle was always an example to all and as a patrol leader he was quite first class, notwithstanding that he had an intuition that he would be hit sooner or later, and quivered from head to foot before setting out on a mission."

Again the records mention Major Young's fine leadership of his Company, and there is a reference to that moment when, through no fault of their own, the tanks were late in support of "B" Company, who were consequently pinned by the machine gun fire. Major Young, at great personal risk, ran across the open to the tanks and directed them forward to the point where "B" Company needed them.

Darkness was falling as the resistance was finally overcome. Some thirty prisoners were taken from the hill positions where the two Companies consolidated, with the remainder of the battalion a thousand yards to the west.

Once again the enemy withdrew during the night.

Chapter VII

THE CROSSING OF THE NOIREAU

REAKFAST was ordered at three-thirty in the morning of 15th August, for orders had already been received that the Brigade would cross the Noireau, a small tributary of the River Orne, on a broad front.

As frequently happened, the move down did not take place for several hours, but Captain J. W. Baden, with Pioneer Sergeant Martin, set off to reconnoitre for crossing places, with a dismounted Carrier section for protection. The road led trough the edges of the Graveyard of the Falaise pocket, strewn with the appalling wreckage of German transport, men, and animals.

On the north bank of the Noireau the country sloped gently upwards to the road down which the battalion would come. A lane ran down the distance from the road to the river bank, and then turned west for about four hundred yards to a large factory on the opposite bank. Behind the factory it forked, one branch going straight on, the other bridging the stream and turning south-west. There was a small village at the road fork.

The gap from the first road bend to the river was one hundred and fifty yards over open meadows, then the map showed a railway line on the far side, and another track running parallel at the foot of high, scrubby, cliffs.

The patrol made its way down the lane which was sunken and leafy, meeting only one obstruction—a large shed which had been dragged across the road. Sergeant Martin explored round it, and under it, for mines, and decided that it could be quite easily pushed out of the way by a carrier. They then reached the bend at the river.

Captain Baden placed the Bren teams out for cover, and started across the meadow with Sergeant Martin. They had gone about thirty yards when a low whistle from Sergeant Martin halted him. He had spotted, on the cliff opposite, a German sentry strolling with his rifle slung over his shoulder, his back slightly towards them. They were not seen, and doubled smartly back to the road.

Now began a tedious crawl along the road to the factory. The hedge was sparse, and only eighteen inches high. The road surface was strewn with mines, poorly disguised under a covering of dust. History will never know what language was used, but the pair crawled the whole way to the village without being seen.

They could now see German sections digging in on the slopes at both ends of the cliff; they were met by a young French workman anxious to give information. He gave great help in indicating that there were mines on the bridge approaches, on the level crossing, and at the foot of the cliff, and pointed to where the bridge itself was blown. He showed how one could still cross on foot at the breakwater.

"Les Anglais, les premiers Anglais" now went in to have a look at the mill which appeared to have been turning out metal barrels of synthetic rubber, or oil. It was quite empty, and they climbed all over it, making a lot of noise over rubble and broken glass. From the windows there was a good view of the river bed, and of the Germans digging-in machine guns in the orchard on the right, and on the bluff to the left. They took off their boots and steel helmets, and paddled the stretch of stream in which they were interested from one end to the other, under the lea of the south bank. It was a firm gravel bottom, and quite shallow. They picked a point about half way along the road where the Pioneers would clear the hedge and cut away the bank for the supporting vehicles.

The Germans either did not see them, or else would not believe what they saw. They possibly took the patrol for a couple of Russian farm workers having a day off!

Back at the mill end Captain Baden chose to have another look at the south side, and they did this from behind a small power house detached from the main building. It was fortunate that they did, because they now saw a much more serious obstacle—a mill race ten feet deep, and ten feet wide, with sheer brick sides, between the river and the railway. They found that the water was only a few inches deep so long as it flowed freely. Sergeant Martin made plans to bridge it by rolling in steel barrels from the factory, until it was filled to ground level—the gaps between barrels, he hoped, would let the water get away.

The reconnaissance was now complete, and they slipped behind the factory to make their get-away. But, no! The village had different plans. Their friend the workman was going to photograph his 'premiers Anglais', and Madame was going to pose with them. The village turned out to watch—this was '*an occasion*'. The hubbub was amazing; every-one seemed to have heard about it, except the Germans. Captain Baden persuaded them to go quietly away, but Madame, who turned out to be 'not at all bad looking', skipped behind the door with more joy than modesty and changed into her Sunday frock. Then she was photographed in front of her house between the two 'Tommies'—not two hundred yards from the Germans. A quick cognac was passed around, and the patrol left by a route which avoided the long crawl.

Captain Baden went round, and collected his covering party from the bend of the leafy lane, and they all got back to the battalion just before two o'clock.

The report was later given to Colonel Nicol. The Commanding Officer promised Sergeant Martin two bulldozers, and a section of sappers for the crossing.

*   *   *

Meanwhile the Commanding Officer had taken a small order group, with another section of carriers for protection, down to the river bank slightly to the left where they observed from behind farm buildings. From here, where they watched for three-quarters of an hour, no enemy movement was visible, but here also they had the greatest difficulty in preventing a crowd of enthusiastic French peasants from giving their presence away.

A Typhoon, swooping low over their heads, released its cargo of rockets dangerously close and scored a hit on some dump just over the stream, for a cloud of smoke rose from the target area. It was decided to return to the battalion.

During the afternoon plans were completed and a hasty meal was dished out. The start line was to be eight hundred yards from the river, and H hour six p.m., by which time it was hoped that the excessive heat of the day might have eased.

A heavy plan of covering fire was arranged from the ridges near the road, including a battery shoot by the Mortars, covering fire from the Carrier platoon Brens, and very heavy overhead support from the machine gunners of the 8th Middlesex Regiment.

Major S. C. W. Young was leading with "D" Company, and they advanced from the start line due south across the fields, using for cover the hedgerows, corn, and a small wooded knoll which was at the left end of the crossing sector. The enemy were now thoroughly awake and a lively fire, with some inaccurate mortar fire, started to come back.

"D" Company had a hard time reaching the factory and getting across the blown bridge, but once they got among the buildings the fighting resolved itself into isolated scraps with snipers and machine gunners. They were able to get across the mill race breakwater and establish a small bridgehead in the orchard.

"C" Company—the next to follow—had come up as far as the wooded knoll and were waiting for "D's" success signal. In this waiting position they were covered by quite a lot of fire from the German spandaus at both ends of the bluff. Fire from heavy mortars was also brought down on them and on the factory. They were not able to fire back, being unable to tell how far on to the south bank "D" Company had penetrated.

"C"—like other companies at this time—was down to two under-strength platoons. Major D. M. B. Durie sent one forward to the mill, covered by fire from the other at the knoll, and then this in turn was helped forward by "A" Company who were next in the advance. They made their way, with difficulty, over the obstacles and across the railway, changing their planned course twice owing to enfilading spandau fire and zig-zagged up the steep cliff in the centre of the battalion front towards their objective, a high piece of ground which lay above and beyond the top of the bluff. The ground on top was rocky, crossed with gullies, and studded with thick gorse. The final slope to the objective was up a 45 degree ridge, and the weather was not noticeably cooler as evening drew on.

"A" Company then moved through "D", at the mill, to consolidate on the right without much trouble. "B" had made a separate crossing well to the left and were going independently for a group of farm buildings. The Middlesex had given a tremendous volume of support in pinning the Germans down, and in the next two days several hundred German dead were counted on the Brigade front. Casualties, so far, had been by far the lightest for any big operation carried out by the battalion.

All Companies now started to dig in under harassing fire on a perimeter which covered about a thousand yards. The enemy had lost heavily and had withdrawn south across some fields to various isolated orchards. The Worcestershires and D.C.L.I. were over the river on our right.

"C" Company could see on their left the farm where "B" Company should be. It soon became evident that such was not the case. Just before dark Company Sergeant Major Trinder arrived at "C" Company to say that "B" had got divided soon after the river crossing and that he had only one platoon with him, he knew some men were lost along the wooded edge of the stream, and that only a few could have followed Major E. R. H. Harvey towards the farm.

In the fading light Major Durie told him to dig in with his men, and send patrols to the farm and the rear areas to try to make contact with the rest of the Company—with the idea of regrouping at first light. It was later found that Major Harvey had reached the farm and held on to it all night with two men, while parts of it were still occupied by the Boche.

Back in the valley the struggle to get the supporting transport up started as soon as the infantry were clear.

Sergeant Martin's pioneers were rolling barrels into the mill race, and standing up to their chests in water as the stream did not get away fast enough. The greater part of the drum dump had been set on fire by shells and as barrels blew up it was frequently necessary to jump into the river to avoid being roasted. A bulldozer was used to push a binding of earth and turf over the barrel bridge, but only a few carriers and anti-tank guns got across before it started to subside sideways under the pressure of water.

An all night struggle went on to keep the bridge in working order and in an effort to get anti-tank guns up the craggy slopes of the hill. The remainder of the tracked transport was able to get over by going west to the Worcestershires bridgehead.

*   *   *

Thus, on the morning of 16th August the position was as follows. Left "B" Company regrouping, and mopping up their farm and the fields around it. Centre and forward on the highest ground "C" Company dug in. Right "A" Company and behind them, still in the village area, "D" Company.

All Companies combed the front with fighting patrols. Corporal Barratt led a particularly good one from "C" Company. A small number of casualties were incurred and Boche L.M.Gs were located in a sunken lane running across the orchards in front.

Major Harvey took out a fighting patrol and cleared the sunken road. By noon we had tanks over the river at the factory and the battalion was ready to push forward.

Orders were issued for an advance by "C" Company to two road junctions beyond the present enemy positions—that is, due south. "D" Company was to move across and clear forward in front of "B". "A" to follow "C" and take over the first of their objectives when they had cleared it.

A troop of Sherman tanks of the Sherwood Foresters was with "C" Company as they moved off at 1.30 p.m., with Fifteen platoon leading. They followed a gully curving to the right which kept them in dead ground, avoided the open fields and orchards, and came up on their objective using tanks and infantry in short bounds of inter-supporting fire and movement from one hedgerow to the next. A small hamlet was found on the first cross roads and the tanks "brassed this up" with their guns from hull-down positions while the platoon went in commanded by Sergeant Richardson.

The enemy retreated hastily, leaving a small amount of equipment.

Major Durie now appreciated that to advance to his second bound would leave his left flank exposed, for he had heard over the wireless that "D" were held up in their attack on the village of Le Canet. He immediately sought and obtained permission to turn left and attack this village with Fifteen platoon, leaving Fourteen to hold the hamlet under Corporal Barratt.

Again tanks and infantry worked well together and the tanks reached the centre of the village near the church, firing freely, before turning south to attack an orchard which contained the majority of the enemy. A running battle lasted twenty to thirty minutes and resulted in a number of Germans killed, and fifteen prisoners.

"D" Company moved in just as the last houses were being cleared and took over the village. A quick conference was held and both Company Commanders agreed to exploit south by different routes—linking at the next road junction. Meanwhile Fourteen platoon at the hamlet had sustained, and beaten off, a small counter attack.

Sergeant Richardson reached his second objective, clearing up snipers with the aid of the tanks which had given first class support throughout. Company Sergeant Major Evans then went back with one man, by an unexplored route, to the hamlet and led up Fourteen platoon; he went back again and brought up the transport, and the day's gains were consolidated a few hundred yards further forward than had originally been hoped for. Here mines were located and an enemy half track was seen withdrawing—Major Durie, to his surprise, found that Corporal Knapp had dragged the Tellermines all clear of the road with the aid of his section, and without pioneer assistance. However the job was completed without accident.

There were still two more roads in front of the leading Companies, one small one to the right of "C", and one, a larger road of some importance, running right across with the village of Le Hamel in the centre, where several of these minor roads converged. Major Durie with one Bren gunner (Lance-corporal Vincent) went out on a patrol of the first road, and returned with twenty prisoners. Then night settled, and other patrols continued to bother the Germans on the larger road till dawn. There were some scraps during the night, and one of "C" Company's wounded was cared for by civilians until they moved up next morning. Le Hamel was strongly held until the small hours, but at 0800 hours on the seventeenth "C" Company moved in un-opposed.

They found the village 'stiff with mines, and enemy dead', and during the occupation took another ten prisoners, all deserters. By ten o'clock the village was consolidated and sappers were busy disarming the mines. Contact was made with the 5th D.C.L.I. who had penetrated to about the same depth on our right.

I must not pretend that this was a model attack; there had been movements of extreme confusion on the river bank, but it was the first clear-cut, self contained, battalion battle and the Noireau crossing had yielded a substantial haul of prisoners, together with the very large number of killed which fell to the Machine Gunners and Mortars. Our own casualties were comparatively light. Major D. B. M. Durie was awarded the Croix de Guerre with Gilt Star, and Sergeant Richardson was Mentioned in Dispatches for this operation.

"This is the pay-off for Dunkirk—traffic roars southwards after the retreating Hun". So wrote Major Young at about this time. Suddenly we were not in the front line at all. The Falaise pocket was crumbling, there was no longer a static front. After these two days of pushing and mopping up fresh troops went through taking all their transport with them. In twenty-four hours there was probably not one enemy still resisting within ten miles of the Somersets.

Within three days of the crossing an ENSA party arrived and gave an open air performance right where "D" Company's bridgehead had been.

But, what of our Frenchman who had witnessed the plan, the execution, and the success of the battle?

Throughout the fight he faithfully performed his self-appointed role of guide and comforter. He, and Madame, and their friends, tended the wounded and opened their house for first aid treatment. Later, when peace returned to the valley, the entente was sealed with a supper party. It is not known whether a bullock was really killed in action, but the villagers soon found one—and no one was ungallant enough to doubt their story.

Among those present were Sergeant Martin and members of the Support Company. The table groaned as it had not done for many a long day with roast beef, fruit, cheese, cognac, and, if memory serves, a bottle of "le bon Whiskey".

Chapter VIII

THE SEINE

HE following account of the initial crossing of the Seine is reproduced by permission of the "Western Gazette"—it is written by their military observer.

"Units of the 43rd (Wessex) Division, it is now announced, were the first British Forces to cross the Seine.

In a brilliantly planned assault, mounted at high speed, the 43rd Division secured a footing across the Seine at Vernon, some 50 miles north west of Paris, on the evening of August 25th. In spite of stiff German resistance, the Division, in a complicated amphibious operation, had established a firm bridgehead within less than 24-hours of the first crossing.

The assault across the Seine was preceded by a cross country move as rapid as anything yet seen in France. The 43rd Division surged forward over a hundred miles in three and a half days. Infantry of the leading battalions travelled some 90 miles in 'ducks' and were crossing to the assault within two hours of arriving in the concentration area.

The enemy had withdrawn from the small town of Vernon to positions on the high cliff on the eastern bank. From here the German machine guns completely overlooked the town and the approaches to the river front. Under cover of a smoke screen laid by the artillery, the infantry began the crossing in storm boats and 'ducks' at seven o'clock in the evening. Steep and muddy banks on both sides of the river, over 200-yards wide at this point, made the approach very difficult. The weeds of a submerged island fouled the propellers of the storm boats. A number of them stuck on unsuspected sandbanks.

With the assistance of the Royal Engineers of the Division, who were already preparing to bridge the river, nearly all the craft were finally launched. Some were early damaged, and casualties were caused by machine gun fire from the opposite bank. As the craft reached the other side many of the infantry found themselves impeded by thick mud before they could fan out to secure the crossing. A wide watercourse, which air photos and reports of local inhabitants suggested was dry, turned out to be impassable with liquid mud. But by darkness four companies were across, and had wiped out a number of German machine guns and pockets of enemy infantry.

The crossing continued under cover of darkness. By 2 o'clock in the morning the infantry of three battalions were on the eastern bank and leading companies were consolidating. At first light a fourth battalion began to cross on the demolished road bridge, on which a footing was just possible. Mopping-up in Vernonnet, immediately opposite the town of Vernon, and along the cliffs began.

During the night an earlier attempt had been made to cross on the demolished bridge. It came under severe fire from machine guns still holding out on the opposite bank. It was well after mid-day before these nests, concealed in the rocks and scrub, were finally eliminated. Our own machine gunners, firing from the houses on the river bank, and fire from tanks also gave valuable support to the infantry from the opening of the assault.

Exposed to direct fire from short range, the Royal Engineers attempted throughout the morning to span the river with a 680-ft long folding boat bridge. The rafts had been completed 200-yards up stream overnight in the face of German machine gun and mortar fire.

At first light they lay hidden under the lee of an island. Working in pitch darkness, a bulldozer had attempted to make an approach way down the steep 15-ft bank for ramps of the bridge. It drew enemy fire, but all preliminaries to the actual fixing of the bridge were finished early the first morning. It was not until 3 o'clock in the afternoon that the Royal Engineers, after a number of gallant earlier attempts, were really able to begin the actual construction of the first bridge across the Seine. At 6 o'clock it was complete.

The first vehicles, Bren gun carriers and supply vehicles of the infantry, followed by two more infantry battalions, began to cross immediately. During the second day tanks were rafted across at the rate of two an hour, and here, again, the mud on the far bank made exits difficult.

Enemy opposition, though patchy had made the river crossing perilous and difficult. Though our leading infantry had secured a firm footing the first night, machine guns on the cliff top, which the ground made it extremely difficult to get at, proved very troublesome. The Germans shelled the town with heavy guns spasmodically throughout the first two days. At mid-day on the second day they scored a lucky direct hit on the bridge. Within two and a half hours the Royal Engineers had repaired it and transport was again crossing. By early evening that day a Bailey Bridge had been constructed by Corps troops alongside the one-way floating boat bridge, and adequate maintenance routes assured.

Leading battalions of the 43rd Division had fought so well that the footing on the east bank was rapidly extended to form the first British bridgehead across the Seine. By the evening of August 27th, 48-hours after the first assault, all infantry units of the Division were across the Seine with machine gun companies and anti-tank and anti-aircraft batteries in support.

Before first light the next morning three Regiments of tanks had been put across. Field artillery were in action from behind Vernon. Within 72-hours the 43rd Division held the villages of Panilleuse, Tilly, Heubecourt, Haricourt, Bois Jerome, St. Quen, and Giverny, Le Pressoir, and Pressagny l'Orgueilleux on the flanks. A bridgehead four and a half miles east had been established. On the evening of August 28th the British armoured columns were moving fast across the Seine to thrust eastwards.

The rapid 100-miles move of the 43rd Division, with the establishment of the Seine bridgehead at the end of it, called for very careful maintenance plans. With bases suddenly 120-miles in rear, normal supply methods were out of the question. Sufficient supplies for some days ahead had to be carried with the Division, requiring extra load carrying vehicles. Some 90,000-gallons of petrol, 150,000 rations, and many thousands of tons of ammunition of all calibres, moved with each assault group. In all some 5,000 vehicles were involved in the swift assault of the Seine."

*   *   *

After its long drive, on 25th August the Seventh battalion was harboured in a wood near Pacy-sur-Eure for nearly twenty-four hours, and moved forward in the afternoon of 26th August to the Foret de Bizy. A meal which was being prepared was consumed hastily as orders were received for the river crossing at 7 p.m.

We crossed behind the 5th D.C.L.I., marching troops struggling in single file up and down the fallen sections of the railway bridge, mended and repaired in places with ladders and planks. The fighting transport used the Class 9 (nine-ton) bridge. During the night guides were busy assisting the 4th/7th Dragoon Guards to get their tanks across on pontoon rafts—a very tricky matter since the river level had been lowered by the Boche, and presented 5-ft high banks of soft mud.

The task of 214 Brigade was to expand the narrow bridgehead which had been gained, with 1st Worcestershires right (south east), 7th Somersets centre and forward, 5th D.C.L.I., left. The battalion marched to its area in the large Foret de Vernon without meeting serious opposition, and fortunately found the track leading up the spur to the north of Vernonnet dry and just passable to motor transport. Positions were occupied, as darkness was falling, in a tight diamond formation with "C", "D" and "B" Companies forward and "A" Company covering the rear. The whole place was heavily wooded with narrow rides and occasional clearings deep in bracken, there were no signs of battle and very few of the enemy. The night was quiet except for various civilian reports of enemy positions and contact was successfully made with the Worcestershires and the D.C.L.I.

At seven o'clock on the morning of the 27th considerable enemy machine gun fire was heard away on the left flank, it was directed against the D.C.L.I. A patrol went out from "B" Company and made a search, but no enemy were found. At eight, Brigade orders were issued for a battalion advance to control further track crossings deeper in the forest as soon as possible. Reports from all sides indicated that the enemy was withdrawing.

It was realised that the first step should be to gain control of an intermediate track junction, some way in front of the forward companies, to secure a firm base for the battalion advance. This task was given to "A" Company, who set out at about ten o'clock.

They reached their area without meeting opposition and sent a wireless signal to this effect, but shortly afterwards some mortar fire came down just south of the farm buildings at their track junction, and was followed by fire from two machine guns whose position they reported.

They were asked to confirm the map reference given, and an artillery concentration was then put down on the machine guns. "A" Company reported that as far as they could tell in the forest it had been near the enemy, but not on them—at the same time a fighting patrol from "C" Company went out and found no enemy in the area.

Meanwhile "D" Company, who were about to move, were ordered to stand fast until the information was checked. It seemed probable that "A" Company were not at the place they imagined themselves to be—and the misplaced artillery concentration rather confirmed it. It was not at all unlikely that this was the true state of affairs as the tracks shown on the map were frequently at variance with those found on the ground—moreover in the dense woods the rides and tracks all looked very much the same.

Hardly had "C" Company patrol reported back that there were no enemy, when "A" Company reported that they were surrounded, and called urgently for reinforcements. A second message stated that things were serious, but that they thought they could deal with them. A troop of tanks from 4th/7th Dragoon Guards had just arrived and these were sent forward at once; "A" Company were told by wireless that they were coming. This signal was not acknowledged.

The tanks went forward and wirelessed that they had reached our troops—it was assumed that they had reached "A" Company. Ten minutes later "C" Company said that a troop of tanks was fighting with them against some more enemy who had appeared, and it was realised that the vital help had not reached "A". The tanks were ordered to go on. A tank commander was killed, and the remaining two tanks got into difficulties. A fighting patrol was now ordered forward from "D" Company with the support of the tanks. This little group soon became involved in fierce fighting, and again the tanks lost contact with the infantry. The patrol was extricated with difficulty after suffering heavy casualties.

After the "C" and "D" Companies actions everything was quiet—nothing more was heard from "A" Company and it became evident that they had been over-run. No further sign was seen of the enemy though an attack flared up against the Worcestershires on the right. Patrols went out to the scene of the "C" and "D" patrol actions and the casualties were brought in.

Very early on 28th a reconnaissance patrol reached the "A" Company cross-tracks, but found no sign of them; they reported seeing only two Germans. The battalion advanced with a squadron of tanks of the Sherwood Rangers later in the day, and secured all its original objectives without any further enemy interference.

From subsequent examination of "A" Company's positions it appeared that the Company, which, like all others, consisted of two platoons, was too widely dispersed in view of the density of the forest.

German machine guns, less than 100-yards from the farmhouse gave covering fire from the German right, and the main attack developed against a gap of 30-yards between the two platoons. This gap was masked by dense forest and could not be adequately covered by defensive fire. Having penetrated the gap the enemy were able to enfilade both platoons from the rear.

Three dead and three wounded were found and civilians reported that between 50 and 60 prisoners had been taken away.

It is more likely that they were surprised by a large body of Germans—themselves retreating than that this loss was the result of a deliberately staged enemy trap. It was a type of operation which was undertaken frequently, and with success, in similar forests during the big withdrawals of the following spring in Germany, but coming after a great advance, and on the eve of the break-out across Europe, it was a bitter blow to the Battalion.

The tide of battle swept onwards, and peace settled on the forest. The armoured divisions were over the Seine, through the bridgehead and galloping across the plains of France and Belgium—some of the battalion transport had been loaned to the spearhead Divisions to help ferry forward their vast requirements of supplies. The Somersets set about making themselves clean and comfortable around the Chateau de Vernon, in the forward edges of the forest, and along the banks of the Seine.

On September 1st, Major L. Roberts arrived with a complete company of the South Staffordshire Regiment, 94 strong, to replace the lost "A" Company. It was cheering to get such a complete reinforcement, and it must be recorded that this Company merged itself with complete success into the life of its adopted Regiment serving with the battalion until the present time.

The fifth anniversary of the war was observed with a Church Service at the Chateau, and on the following day the Divisional Commander held a parade at which he decorated the following members of the battalion:*

Military Cross	Major S. C. W. Young
	Captain W. H. Goudie
	Lieutenant P. A. Eves
Military Medal	Private J. E. Gant
	Private L. Carpenter
	Private G. Barrell
	Private R. Homer.

* These were only the first of the Normandy decorations to come through—a complete list of awards and citations will be found at the end of the book.

On September 7th Lieutenant-Colonel H. A. Borradaile took command of the battalion. Games, football matches and recreation were arranged, and there were swimming parties in the Seine.

A number of men were lucky enough to get day trips to liberated Paris, where they were among the first British troops to be seen, and were given a great reception. It was strange, coming straight from the battlefields, to be in a great and busy capital city, among famous buildings and lovely gardens, gay boulevards, and pretty women; to be able to drink in a cafe, to walk the thick pile carpets of the Galeries Lafayette, choosing powder and perfume, and trying to look wise over the purchase of flimsy silken knick-knacks and fine silk stockings (at fine prices) to be sent home to war-weary England.

A battalion dance was held at the Salle-des-Fetes in Vernon.

With one eye on the canals and great rivers of Holland, trials were carried out in loading and rivercrossing in amphibious "ducks", and "D" Company gave a Brigade demonstration as a result of these experiments—for it was realised that with the swift advance of the Army into Belgium, our turn to move would call us forward into country of a very different nature and requiring a very different technique from that which had, so far, been experienced.

Holland

AND THE

Great Rivers

Chapter IX

DEVIL TAKE THE HINDMOST

Being an account of how the Somersets raced across the battle-fields of the past, in an endeavour to bring help to the Armies of the future. And of how the enemy was sometimes in their rear.

ORNING in September. Seven o'clock, and the date the fourteenth of the month. There is a crisp dew on the bracken of the Foret de Vernon, the air has the sharp tang of early autumn, and the promise of burning sunshine before noon. Wisps of mist in the hollows are stirred by the throb of warming engines. The lovely stillness is rent by the clatter and excitement of a battalion under orders to move.

Carriers, trucks, and guns pulling into place in the waiting column, spanners and hammers clanking over final adjustments, Sergeant Majors bawling at slow platoons, platoon sergeants hustling laggard men, cooks and Colour Sergeants hastily washing out the breakfast dixies, and loading cookers back on to the trucks, motor-cycle policemen chasing vehicles into their correct place, the R.S.M. getting marshalling reports from his police. Signal microphones nattering as the operators set up their "net", the Adjutant standing near the command set, ticking off completed serials against his march table. For in half-an-hour's time the Seventh Battalion will lead the Brigade, and "D" Company must be ready before then to lead them to the start point.

Speed? The best that can be made. Destination, Belgium and beyond.

Before the sun was hot, they had left behind the wooded Seine country, and the orchards, and the stubble fields. Over the Somme bridge, and across the plain to Beauvais.

A Frenchman asks for a cigarette—someone leans out from a Lloyd carrier and gives him a Player. He looks at it, without enthusiasm, puts it behind his ear; takes a packet of Camels from his pocket, lights one and saunters away.

Now Albert and Vimy are ahead, and the column rolls between the endless cemeteries of those who gave their lives that this day might never happen. There stands the Canadian memorial—the crosses are white and regular in the clear air. On again to the French border, in every little village halted vehicles are instantly covered by a swarm of cheering civilians. A carrier stops here and there with a broken track pin, or an over-heated engine. Drivers try to carry out repairs under a bombardment of fruit, flowers and small children. The clank of steel over the cobbled streets of Valenciennes.

Into the coal belt now, pitheads and slag heaps the main features of the scene. Cheering and singing mounting to a roar at Mons, tram bells clanging in unison in rows along the streets. People reaching up from the road to touch, if only for a moment, the hands of the passing soldiers. Not a few, I think, of those soldiers must have been near to tears that such a moment should be theirs. Somehow, in that moment, they felt rewarded for all the bitter weeks they had known since leaving home.

On through Nivelles, and towards the outskirts of Brussels. Was it too much to hope that the citizens of the capital should touch hands with the men of Yeovil, and the Mendip Hills? Just a few fields off the road lay the village of Waterloo. Flowers, apples, pears and plums—hands and baskets-full at every hamlet held up to be taken or tossed gaily into the interior of the trucks. Eight miles from Brussels, and the road forked away to the east into the lovely woods of Soignes, where Belgian nobility in its carriages used to drive on summer evenings. It was pleasant here to run for a while under the welcome shade of the trees.

Into historic Louvain in the late afternoon. Louvain decked with flags, and thronged with cheering crowds. Somewhere, on some street corner one caught a glimpse of Brigadier Essame, standing up in his car, beaming pride, and encouragement, to the passing troops. A group of nuns caught the column at a temporary halt, and went up and down handing up cups of tea.

A last stretch of eighteen miles, and the battalion pulled into a harbour near Diest. Speedometers had clocked one hundred and eighty five miles for the day.

✳ ✳ ✳

Next day saw only a short move—to a concentration area just north of the Albert Canal, near Bourg-Leopold. The same evening a lone German bomber dropped one bomb which fell in the middle of the battalion area. Corporal Picton of the Anti-Tank platoon and Private Saunders of the Pioneer platoon both received severe wounds which proved fatal. Private Boreham, of the Anti-Tank platoon, relates how he was working on his gun when he heard the bomb coming. He started to run for a slit trench, but fell over the trails of his gun, he got up, ran a few yards, and fell over a tent rope. He was still lying there when the bomb landed.

The tremendous plan of the coming days was made known to everyone. Three airborne divisions were to be dropped on key points commanding the road to Northern Holland. 30 Corps on the ground would be the spearhead which would link up with them. Guards Armoured Division leading, followed by 43rd Division. The Seventh Somersets would be the leading battalion of 214 Brigade. They would ride in amphibious "Ducks".

The Corps task was to force a way through to the Zuyder Zee, and thus cut off the 300,000 German troops reported to be in Western Holland. The role of 214 Brigade was to seize and hold an area in the forest north of Apeldoorn.

Sunday 17th September was a brilliant day, the Airborne drop began shortly after noon. There started probably the first battle in history to be watched, minute by minute, by the entire world.

17th September	101st U.S. Airborne division capture Eindhoven, and secure the Maas bridge, at Grave, intact.
	82nd U.S. Airborne division dropped on the southern outskirts of Nijmegen on the river Waal.
	1st British Airborne division dropped west of Arnhem on the northern mouth of the Rhine.
18th September	Guards Armoured division link up with U.S. 101st.
19th September	British spearhead crosses the Maas bridge at Grave, pushing for Nijmegen.
20th September	Guards reach U.S. 82nd Airborne division at Nijmegen.

In the evening of 20th September the Somersets moved with their special column and travelled seventy miles through the night, "D" Company again forming the advance guard. Daylight found them between Grave bridge and Nijmegen. Though they did not know it then, the corridor up which they were driving was scarcely eight hundred yards wide. There was no time to extend the flanks while the task was to run a life-line up to Arnhem. Often odd parties of enemy were to cut the road behind them, and desperate local battles began between gunners, supply units, and groups of raiding Boche.

During the morning 21st September they passed small groups of Americans holding their original objectives, they saw airborne reserves dropping on Nijmegen, windmills, and the small, neat, houses of Holland with spotless curtains and crystal-clean windows.

The Commanding Officer went forward to find out about the Nijmegen bridge. This was intact, but under very heavy shellfire. American paratroops had a small bridgehead on "the Island" (as the land between the Waal and the Neder Rijn became known), and a Guards Sergeant in a single Sherman tank had rushed the four hundred yard long bridge in the face of enemy fire. We moved into the city in the early afternoon with orders to attack over and beyond the river.

The plan was for 129 Brigade to advance up the main road through Elst to Arnhem while 214 Brigade moved on their left via Oosterhout, Valburg and Driel. The Somersets were to lead on this left route, and to their column were added two "Ducks" specially loaded with reserves for the Airborne—particularly medical supplies, and ammunition.

Nijmegen had two bridges—the road bridge to the east allotted to the Guards, and the railway bridge, also suitable for road traffic, by which we were to cross. 130 Brigade were already in a tight bridgehead on the far side with Fourth Dorsets on the river bank, beyond them was an American airborne battalion. We were told to wait and take cover in houses. There was very heavy shelling at the bridge approaches. The city was in a turmoil of excitement and confusion. In the town there was cheering and kissing at one end of a street, and shooting at the other.

Lieutenant-Colonel Ivor Reeves, who commanded the battalion some time later, wrote this account of an Order Group in a liberated town—not Nijmegen, though it draws the scene equally well.

"The difficulty of collecting one's Order Group, of thinking and giving out orders, of making oneself heard and linking the various sub units of supporting arms together—amongst the mass of the populace still crowded round, still cheering, still flag wagging, still thrusting plums at you, still kissing you and asking you to post a letter to America for them, or give them some petrol, or to come to their house for a drink, offering you information about the enemy, or inviting you to kiss the baby—has to be seen to be believed."

In the confusion at the bridge approaches and the distraction of the shelling the battalion column got broken and Captain H. J. R. Catford (Commanding "HQ" Company and "A" Echelon) found himself in charge of a portion of it which was waved-on across the road bridge behind the Guards. When he checked up he found he had with him a section of carriers, the pioneers jeeps, the two "Duck" loads for Arnhem, various odd Gunner vehicles, five cooks trucks with C.Q.M.S.s and cooks, part of the R.A.P., a troop of seventeen pounders and a troop of R.Es. He deployed them for local protection, and went back to try and find the battalion. It is a long story, and has lost nothing in its frequent re-telling. The outcome of it was that the cooks prepared the evening meal on the wrong side of the bridge, practically in the front line, and took it back to their Companies. But Nijmegen is a big place and they couldn't find the battalion, which, meanwhile, had cooked and eaten its reserve compo ration. "A" Echelon settled down to hold its piece of the Island with the troops who were already over.

The Welsh Guards, from their bridgehead, were held up by strong enemy positions at the village of Oosterhout. Their tremendous drive had spent itself at last.

It was now getting dark and it was clear that the "Island" could not be rushed. Lieutenant-Colonel H. A. Borradaile went over the railway bridge twice during the night on reconnaissance, and an attempt by the battalion to reach the Rhine, after clearing Oosterhout, was ordered for 0700 hours 22nd September.

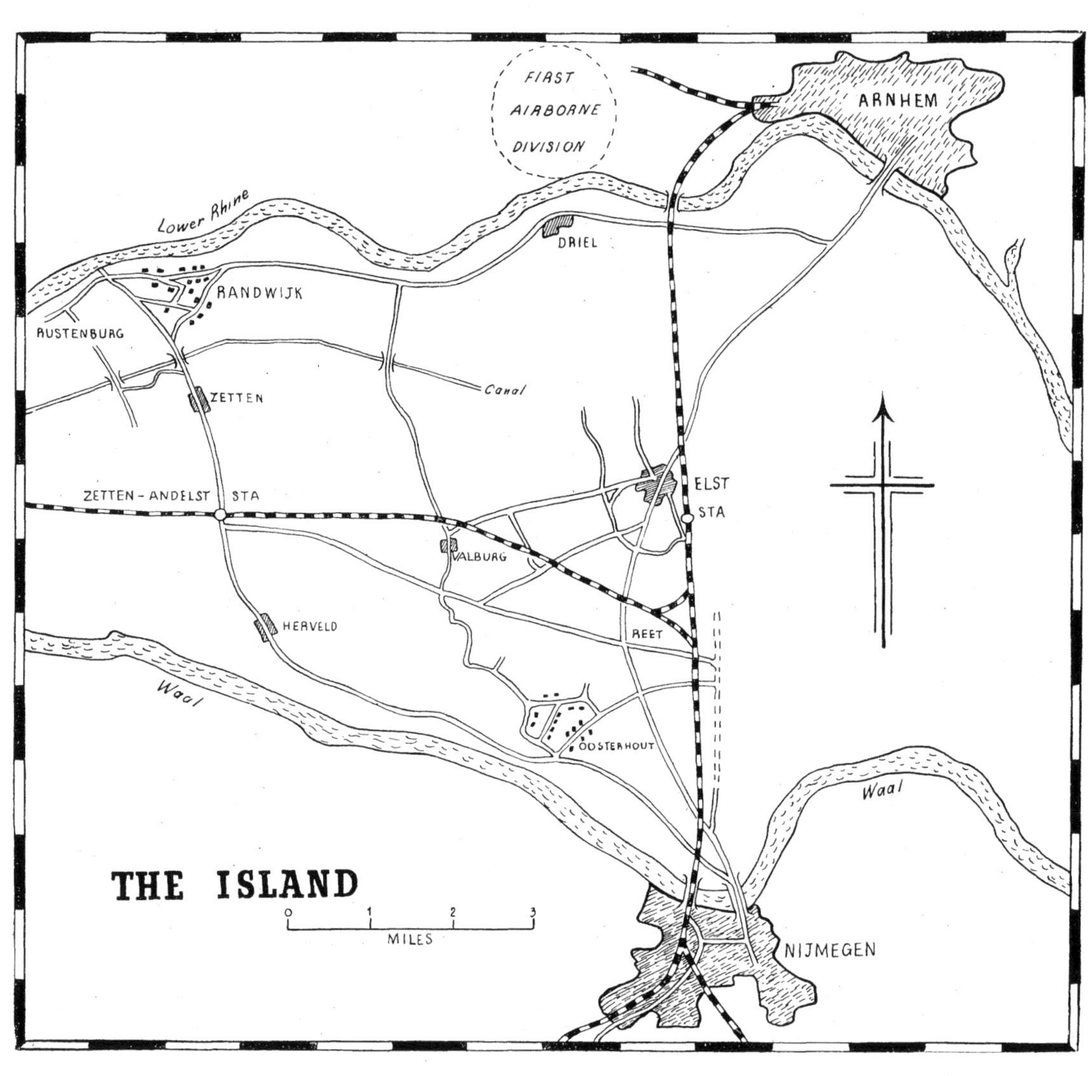

FIRST AIRBORNE DIVISION
ARNHEM
Lower Rhine
DRIEL
RANDWIJK
AUSTENBURG
ZETTEN
Canal
ZETTEN - ANDELST STA
ELST STA
VALBURG
HERVELD
REET
Waal
OOSTERHOUT
Waal
THE ISLAND
0 1 2 3
MILES
NIJMEGEN

Chapter X

"THE ISLAND"

Phase One · OOSTERHOUT

THE battalion crossed Nijmegen railway bridge at 0700 hours, with Major S. C. W. Young's "D" Company still as vanguard. They had under command the tanks of "A" Squadron of 4th/7th Royal Dragoon Guards, a troop of seventeen pounders, machine gun and mortar platoons of 8th Middlesex Regiment, and in support of them 179th Field Regiment R.A., and one battery of self-propelled twenty-five pounders.

The bridge bore evidence of the bitter struggle that had taken place—dead American parachutists, dead Germans and smashed machine gun nests. It was slightly damaged, and under fire from the German guns.

The battalion recce group had already made contact with an American airborne battalion who here holding the bridgehead and were to withdraw as soon as the battalion passed through them.

Shortly after the battalion started, elements of the Corps Armoured Car Regiment started to pass it, following one troop which, in the early morning mist, had already that morning passed along that road and succeeded in reaching the Neder Rijn. At 0945 hours the leading car was knocked out and "D" Company was held up by fire from a tank and some infantry just outside Oosterhout.

An attempt was made to deal with this with P.I.A.T.s, but the leading troops were unable to make any headway, being pinned to the ground some seventy yards from the enemy. The leading platoon commander, Lieutenant W. Tharp, was wounded. Major Young was severely wounded by a shell whilst making his reconnaissance.

The Commanding Officer came forward and ordered "D" Company to make use of smoke to endeavour to withdraw the forward platoon, so that artillery fire could be brought down on the enemy. On his return to battalion headquartiers he ordered "C" Company

Group, including one troop of tanks, to move (right flanking) to an area north of the village. "C" Company moved off at 1100 hours, but by 1220 hours was held up by heavy mortar fire from an orchard.

They had, by this time, reached a position about level with the village and three-quarters of a mile north of it. They were joined by a Dutch policeman in full uniform who jumped into a ditch with the Company Commander, and sketched plans of the German lay-out as he knew it. He stayed with the Company as they attempted to work their way forward along the dykes, and waved happily to Dutch civilians who peered from their houses, watching the attack.

A number of young prisoners fell to "C" Company—so young that they must only recently have been transfered from the Hitler Youth. The Dutchman interrogated them, waving his revolver so violently that they were terrified, as also was Major Durie who expected to see them shot at any moment. "For four years" said the policeman "I have been ordered about by these young so-and-so's. Now I am going to do the talking".

Information wrongly reached battalion headquarters that "C" Company had had severe losses. In fact they were only firmly held up, and later were able to move up to consolidate beyond the village.

In the meantime "D" Company (now commanded by Captain N.H.J. Cox) had succeeded in withdrawing their forward troops, and were preparing to send out a tank-hunting patrol to deal with the enemy tank.

The battalion found itself in the unenviable position of being strung out along a dyke road, its transport spaced at regular intervals with practically no cover. Solid shot from enemy 88's was whistling viciously across the road.

At 1300 hours the Brigade Commander visited the battalion, and it was decided to put in a battalion attack, supported by most of the Corps Artillery. The attack was made left-flanking by "A" and "B" Companies, each with one troop of tanks in support, who formed up under cover of the dyke road. "A" Company right, "B" Company left, the dividing line between them running due north from the bend in the road south-west of Oosterhout, and therefore diagonally opposite "C" Company. The attack was supported by four Field Regiments, one Medium Regiment and one Heavy battery, besides the 4.2 mortars and our own 3-inch mortars.

The fire plan was on a time basis, the concentration starting at H-15, and lifting three hundred yards at H. and at H+20. The timed fire plan ceased at H+40.

H hour was fixed for 1430 hours, but had to be delayed to 1520 hours in order to give the artillery time to get ready.

74

The attack went in according to plan. Resistance was not heavy, and was quickly overcome. By 1615 hours both forward Companies were on their objective and mopping up was being completed. By 1700 hours the village was clear, and "C" Company was ordered to move to the area of the church. "D" Company had already moved up with battalion headquarters.

During the mopping up prisoners were coming in so fast that they were sent running down the road to headquarters without escort.

The total bag for the day was one hundred and thirty nine prisoners, one Quartermaster's stores completely equipped, one Mark III tank (undamaged), one 88 mm gun, and five small A.A. guns. Our casualties were nineteen wounded.

The most bitter loss of the day was that Major Young, after leading the vanguard all the way from the Seine, died of wounds while under operation two days later. Of him Colonel Borradaile said—"Without a doubt he was the most popular officer in the battalion — the men have felt his loss tremendously. As a Company Commander, with his experience and knowledge of battalion affairs, he was all that a Commanding Officer could wish for".

It was later learned that after the Oosterhout attack the ammunition immediately available to the Corps Artillery was down to three rounds per gun — so difficult was the task of getting reserves up the dangerously narrow corridor.

The Military Medal was awarded to Lance-corporal A.L. Cockayne for bold leadership of a section of "A" Company. His task was the local protection of Company headquarters which was hindered by heavy small arms fire in a closely built up area. The section carried out its task with marked success, and later carried out an attack which resulted in the capture of twenty prisoners.

The battalion received a personal message of congratulation from the Corps Commander after this battle.

The Brigade Commander had already dispatched the 5th D.C.L.I., who had taken over our two "Ducks" of ammunition, to pass trough us and continue the advance. The same evening they reached the river bank at Driel, almost opposite to the woods where First Airborne were making their desperate stand.

Phase Two · Battle report · E L S T

Next day, the morning of 23rd September, the battalion was still in Oosterhout. At 0530 hours orders were received that the battalion was to move to the area of Molenhoek and to be clear of Oosterhout by 0630 hours. This was not possible and the head of the column moved off at 0630 hours. The tail came under some enemy long range small arms fire (probably from a tank) as it left the northern outskirts of the village. The area indicated proved unsuitable on recce and by 0830 hours the battalion was concentrated just south of Valburg.

In the meantime the Commanding Officer had gone to Brigade 'O' Group at 0730 hours. On his way back the jeep was shot up by an enemy tank which had moved back into the outskirts of Oosterhout. Both the driver, Private Setter, and the Intelligence Officer, Lieutenant Doran, were wounded; Private Setter died that evening. The Commanding Officer escaped with a scratch and was able to get back to the battalion and issue his orders at 1030 hours for the attack on Elst in conjunction with the 1st Worcestershires.

The battalion objective was the southern half, the 1st Worcestershires being responsible for the rest of the town to the north. The route was via Valburg. A squadron 4th/7th Dragoon Guards was in support of the battalion and the Divisional artillery was available to support the Brigade.

At 1155 hours the operation was delayed half an hour as 130 Brigade were occupying the road during their move north to the Rhine bank.

At 1430 hours, after the Commanding Officer had attended a further Brigade 'O' Group, the battalion objective was changed to the cross roads south-west of Elst. The road was still occupied by 130 Brigade, but in the meantime all rifle companies were to move across country to secure the start line and to act as a block to enable the Divisional Commander to move north on his recce. The leading Company moved off at 1455 hours and by 1600 hours all Companies were in position. About the same time the tail of 130 Brigade cleared the road and zero hour for the attack was fixed for 1700 hours.

The battalion moved off as planned and "C" Company reached the objective with no opposition at 1700 hours. "D" Company was immediately pushed on to secure a road junction astride the main road. It met slight opposition but gained its objective just as light failed, taking ten prisoners.

All Companies were now in position, eight hundred yards south-west of the town, in a compact lay-out with the battalion right covering the main road running north to Arnhem.

Now "D" Company, who had got on to the main road unbeknown to the enemy, were having a good time. Within the next hour the bag consisted of two DRs, one 20 mm A.A. gun complete with crew and towing vehicle, one artillery officer complete with car and one ration truck which was hit by a P.I.A.T. Most of this traffic was going from north to south where the enemy was still holding up 129 Brigade in the area of Reet.

However, well after dark, one tank moving in the opposite direction managed to crash past them.

At 0330 hours "D" Company reported a considerable number of enemy moving north along the road. Artillery fire was brought down, causing a certain number of casualties but the majority did succeed in getting by and moving into Elst.

Editor's Note.

"I am quoting the battle report as closely as possible here, omitting only map references which would not be of interest. The night was for "D" Company what they themselves would call 'a bit of a party'. They were alternately fighting the Boche who were trying to withdraw from Reet to Arnhem, and those who were trying to get reinforcements from Arnhem to Nijmegen. It is evident that several times in the night they were out-numbered, and it was inevitable, for they had only moved in at dusk, that their defences were not as co-ordinated as they would normally have been. The saving factor was that the enemy's information was chaotic."

At 0730 hours on 24th September, "B" Company moved forward supported by one troop of tanks and against slight opposition occupied another sector of the main road.

At 0925 hours, as a result of orders from Brigade, "A" Company was instructed to cut across the main road and move due east to the railway line. While the Commanding Officer was giving these orders, the Company area was strafed by German fighters but there were no casualties. By 1030 hours "A" Company with one section Anti-Tank guns were in position, having taken two prisoners belonging to S. S. Waffen.

The rest of the day was quiet on our front while the Worcestershires tried to get on, having been held up on the northern road by considerable enemy opposition.

At about 1830 hours, however, orders were received for a Company group to occupy the station. "A" Company were ordered to move there but within two hundred yards were held up by enemy machine gun fire. As it was then dark, the Commanding Officer ordered "A" Company to return to their original positions and to maintain contact by patrols.

On the morning of 25th September "B" Company were ordered to attack and secure the area of cross roads in the middle of Elst, as the Worcestershires were still held up to the west.

The Company supported by a troop of tanks moved off at 1000 hours. One platoon moved on the right of the main road and one on the left, through very thick, enclosed, country with many houses and small orchards. One tank which tried to get through this country was immediately ditched and the other two had to move up the main road.

The platoon on the right was soon held up by machine gun fire across the open ground. The advance on the left of the road, supported by our mortars continued without opposition up to about three hundred yards from the objective. Here it was held up by machine gun fire and snipers at very close range. Just before this, both the remaining tanks had been knocked out by an Anti-Tank gun from the area of the cross roads. The Company signallers had both become casualties and so the Company was out of communication. The Commanding Officer moved forward to discover the situation and finding that the Company was pinned by close range fire, ordered them to withdraw three hundred yards in order to allow artillery fire to be brought down on the enemy. This was done, the artillery fire including one Medium Regiment and also the 4.2 and 3-inch mortars was brought down at 1500 hours. The Company moved forward and took its objective, and the offending Anti-Tank gun, without further trouble.

In the meantime "C" Company had moved up west of the town to relieve a Company of the Worcestershires for a further attack. At 1330 hours "D" Company were ordered to move up to occupy "B" Company's original position.

The Somersets consolidated in the new positions, and the Worcestershires came up on their left without further trouble. It was evident that the Germans had decided to abandon Elst; four companies of them, with ten tanks, were seen by the D.C.L.I. heading back for the Rhine. They were attacked by Typhoon fighters in addition to being engaged by our machine guns and artillery.

From Elst it was four and a half miles by road to the bridge at Arnhem. The German air force was making repeated efforts in our rear to destroy Nijmegen bridge.

Phase Three · RANDWIJK

The Fourth Battalion The Wiltshire Regiment took over Elst on 26th September, and the Somersets went into reserve. One night was spent in the (comparative) rest area of Herveld.

At noon the next day information was received that the enemy had crossed the Rhine, in some strength, west of Arnhem and had pushed back our armoured car screen at Randwijk. This was thought to be a diversionary attack and the battalion was ordered up to restore the situation.

At 1215 hours the Divisional Commander arrived and shortly afterwards Brigadier Prior-Palmer, Commanding 8th Armoured Brigade, who had been given the task of containing the enemy. The situation was as follows—One Company of the Seventh Hampshires supported by tanks had been fighting in the eastern outskirts of Randwijk but had not been able to occupy the village and were then back in their original position. Stops, consisting of 43rd Recce and 12th K.R.R.C., had been established along the line of the canal. These were not in touch with the enemy, whose numbers were estimated somewhere between three hundred and six hundred.

The Commanding Officer decided to move along the two roads leading north from the 'stops' to Randwijk and Rustenburg. "A" Company on the right, "C" Company on the left, each with one troop of tanks in support and with one section Anti-tank, one section Mortars and one section Carriers under command.

These Companies were to use their tanks etc. for a quick lift up to the line of the 'stops'.

Again the column was confined to the dyke roads, and tank movement was restricted by deep ditches.

THE RUSTENBURG BATTLE. Major D. B. M. Durie M.C. writes—"For C. Company, in particular, the Rustenburg battle was a 'War of Nerves'. We were all in good form on the evening of 26th September at Herveld, for Dutch hospitality was up to the usual high standard. We had just come out of smouldering Elst following its final capture after some days of bitter fighting.

Our mental state was unprepared next morning to receive the news that the Germans had crossed the river Lek at Rustenburg with between three hundred and six hundred men. However, having received our orders we proceeded up the road with a troop of tanks in support to capture the dyke road commanding the ferry that the Germans had used for their crossing.

We debussed from our tanks at Hemmen canal bridge and passed through the 12th/60th Rifles who had no definite information about the enemy. A. Company were on our right moving on a road parallel to our route, but on our left there was nobody for approximately two miles.

Our route was the usual Dutch scene—ditch and willows on either side of the road with occasional lone farms, houses, and orchards. The Boche were well dug in and concealed, and we soon found that the best method of dealing with them was by moving up the wet ditches rather than flanking attacks over the very flat ground on either side of the road. Sergeant Woods and Private Pomeroy (of 13 Platoon) firing Bren guns from the hip played a big part in clearing one of the toughest strong points, killing three of the enemy and taking twelve prisoners. During this battle we were attacked by approximately fifteen to twenty low flying German fighters, but had the good fortune to suffer casualties neither to men nor vehicles.

By 2030 hours we were approximately five hundred yards short of the apex of a large triangular orchard, the base of which ran parallel to the dyke road flanking the river. We could see the high ground on the opposite side of the river and movement forward had to be very stealthy. The light was beginning to fade and our troop of tanks had orders to return to their forward rally. Owing to the heavy rain and movement along the ditches the No. 18 wireless set had got damp and ceased to function. The Company Commander, therefore, decided to consolidate short of this orchard and locate enemy positions in the orchard and dyke road with a view to final attack at first light.

At about this time the enemy increased his mortar fire (two of our Anti-tank section were killed) and started firing Anti-tank solid shot, smoke bombs, and parachute flares. It was all rather weird and we speculated on these somewhat new tactics. We surmised that he was probably pulling right out of his bridgehead.

The Commanding Officer arrived and told Major Durie that it was imperative to secure the ferry crossing that night. By the light of the burning farm buildings a plan was made over rain-soaked maps, to put in a night attack to clear the orchard and capture the dyke road.

The Divisional artillery saturated the forward side of the orchard, later lifting to the rear and finally on to the area of the road. The Company took full advantage of this barrage by 'Leaning on it' so closely that at times the mediums were falling behind us. The barrage was apparently too much for the Boche for we found the many newly dug weapon slits empty. The Company carried out a tight consolidation with great speed and supporting arms were up and in position less than ten minutes after the objective was taken. Local patrols up to the river bank failed to make contact but the whole Company stood-to at full strength until dawn.

As dawn broke we could see that our positions were completely overlooked from the high ground on the opposite side of the river and movement by day forward of the dyke had to be ruled out. However, we held the initiative and spent the day showing our strength by hitting every sign of enemy movement with either artillery, three-inch mortars, or small arms. Lots of demoralised Boche came in to surrender, but one S. S. officer crept up to 13 Platoon's weapon slits and wounded three men with his pistol before Private Bennett (the carrier driver) riddled him with a Bren".

During the night there was one other incident worthy of mention. The Intelligence truck was, for some reason, used to take up "C" Company's food. On leaving the Company for the return journey, the driver took the wrong road and went off along the dyke. On passing Randwijk, still held by the enemy, it was fired on. The two men in it 'baled out' and managed to reach the 7th Hampshire Company on the right, from which they were returned the next day. The truck was also recovered the next day undamaged and with its contents intact.

Major L. Roberts M.C. with "A" Company had launched an attack on Randwijk at the same time. He says—

"Pitifully exposed to torrential rain we made the journey to the canal on Sherman tanks and carriers. There the situation was as the Commanding Officer had described—a flat expanse of marshy ground up to the southern fringe of Randwijk village, visible some eight hundred yards away, and completely dominated by the high ground the other side of the Lek.

Artillery smoke was bravely trying to conceal our nakedness, but judging from the 88 mm reports it was obvious that the tanks could not cover those eight hundred yards unscathed, and that they would have to support us from the canal area with indirect fire.

A very bedraggled 9 Platoon, commanded by a Canadian officer, Lieutenant W. B. Mottrom, went forward as vanguard, hugging the hedgerows. The eight hundred yards were covered without incident other than random shellbursts, and the platoon made the right-angled turn along the road skirting the south of the town. Then began a nerve-racking advance past the byroads which ran into the maze of houses of the village, which might easily pour forth enemy ambush parties into our flank or rear. The rear platoon dropped off pickets to deal with this risk. We advanced some hundreds of yards, but made no contact. All the time it was pouring with rain, the 88s were sharply barking from the opposite bank and shells would explode near us, but mainly behind us at the turn, where I could see some carriers which had run the eight hundred yards gauntlet and were now prancing out of the way of the shells.

Suddenly, as if to add to our discomfort, two Messerschmitts swooped down from nowhere and strafed the road with machine gun fire. It's quite remarkable how troops disappear on such occasions. Ditch or hole leap to the eye—legs propel with piston-like urgency—a flying leap, and you wait and hope panting with fear and thrill.

On for another two hundred yards—when should we bump the enemy? Perhaps they weren't there at all? Such thoughts had begun to seize the mind when the expected spandau trilled into life. Down went the section leading on the left of the road, one man severely, another slightly, wounded. They disengaged and returned the fire, which came from behind a knocked-out tank some three hundred yards to our front. The business of accurately locating and estimating the positions and strength of the enemy was now brilliantly done. Lieutenant Mottrom, who had regrouped his whole platoon on the more covered right of the road, passed information over the No. 38 set, which I passed verbally to Captain Ian Bridges, R.A., who in turn passed it back to the guns over his set, which was in a 15-cwt truck.

A 15-cwt truck—how everything conspired against us!

The salvos of shells were corrected amid exchanges of machine gun fire with the aplomb of a Salisbury Plain artillery exercise. It was interrupted by an enemy burst of fire smashing through the windscreen of the truck and between Captain Bridges, his driver and myself, all standing behind. The driver fell, wounded by a bullet and was evacuated. At last Lieutenant Mottrom announced triumphantly that the shells were plumb on, and that the enemy were at least a platoon strong on the right of the road with more on the left. Meantime Corporal Pete Maskell was back from a patrol I had ordered out to find the enemy's right flank. Despite heavy fire—I learned later that a German had put a bullet through the side of his steel helmet at point blank range—he brought back the exact position of the enemy and estimated their strength left of the road to be a strong platoon. At this stage therefore we had the enemy's exact position and flanks, had registered the artillery, and could safely say he was in company strength.

The time now seemed ripe for an attack—company against company—but there were many considerations which made it also seem untimely. My set to the Commanding Officer had been rendered unuseable long ago by the rain, it was now quite dark, I knew nothing of C. Company's whereabouts, and my own men were extremely tired, wet and hungry. I therefore decided to make a company strong point some two hundred to three hundred yards from the enemy locality in the shape of a triangle with 7 Platoon as the apex on the road, 9 Platoon back on the left and 8 Platoon and Company Headquarters back on the right. But how to get back the 15-cwt with its precious wireless set, and the road under direct fire? The only way was to shell the enemy, and under this cover Captain Bridges turned the truck round in the narrow road and drove it back safely.

That night, in the pouring rain, we shelled the wretched Germans mercilessly whenever they made the slightest noise. One single mortar bomb would be answered by the troop, battery, or the whole regiment. We dished out dinner, held an order-group for a dawn attack.

The Commanding Officer came in the early morning and he approved the plan, saying we would be supported by the divisional artillery.

We dished out breakfast. The risks and the difficulty involved in doing this were very great, but they had to be taken. While still dark a patrol was sent to find out if the enemy, now quiescent probably through our shelling, was still there. Its fire was returned in good measure.

At 0630 hours the attacking Platoons, 8 and 9, went forward from their overnight positions, supported by a divisional concentration and the three-inch mortars to keep the village of Randwijk quiet, and, more closely, by 7 Platoon who thickened the covering fire with guns moving along the flanks of the attacking troops. The attack was a huge success mainly owing to the tremendous weight of artillery. The enemy in their slits in the wood must have experienced a foretaste of hell, for several slits had direct hits and many Germans were totally dazed. We took more than our own numbers in prisoners alone, and forged on to link up with C. Company who were now on the river at the ferry. The battle was not quite over, however, for some S.S. who had evaded our mopping up waylaid our transport as it came up with the ammunition. A lively battle was waged by the drivers, and the S.S. finally escaped into the village. Randwijk was later mopped up, after a gun duel around the church.

The enemy's total casualties were six killed and some one hundred and thirty prisoners, casualties inflicted by a Company which had already fought that week actions at Oosterhout and Elst, and was then only seventy men on the ground. Our casualties were two killed and five wounded.

So much for the success of this German attempt to distract 43rd Division's attention from the rescue of the Airborne Division".

*   *   *

The two Companies had taken well over a hundred and fifty prisoners. The men of Wessex were now all over the "Island", and the Fourth Battalion Dorset Regiment, together with Polish Airborne reserves had already crossed the Neder Rijn and reached First Airborne.

Some supplies were ferried across, but the vital bridges were in German hands, and it was becoming evident that the Rhine barrier would not be crossed without another major operation. When the orders were finally given for that gallant band to withdraw, it was the 43rd Division which covered them over the river and brought them back to the Allied lines.

Chapter XI

WHICH TELLS OF A DREARY MONTH
AND A MAD MINUTE

*F*OR six more days we remained on the Island, doing alternate spells of 48-hours on the river line, in the Randwijk area, and 48-hours resting a few thousand yards back, around Zetten and Zetten-Andelst. They were days of settled autumn weather and life was pleasant among the immaculate fruit farms. The Dutch people were warm hearted and kind, though their villages were well within range of the German guns. We were billeted with their families and lived in schools and farms, bakeries, cottages, and butcher's shops—every house which had room for some "Tommies" was thrown open. Battalion headquarters was in the four-storied school at Zetten which commanded a fine view up and down the Rhine—for some reason unknown it was never hit by shellfire.

Meanwhile the long corridor up from Belgium was being broadened to a wedge. At its base the Americans were in Luxembourg and Aachen. The line of the Maas formed its right with our half of the Island as the apex, plus a small area round Nijmegen; on the left British and Canadian units were expanding to the Belgian coast, and the port of Antwerp. Much later it was further widened to take in Northern Brabant (strongly contested at s'Hertogenbosch), and the Zeeland islands at the Scheldt estuary.

On 3rd October we were relieved by a unit of 82nd U.S. Airborne Division and moved back to Ewijk a few miles west of Nijmegen. We left the Island during an air raid on the new pontoon bridge put up by the Engineers—one span of the railway bridge having collapsed into the river as a result of the German attack by long distance Olympic swimmers. Ewijk was full of refugees from Nijmegen, but again our reception was most friendly. Our stay there, six days, was mainly a rest, but included, on the seventh, a spell of flank protection for the gun area which was established at Deest, covering the left sector of the Allied "Island" line.

South-west of Nijmegen is an area of sandy wooded hills which had been the dropping area for the American 82nd Airborne. It stretches some ten thousand yards away from the town, and the main road south runs down the right, along the Maas bank to Mook; in the centre where the woods end is Groesbeek, and on the left the marshes of the Waal. Across the flat farm country below Groesbeek, at a distance of less than three thousand yards, lies the German border; beyond that one can see the pines of the Reichswald forest. The railway line to Germany runs out of the woods at Groesbeek and across the open towards the Rhine.

To Mook the battalion moved on 9th October and for exactly a month we held the area, doing periods of from five to eight days in the line, and similar periods resting in Mook and Malden. There were always two brigades in the line and one in reserve; it also happened sometimes that we were the reserve battalion of a forward brigade.

The slit trenches which were taken over were roofed and revetted with parts of broken gliders; more than a hundred abandoned gliders dotted the open fields in front of the line.

Movement in the open was impossible by day, and the lengthening nights were busy with the movement of supplies, visits of the Commanding Officer and support platoon commanders around the companies, and by the company commanders around their scattered platoons. The lines were long, and a thorough tour usually occupied most of the night. Aggressive patrols from both sides prowled the area of no-man's land.

Very heavy harassing fire was put over from time to time by our guns, and at long range one could shoot with small arms fire into Germany. The sandy hills behind Groesbeek were higher than the ridges of the Reichswald, and it was possible to see for great distances over, and beyond, the frontier.

Sergeant Woodhouse was still in command of the sniper section. He was an old soldier of many years service, a boxer and heavily built, rather bald, and with a slight stoop. Fear was a peculiar complaint which sometimes affected other people—he didn't know about it. His patrols were among the best of many at this time.

On one occasion the patrol he was leading came under the fire of three machine guns in a forest ride. Sergeant Woodhouse stood in the ride and fired ten shots from the hip while his men got under cover, then he himself withdrew.

In a lighter moment he was chasing two pigs which, thoughtlessly, ran into a wood in the enemy lines. His men could hear the Germans laughing at him—so similar, at times, were conditions to those of the last war.

He was also a heavy snorer and for this reason could seldom find anyone to share his slit trench with him. I tell this incident without vouching for its accuracy, as it was told to me. One night at Groesbeek a Boche patrol crept up to his trench, attracted by his rhythmic snores. A burst from a Schmeiser was fired into his trench, but he was not hit. Nor, for that matter, did he wake up.

He was a great loss to the battalion, both as a soldier, and as a cheerful companion, when he was wounded in the shoulder by a grenade a few weeks later.

Three-quarters of a mile in front of Groesbeek was the village of De Horst, the most forward company position in the line. At one time "C" Company took it over and held it for a period of five days. The platoon and section posts were so far apart that the company commander began to wonder whether the guides had lost their way. Section posts were sometimes three hundred yards apart, and platoons up to three-quarters of a mile. It took three hours to visit a whole company area at night, and moving between posts was like doing a patrol. Platoons, too, were still below strength, and in need of reinforcements. When positions were taken over there were a great number of traces and maps to be mastered, plots of defensive fire and S.O.S. tasks, traces of minefields, locations of trip-flares, and lists of target code-names.

Rations were carried up to forward companies at night, and the carrying parties themselves needed strong escorts. Breakfast was eaten before daylight, at 5 a.m., and dinner at 10 p.m. On some nights nothing broke the eerie silence, and on others the sentries would be kept on tenterhooks all night by sharp exchanges of fire.

In this way one section of "B" Company lost Private Barrall, killed by a sniper, and another section lost the two men on its Bren gun. This section was only five strong, and the Bren team was holding the post before dawn while the remaining three carried up the containers of breakfast rations. An enemy patrol, which perhaps had been watching their routine for some time, got in behind the post and captured the two men as well as the Bren gun with ammunition and magazines.

Incidents, such as this, happened more than once. Major Durie, going round the posts of "C" Company after dark, approached Lieutenant Eves on a lonely stretch of road. Each saw the other shadowy figure at the same moment and dived for a ditch on opposite sides of the road. A short pause, while revolvers were pulled from their holsters. Then a head came up. "Psst ... Who's there?" Head down again in case the answer should be bullets. No answer. Another pause. Head up again "Psst ... Who are you?" "British." "Then what's the pass-word?" And then they recognised each other and walked off together down the road, laughing (but not very loudly).

At another forward village, Nijerf, the church was set on fire by German bazookas while Fifteen platoon were taking over. The enemy were dug in on one side of the street, and our positions were on the other. The incoming platoon had to crawl the final few yards to the slit trenches, through the circle of light thrown by the blazing church, and the trenches themselves were in the church yard. Platoon headquarters was in a back room of the vicarage, and was lit by some enormous altar candles salvaged from the blazing church. They stayed in their positions in the graveyard for three days—moving only at night, and then with extreme stealth.

Every noise on their part brought a volley of fire from over the road, and they, similarly, fired at any German movement. Sergeant Richardson asked the Company commander to let him have a field telephone without a bell because every time the bell rang his headquarters was peppered by the enemy, and grenades were exchanged across the road. The rubble and broken glass around the houses made such a noise that, on our recommendation, when the Fourth Somersets took over, their whole platoon arrived in gym shoes.

Another difficult position was held by "A" Company on the main road due south of Mook. They were on a high wooded spur immediately above the left side of the road, and well forward of our main line. In their left rear was a German company, and there were also enemy further down the road. The houses on the road were in no-man's-land so that the nearer ones had to be searched every morning, to make sure that the enemy had not infiltrated. The policy was to hit hard so as to give the impression that we were very strong. As many as two hundred two-inch mortar bombs, and fifty P.I.A.T. bombs (fired high-angle) were used each day by the Company. The three-inch mortars were used liberally on pre-arranged tasks. Major Roberts had one two-inch mortar permanently trained on the enemy, from which he encouraged any man who visited his forward HQ to fire a few bombs. Showers of rifle grenades used to drop on them from the enemy's left position, and these were always answered by a heavy "stonk" from our guns. With the falling of the leaves, constant renewal and alteration of our camouflage was necessary.

It must be truthfully admitted that by the end of eleven nights of such strain morale was lower than it had been at any time during the campaign. Such is the effect of defensive war. It was then that Brigadier Essame ordered a "Mad Minute".

At 7.14 p.m. on 21st October all was quiet. At 7.15 hell was let loose. Every rifle, Sten, Bren, Mortar, and pistol was fired as hard as it would go. As someone has, unkindly, said "Even the cooks fired their rifles". The Artillery of all calibres fired rapid, Bofors A.A guns, machine-guns and tanks raked the back areas. On to trenches, gun areas, and supply lines it went—into Germans or Germany, it didn't matter which. At 7.16 all suddenly stopped;

and in the deadly hush everyone felt much better, even though they waited for the answering "stonk" which they knew would surely come.

It was an expedient which was often used later, but was never more dramatic than this first time.

And so the month passed, and October gave way to November. The nights grew longer and colder. The dry autumn ground turned to heavy mud, and the Germans added more and more strength to their winter line. Casualties were not heavy though they occurred in a steady trickle.

On November the tenth the Somersets pulled out of the Mook sector, and made a five hour journey to Schinnen at the extreme southern corner of Holland.

THE

Winter War

AND THE TURNING OF THE

Siegfried

Chapter XII

NIEDERHEIDE
AND HOCHEID WOODS

THE reason for the long move south was that the Americans were about to launch a renewed attack beyond their Aachen salient towards Cologne. Their first objectives were the towns of Duren and Julich. The task of 43rd Division was to secure the American left flank.

From Schinnen we moved on 12th November to the towns of Kling and Brunssum where detailed plans and reconnaissances were made. Brunssum contained a huge state coal mine which was able to provide the luxury of unlimited hot showers for the troops. Again much trouble was taken by the inhabitants that everyone should be comfortably billeted.

Planning was carried out in great detail and briefing was done on an excellent sand table model, with the aid of maps and first class air photographs.

In rough diagram the lay-out was:—

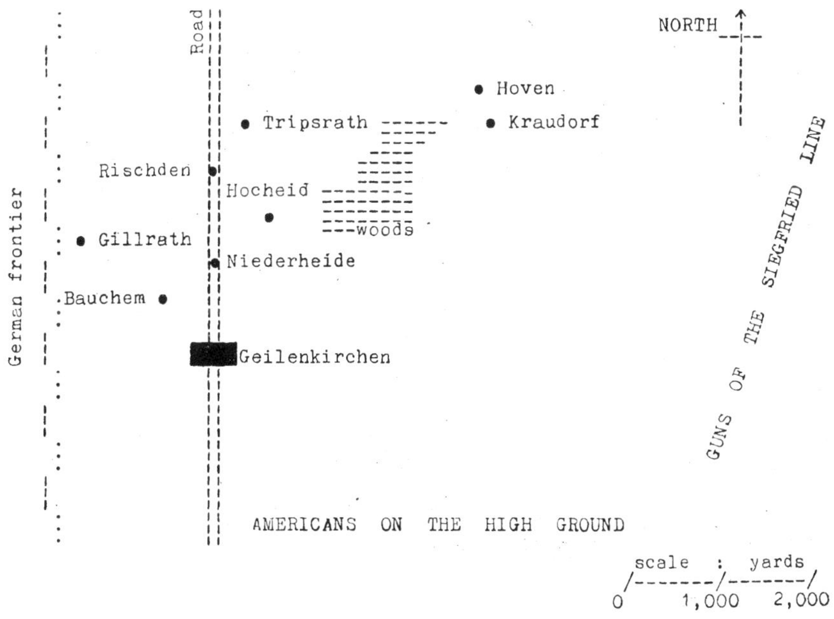

The task of 214 Brigade was to cut all exits from Geilenkirchen which was an American objective. For this task 5th Battalion The Dorset Regiment was put under command of 214 Brigade. 129 Brigade were holding the start line which included the village of Gillrath.

Objectives were: First, 7th Somersets to take Niederheide. Second, 1st Worcestershires to Tripsrath area. Third, 5th D.C.L.I. the village of Hocheid (and later Hoven). Fourth, the Dorsets to secure Bauchem.

On 16th November Colonel Borradaile took his recce group up to the brickworks at Gillrath from which it was possible to have a good look at the two thousand yards of flat shell-torn country which divided the start line from Niederheide (of which eight hundred yards was completely open). Mud was everywhere, but a tank officer had been taken out on patrol and was of the opinion that going, in the open stretch, was possible for tanks. A mine reconnaissance had also been carried out. From the O.P. it was possible to see away on the right to Bauchem and Geilenkirchen.

On 17th November the Colonel gave out his orders on the sand model; later all platoons were brought in to see it by their commanders.

Niederheide was a straggling village with a thickly wooded approach on the north and west sides, it extended on both sides of the main North-South road. The attack was to be made frontally with two companies up, "D" on the right and "B" on the left. A track running due east from Gillrath was the inter-company boundary. Planning was largely done from air photographs.

"C" Company were ordered to follow up ten minutes behind the leading companies to mop up in the thick country on the "B" Company front. "A" was in reserve to move under orders of the Commanding Officer. The carrier platoon was to provide right flank protection for all troops advancing over the open ground.

"A", "B" and "D" Companies each were allotted one section of anti-tank guns, and under command of "B" and "D" were placed assault sections of the pioneer platoon to deal with mines, pillboxes and barbed wire. From "A" Squadron 4th/7th Royal Dragoon Guards the Commanding Officer placed one troop in support of each of "B", "C" and "D" Companies.

The start line was the Gillrath-Bauchem road, and the forming up area two huge sand quarries near the Gillrath brickworks. All fighting transport was grouped under Captain R. P. Townshend who had made plans to rush the open ground as soon as the infantry were well into the Niederheide approaches. In order to free the road for the Dorset attack on Bauchem, all transport had to be clear of the start line by 1415 hours 18th November.

The Niederheide attack is of special interest for three reasons. There was plenty of time for detailed preparations and planning. It was the first attack launched wholly on German soil by any British battalion. And because it went exactly according to plan.

The battalion left Brunssum at 8.15 a.m. on the eighteenth November, riding on the backs of tanks and in T.C.Vs. The approach route was through thick woods and over rough tracks cut by the Royal Engineers, and named "Bond Street", "Regent Street", and "Strand". The attack was treated as a gala occasion by the press who milled up and down the column in their jeeps, and later described some parts of the assault. Reporters, photographers, and news-reel operators were all there, and were favoured by the weather with a crisp cold day of brilliant sunshine. The results of their labours were featured in several of the weekly illustrated papers.

The thunderous artillery preparation started at eight in the morning, and was a continuous rumble until late in the afternoon. Typhoons were searching over the enemy lines, swooping, now and then, to release their cargoes of deadly rockets.

We were ready in the assembly area by 10 o'clock, where hot tea and rum were served. There was plenty of time to ensure that every sub-unit knew its job and was ready to move up to its correct place over the start line.

At 1100 hours "B" and "D" Companies left the assembly area, followed ten minutes later by "C" Company. "A" Company and "F" Echelon transport remained in assembly area until 1230 hours, at which time "B" and "D" Companies crossed the start line, again followed ten minutes later by "C" Company.

The tanks almost immediately started to have difficulty with the going, and eventually only one got through with "D" Company, none at all with "B" Company and three with "C" Company.

Artillery support was provided by four Field and three Medium Regiments. The support consisted of a series of concentrations on known and suspected enemy positions. The speed of advance was timed for one hundred yards in two minutes over the open ground and one hundred yards in three minutes thereafter.

Throughout the advance Bauchem and Geilenkirchen were screened off by a smoke screen. The fire programme for the subsequent attacks dealt with Rischden and Hocheid immediately Niederheide was finished. Bauchem was also dealt with throughout the whole period by the mortars of 129 Brigade who were holding the line.

The Companies maintained their irregular line ("orderly disorder", designed to minimise losses from shellfire), and the advance carried them on to their objectives as planned. There was some delay on the "D" Company right flank where the right hand platoon had to get enemy out of dug-outs with phosphorous grenades before reaching the village. Such trenches as were forward of the woods were waist deep in water, and the Germans surrendered freely after some hip-firing on our part. Corporal Biggs, who had always shown himself well to the fore, merits a special mention here for he refused to leave his section, even though wounded in the leg and back. The right forward platoon was again held up by machine gun fire just short of the objective, and the Corporal received a third, and fatal, wound while leading his section to crush this post.

Fourteen platoon of "C" Company were similarly delayed by spandau fire in the wooded area. Eventually Lance-corporal S. Shepperd located the spandau with his Bren group, but his Bren gunner was killed. He seized the gun and walked into the centre of a ride, firing from the hip. He killed the German gunner, and freed his platoon to continue their advance. For his brave example here and under the subsequent shellfire Lance-corporal Shepperd was awarded the Military Medal.

Mopping up was completed by 3 p.m.

Very different were the results of the plans for the fighting transport. The going proved considerably worse than had been feared and before they were half-way across the ground the majority of them were hopelessly bogged, and buried above their axles. The movement of tanks behind the D.C.L.I. advance had broken up the only track. But for the continued smoke screen they would have come under direct fire—as it was they were heavily shelled.

The mortars arrived safely, but Battalion headquarters transport except for the Scout Car (and that got bogged half-way along) did not arrive at all. All the rest was bogged down with the fighting transport and Captain Townshend.

Battalion headquarters arrived in the shape of the Adjutant (on his feet) carrying in one hand a sign "67 HQ", in the other a roll of signal cable, maps, codes, a bag of papers, and a tin of bully beef. The Signal Officer was even more loaded, and fell flat on his face in a trough of liquid mud.

No food could be got up, but carrying parties were sent back to Company "F" echelon transport to collect items of compo, so that the majority of troops got something to eat.

The tremendous artillery cover had not improved the amenities of Niederheide, there was not a whole building left in the village, and shell craters were nowhere more than six or nine feet apart.

There was no counter-attack, though there was a fair amount of shelling.

The Battalion suffered twenty one casualties and took over one hundred and twenty prisoners.

THE ATTACK ON HOCHEID WOODS

The attack on Hocheid Woods next day was a very different affair in its inception. It was laid on at great speed, there was no recce of start line or forming up point, all of which were selected off the air photographs, and there was some doubt as to whether the battalion could reach the start line owing to the confused situation in Tripsrath.

Orders were given out by Colonel Borradaile at 1.30 p.m. His plan was simple. The attack was to be with two companies up, "A" on the right and "C" on the left. Fire support was laid on by four Field Regiments of guns firing block concentrations with a lift of three hundred yards between each; a hundred yards in each five minutes was allowed for the advance. Objectives were "A" Company the north east corner of the southern part of the wood—"C" Company the neck of wood joining the southern and northern halves. "B" and "D" Companies were to wait in the forming up area and to move up as ordered for close consolidation.

This attack was not meant to be carried out until the woods west of Tripsrath had been cleared, but while the troops for this task were passing through Niederheide, orders were received to carry it out at once.

Pioneers, carrier platoon, and anti-tank platoon were left to hold Niederheide in the meantime, for there were still enemy in Geilenkirchen.

Companies moved off within thirty minutes and the leading Companies crossed the start line at 1530 hours. Once again the attack went according to plan, all Companies being in their appointed place by 1625 hours.

The battalion had nineteen casualties and took a further forty prisoners.

The real difficulties then commenced.

There was only one muddy, sloping path, by which even tracked vehicles could reach the forward Companies, and this led outside the wood and was in full view of the enemy. In addition it was very slippery and bordered by deep ditches.

The Commanding Officer and the R.A. Battery Commander were the first to come to grief, the Commanding Officer's carrier falling into the ditch on the way up to see the forward Companies, and the Battery Commander's half-track following suit on the way back while being pursued by enemy mortar bombs.

During the night, when attempts were made to get Anti-tank guns, company carriers and food up to all Companies, the toll of the ditch mounted, till some eight vehicles were hopelessly bogged—including a jeep and a German horse-drawn cart found in Hocheid.

This cart had been harnessed and loaded with containers of food, but even the pair of horses were unable to keep it from slithering away sideways to join the rest in the ditch

The track was by then impassable to any traffic, six inches deep in mud. During the following two days in pouring rain and accurate enemy fire a track was cut by the Pioneer platoon through the middle of the wood. Soon this gave out, and food, greatcoats, and blankets had to be carried through a thousand yards of accurately registered wood. It was not until the end of the second day that regular maintenance traffic was established by the arrival of four "Weasels", which between them supplied the rifle Companies and evacuated all casualties.

These "Weasels" were the real life-savers of the situation. Built like a high-sided metal boat with propellers and rudder high off the ground, they slid over the mud with their broad, lightly-built, tracks running on rows of small rubber bogey wheels. They were driven by battalion drivers who had never driven a "Weasel" before, and were worked night and day till the drivers were on the point of exhaustion.

Until their arrival stretcher cases had been carried by hand a half to three-quarters of a mile, with the bearers sometimes knee deep in mud. The Medical Sergeant established a forward Aid post with "B" Company so that casualties should get speedier treatment.

The stay in Hocheid woods lasted only three and a half days, but the memory of it has left an indelible impression on those who were there. The gloom of the dark trees, the dripping rain, sodden ground, and roofed dug-outs with six inches of water on the floor, were only the discomforts which nature provided. The dominating interest was avoiding the Boche shellfire. The Germans had that wood registered accurately from every angle. Huge shells from the emplacements of the Siegfried line roared overhead to the back areas making a noise like express trains. Smaller shells burst in the tree tops and ripped the cover of the slit trenches, finding every little crack that was not properly roofed. I have heard one soldier asked whether Hocheid was worse than Normandy. "No", he replied, "I would not care to say that anything was worse than Chateau de Fontaine, but it was certainly as bad!" The probability is that for sheer concentration it was worse, and certainly seemed so under the conditions of damp gloom and lengthy nights.

The anti-tank guns were dragged into position with the forward Companies, and there they and their Lloyd tractors stayed. Two months later when the battalion was again in the line at Hocheid the same guns were still there, their wheels and trails frozen solid with the mud, but still clean and still fired by all their intermediate owners. The six Lloyds had to be left too, two burned out, one shelled beyond moving, and three in the all-devouring ditch.

Anti-Tank platoon headquarters were more fortunate, or so they thought, to find a cellar under a small and much battered house in the village. They were not there very long before an enormous explosion practically deafened them, and covered them with debris which cascaded down the cellar steps. A Sherman tank shooting round the corner of their house at enemy in Tripsrath had decided that it would be better covered if it pushed its seventeen-pounder gun in through one gaping window, and fired out through the other. One shot, and the terrific muzzle blast had brought the house down in a neat pile of steaming rubble. The members of the platoon dusted themselves off thoughtfully, while Captain Townshend addressed the tank's crew—tracing their ancestry for them individually and collectively.

"D" Company was, at one time, put under command of 5th D.C.L.I., for a further attack (on Hoven woods and Hoven village). In the first phase they were used to secure the start line, and the D.C.L.I. succeeded in getting into Hoven village. "D" Company were then called on to pass through the neck of the woods and follow up. At the neck they were held up by very heavy mortar fire and close range machine gun fire; casualties were severe. Major Cox went to get further orders, and while he was away the order came to withdraw the Company from that sector. All other officers, and the Acting Sergeant-Major had become casualties, so Sergeant F. Wheeler took command and extricated the Company—platoon by platoon—from its very difficult situation. For this, and for his fine example throughout the Niederheide battle in which he commanded a platoon, Sergeant Wheeler was awarded the Military Medal.

The Company strength was down to thirty-five at the end of the third day. Battalion casualties were suffered at the rate of nearly forty a day—almost entirely due to shellfire.

To the mud there was really no answer, but to wait for the frost or the spring. The Anti-Tank platoon marched out of Hocheid woods as infantry—carrying the kit from their carriers, their Bren guns, and two-inch mortars. The whole advance from Gillrath had covered four thousand five hundred yards and it was a credit to the planning and to the infantry that it succeeded. No better results were achieved on any of the winter fronts, and it is significant that two months later the front had not materially changed.

The Americans had, meanwhile, taken Geilenkirchen, and the battalion moved in to occupy a part of the town on 23rd November. There was a short rest at Teveren on the twenty-fifth. Four days were allowed to rest, bathe, re-equip and reinforce the battalion. Teveren was a rest area only in the sense that it was out of range of enemy close range fire.

On the twenty-eighth we were back in the line in the Gillrath sector.

Chapter XIII

ALL IN THE DAY'S WORK

I have found myself, at many turning points of this story, wanting to give a more detailed account of those services within a Battalion which are such a vital part of its daily life. Yet the inclusion of them battle by battle, in the exact place at which they occurred, would have the effect of confusing the decisive issues of the day.

In the story of a Battalion's life it is not possible to dwell on the local conditions and human anxieties which, alone, can make a story vivid. To take a classic example—"Journey's End" drew an unforgettable picture of one aspect of the first Great War because it confined itself to one small part of space and time, and to a group of men—their background, their families, their hopes and fears.

It has been necessary here to describe conditions in general terms, and for that reason you will find no special emphasis laid on the horror, and the suffering, the exhaustion and the unrewarded courage which is left in the wake of battle.

Without some account of the work of those who served in, or just behind, the line the story would not be complete. One part of that account is here—the other comes later when the story is near its end.

*　　*　　*

In the early days it was quite common to see an Aid Post, or a Dressing Station, pitch its tents right in the firing line. Shells never for one moment prevented the ambulances from running their errands of mercy.

Time and again one wondered at the courage and endurance of the Medical Officer, Captain H. E. S. Marshall, and the selfless service of the Stretcher Bearers, whose work called for a special form of courage since it was their job to save life without the comforting process of being allowed to hit back.

The following account by Stretcher Bearers, Lance-corporal Barrell and Bandsman Board is reprinted in their own words.

"The battalion had just finished its first attack into Germany at Niederheide, when it was ordered to attack the woods at Hocheid. We were acting as stretcher bearers to 'C' Company who were to be the leading company on the left.

Moving up to the starting line we had a fairly warm time with snipers and machine gun fire, except for one moment when we dived for cover in a ditch—three or four feet deep in water. That cooled us off a bit. However we got there O.K., and the attack started.

The Company had advanced about five hundred yards when suddenly a shout came back for stretcher bearers. We immediately hurried forward to find that the leading platoon had shot and wounded two Jerry snipers. We attended and dressed their wounds—but by the time we had finished the Company had advanced out of sight. So, leaving the Jerries to be picked up and evacuated later, we hurried forward to rejoin the Company as fast as we could. It was quite a difficult job as the wood was thick and daylight fading fast. We had been tearing through these woods for what seemed ages without getting any sign of the Company except to hear occasional rifle and Bren shots, which we tried our best to follow, when suddenly, and before we realised it, we came slap into a section of five Jerries (15th Panzer Grenadiers) one of whom—(obviously an NCO, although we couldn't see any badges of rank as they were wearing camouflage capes)—soon made us realise we were prisoners.

Being able to speak and understand English, he told us to attend to his wounded who were lying around the area, having been hit by shrapnel from our own shells which were still falling around. We attended to the wounded—some were past our help.

The NCO now ordered his men to pick up and help along the wounded, one of whom was lying on our stretcher. Picking up and taking as many of the wounded mens' arms as he could carry, he then started to go back to his HQ taking us with him. The prospect, apart from the actual fact of being prisoners, got us scared, so we decided to try and use some persuasion.

We told them how hopeless their position was, that they were almost surrounded and that they themselves would be taken prisoner, or killed, soon, so it would be far better for them to surrender to us now—but it wouldn't work.

We don't know what we would have done with them had it worked as we had no idea at that time, as later events proved, where our own lines were. It seemed that we were doomed to be prisoners. However, not giving up hope, we tried to appeal to their humanitarian feelings, if they had any, explaining our job was saving life and not killing, and that there were others lying around in that wood who would perhaps die unless we could attend to them.

After a hell of a lot of talking it worked and they let us go, going off themselves with their wounded.

We were soon gone and started to get back to our own lines, but it was impossible in the darkness of that wood. We soon realised that we were hopelessly lost, as we later found out we were more than a mile forward of our battalion positions, and with our own shells 'stonking' the whole area we decided the best thing to do was to find a trench or hole in which to take cover until daylight.

We had been looking everywhere without success when suddenly we saw a break in the blackness with the artificial moonlight shining through. We made for this and found ourselves out of the wood and in what looked like a large clearing. On going across this we discovered a stack of straw bales. The going was very heavy—it was now pouring with rain and we were wet through—so stacking the bales around us we decided to stop there to rest and decide what next to do as this clearing still seemed to be surrounded by woods.

We stayed there all night, shells passing over our heads both ways. Jerries from in front of us—ours from behind. We could distinctly see one of Jerry's mortars firing from just inside the edge of the wood.

We kept alert but no patrol came near us. We were hoping against hope that one of ours would come. When morning came we decided we would have to make another attempt to get to our own lines. Peering just over the top of the straw we could see that the ground was on a slope, with one corner leading to a break in the woods, in the direction of our lines, through which, in the distance, we could see a town. It was receiving a lot of fire from Jerry's guns so obviously, we thought, it must be occupied by our own troops.

Getting up a bit of extra courage, we decided to make a run for it as far as we could in that direction. We jumped out over our hideout, expecting every minute to be fired at, and started to run. We didn't run very far, however. The ground was in a terrible state and we were soon over our ankles in mud—it was still raining and had been all night. Not expecting to make this town all in one go, and with a fairly continuous 'stonk' still falling around, we thought about going into the wood again as it afforded more cover than this open ground, when suddenly on reaching the crest of the slope, we saw immediately to our left and not more than three hundred yards away, a village.

We studied it for a moment and seeing no movement there decided to take a chance and get to the first house we came to. We got to the entrance OK without hearing a sound, but half expected to be prisoners again as soon as we stepped inside the house.

It was completely empty, however, but as there were German uniforms, helmets, ammunition etc., lying around, we didn't know if it would continue to be so.

Not waiting to find out, we did what had become practically second nature on entering a house—we looked for the cellar. We first tried the pump for water as we were by then very dry inside—though not outside. The pump proved, however, to be dry also. We soon found the cellar and very warily descended the steps. On getting to the cellar, which was about nine feet square with a small window on the ground level, we relaxed for the first time for days, and felt temporarily safe.

We stayed there all night, during which we once heard movements above. We kept as still as mice and, although it might have been our own patrols, we decided it was safer not to investigate.

Quite early next morning, just as we were thinking about making another move but before it could materialize, a terrific barrage came down on this village. The house received four direct hits. The barrage had been going on for quite a while—the shells now going over our heads and landing slightly forward of us, when all of a sudden guns started firing at this house from all angles and at quite close range. It seemed to us from just outside, and we could recognise the 'Besas' and 6-pounders of tanks above us. From the noise and crashes it seemed as if the whole house was being torn apart—the cellar was filling with dust and fumes, although it still remained in one piece.

Suddenly above the noise we heard an American voice shout 'Tank commander, hold your fire.'—it was a great relief.

The firing stopped and we could hear a lot of shouting, but before we could come up from the cellar it started again—this time immediately above us in the house itself. It didn't take them long to find the cellar either and bullets started whizzing down the steps hitting the floor and wall immediately below them. We realised something had to be done quickly before they hit us too, so we started shouting everything we could think of—'English', 'Red Cross' etc., thinking the firing would stop. It did, but instead down came a grenade along with some words in German and cries of 'Come out, you bastards.'

We heard the grenade hit the ground about two yards from us. We couldn't see it as it was dark in the cellar, but as soon as we heard it hissing we realised what it was.

I think those few seconds before it exploded must have been amongst the worst in our lives.

It exploded with a bang and flash in that confined space, blinding us momentarily. Luckily it was a blast grenade and we were both still in one piece. Anyway, not stopping to think whether it was blast or otherwise, or to recover from the shock completely, we raced up those steps to be met at the top by an array of pointed weapons and a crowd of grim, determined Yanks. We were questioned in German and English, protesting our innocence all the time. They wouldn't believe it; our story was met with the language reserved only for Jerries.

A couple of weapons were now shoved into our backs and we were marched outside, hands above our heads. An officer was sent for—but he was the same. The German equipment lying around probably didn't help our story. We were by now really scared and almost frantic trying to convince them. Probably the officer began to think there might be something in our story—anyhow he said 'I'll soon prove whether you are English, and took us over to the tanks. We had noticed them, four of them, facing the building, but hadn't realised they were English. When we saw their crews we were quite relieved.

After hearing us and asking a few questions they soon convinced the Americans, who said 'Sorry chums, but we can't take any chances, you know.' We certainly don't think they did.

Being in the middle of an attack, they couldn't help us except to say that their HQ was about a mile down the road, and as Jerry was sending back quite a lot of fire, we decided to go back to the cellar until things quietened down.

The house was then attacked again by the follow-up Company, so we ran out to meet them. They believed our story, but would not believe that the house was clear, so they attacked it all over again using vast quantities of ammunition.

We watched for a while and then went back down the road to their HQ.

A number of bombers which were passing overhead, they explained, should have bombed our village before the attack; but had arrived too late—not too late for us!

They also said that they had taken thirty prisoners from a building one hundred yards from our cellar.

They put us in touch with an officer of our battalion, and we reported back next morning."

✳   ✳   ✳

From a Company Commander comes this detailed account of the journey from a slit-trench in Normandy to the clean white sheets of an English Hospital.

"I was wounded on the top of Mont Pincon—a shrapnel wound in the chest—from a shell which wounded other members of my Company, and killed Lance-corporal Reilly and Private Oldfield of the Mortars. I thought I was going to die. All wounded people, I am told, are the same. The shock stuns their senses and makes them silly. I wanted someone to be firm and kind with me.

I went and sat on the edge of my slit trench and very soon our Stretcher Bearers arrived. They bound me up and, at once, I felt much better. They were a most comforting pair of men—methodical, efficient, and stern.

Shells were still raining down but I found that a jeep had arrived, it was driven by Private House of 'B' Company. Two stretcher cases were lifted up on to the supports fixed above the body and the wind-screen, and four of us were helped on to the floor of the jeep.

It was a vile journey: bumpy heather, and sandy ruts leading down over the back of the hill. We groaned and thought it would never end—yet it was only a mile.

Eventually we reached the lower slopes, and came down on to the road. 'Thank God', we muttered, 'a smooth run back now'. But it was not to be. 'D' Company jeep and ours came to a standstill before three 'brewed-up' Sherman tanks exploding violently on the main road. How to get by? An exploding tank is a strange sight. As each shell explodes it leaves a 'Smokers ring' of quivering smoke about it. It is frightening too. We wounded cared not a bit: wounded never do. But the drivers did and they got us through somehow, and very gallantly, by threading their way through a bit of a hedge, a cabbage patch, and between two of the burning tanks.

The R.A.P. was a haven of rest. The M.O., cool, but obviously upset at his casualties, settled us in. It was a big barn and the shells were pitching down occasionally outside in the field. Tea was being made and brought round the whole time. Somebody brought me an egg and a sausage: no-one had eaten since dawn, some twenty miles back. It was amazingly calm and very comforting.

Padre Richards was moving around, being kind and sympathetic, steadying us with just the right words, for he knew each of us so well.

An ambulance arrived, and we went off down the bumpy red lanes to the rear areas. We passed through a variety of medical posts, where M.O's looked at us and orderlies brought us tea and cigarettes before we moved on down yet further bumpy dusty roads. An ambulance is never comfortable, and it is always beastly being lifted in and out. At length we came to a vast green meadow, spotted with white marquees.

The night was spent here with yelling Germans on either side. We were all surprised how badly Germans stand up to wounds: our own wounded are so patient: Germans yell with fear.

At dawn I was moved to a final Base Hospital, somewhere near Bayeux. A few days I stayed here, and then one morning an ambulance came to the door and we were taken off on the last lap to the U.K. It was a wonderful, sunny, peaceful day, but the roads were as rough as ever and the bumps jarred one damnably.

We reached an aerodrome somewhere near the coast and were hoisted into a Dakota—very comfortable, with a W.A.A.F. orderly dishing out lemonade. I did not notice the take-off—so smooth it was—and fell asleep at once, till a slight bump woke me up in England. Where we were I do not know, but we spent a miserable couple of hours in a hutted R.A.F. camp. Someone gave us a slimy stew and then, after an icy drive through the night in yet another ambulance, we reached a railway station.

We were trundled aboard a train and steamed off into the night. No-one knew where we were going—there was a pleasant feeling of irresponsibility.

Dawn found us, so we were told, at Wolverhampton where N.F.S. men unloaded our exhausted bodies for yet another, but final, trip in an ambulance to the Hospital. It was a wretched drive: cold, jolty and tiring.

But, Oh, what delight to be carried by Boy Scouts up the Hospital steps, to be greeted by a Matron, calm and presiding in a white cap and spotless uniform, to be sailed upwards in a lift and finally deposited, exhausted and feverish, in a clean white bed, covered with blankets and filled with hot water bottles: To be able to sleep—and sleep—and sleep."

* * *

And from a Base Hospital I have this thumb-nail sketch, taken from the letter of an officer who later commanded the Seventh Battalion in the last of its winter battles.

"I am in a different hospital block from the one which I was in before, and like it even better.

I had three slits in my thigh, one on top, one on the side, and one underneath, each about five inches long and two inches wide, through which the muscles seemed to be making a good effort to pop out and go for a walk! On the 14th they sewed up two of the wounds, but there wasn't sufficient skin round the thigh to sew up the third. So I shall have to wait till the bruises are sufficiently healed to take a skin graft—which I hope will be early next week.

I have sampled the usual agonising half-hour when a nurse who is called 'staff' comes along with a young travelling operating theatre, and proceeds to strip off all the old congealed bandages, lint and gauze which have stuck like concrete; while one lies and sweats, and twists the bed rails into weird shapes and shouts ones head off. At last it ends, much to the disappointment of several little learners—future 'staffs'—who have stood around with expressions like terriers watching a rick being thrashed.

The food is good, the service quick and cheerful; everything is absolutely first class".

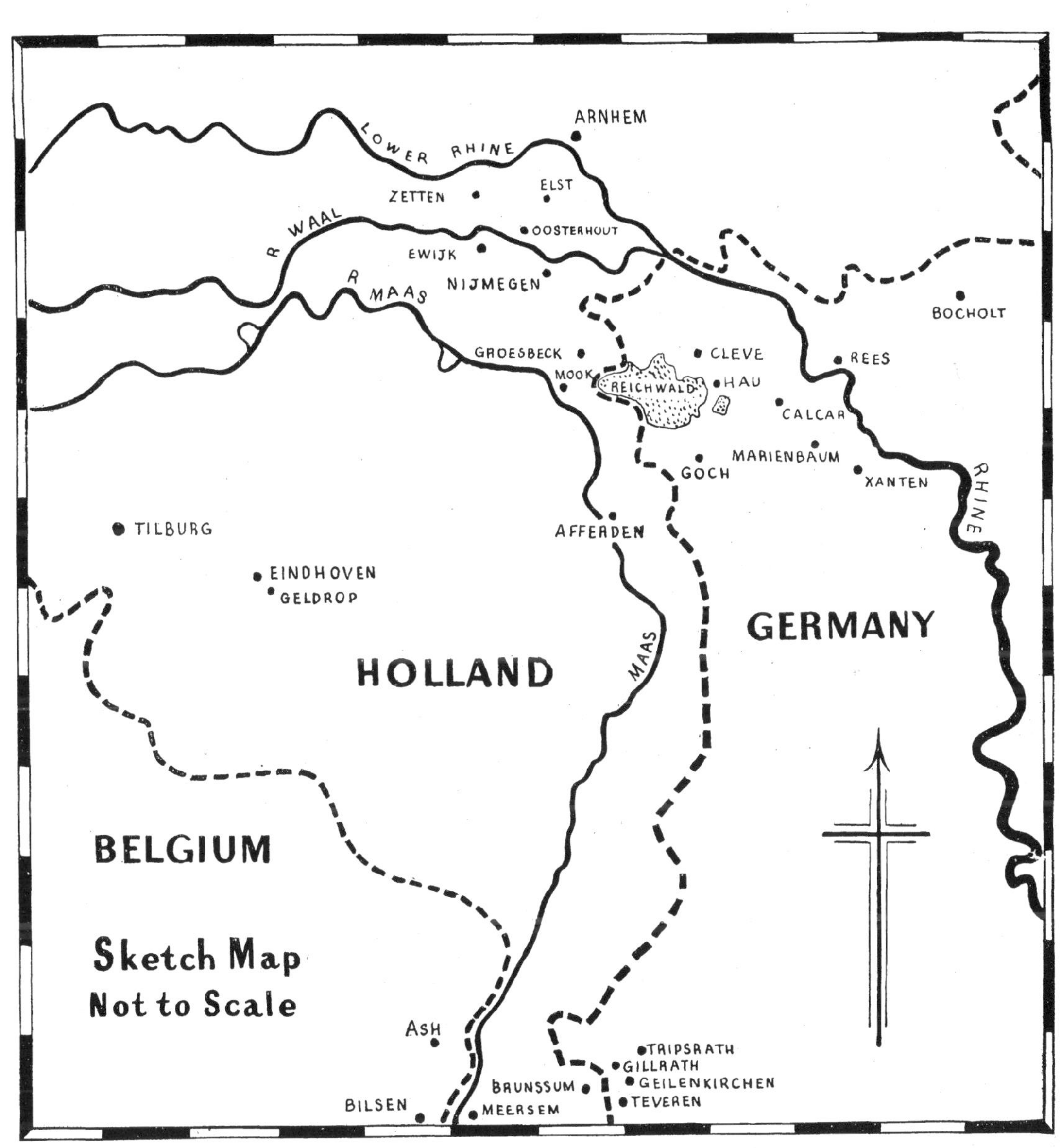

ARNHEM
LOWER RHINE
ZETTEN
ELST
R WAAL
OOSTERHOUT
EWIJK
R MAAS
NIJMEGEN
BOCHOLT
GROESBECK
CLEVE
REES
MOOK
REICHWALD
HAU
CALCAR
MARIENBAUM
GOCH
XANTEN
TILBURG
AFFERDEN
GERMANY
EINDHOVEN
GELDROP
RHINE
HOLLAND
MAAS
BELGIUM
Sketch Map
Not to Scale
ASH
TRIPSRATH
GILLRATH
BRUNSSUM
GEILENKIRCHEN
BILSEN
MEERSEM
TEVEREN

Chapter XIV

DEEP, AND CRISP, AND EVEN

NIEDERHEIDE was the first of a number of periods in the line on this southern sector. For more than two months we kept making return visits, and each time winter took a stronger grip on our experiences. The rain of November gave way to frost which turned the roads to ice and the fields to ridges of iron mud. Then the snow came, and before we pulled out for the last time the whole country was cloaked with a deep mantle of virgin whiteness, and the trees glistened and drooped their loaded boughs to the earth.

Teveren was dreary, battered, and windowless. It was only a few miles out of the line, but it served as a rest area for want of a better place. We stayed from the 25th to the 28th of November, and again on the first of December, and yet once more on December the sixth. A section which found a whole roof or a cellar and a stove was well off. Fortunately coal was plentiful—for this was Germany.

From 28th to 30th November we were again in the line at Gillrath with three Companies forward in the woods, and on the night of 28th a composite battalion of 30 Corps Services troops came up to take over. It was a strange job for them (all officers and drivers of the R.A.S.C.), but they made up in willingness what they lacked in experience. Our Support Company stayed in the line with them while the Rifle Companies rested. It was an attempt to take advantage of the stalemate period which had settled down on the front, so as to give more rest to the infantry battalions.

A long period was spent at Teveren (from 6th to 15th December) while preparations were going on for an attack on Heinsberg. The whole Army was really waiting for the hard weather which would again make tank movement possible. In anticipation of the attack the Mortars dug positions up in the line, but returned and continued to live at Teveren.

We were among the very fortunate units which were called away from the line for Christmas. We spent two days at Meersen, near Maastricht in Holland, while recce parties went right across to Tilburg beyond Antwerp to plan the battalion rest area. It was expected that we should have a month out of the line devoted to training.

The same day came the news that Von Rundstedt had launched a full scale mechanised offensive through the Ardennes, aimed at splitting the American 9th and 1st Armies, and cutting across the south of Belgium. New orders came, and the nineteenth saw us switched to Bilzen in southern Belgium, while frantic orders were sent out to cancel the Tilburg recce parties. We settled down in houses and schools, among people who were kind but extremely scared by the Ardennes news. We ourselves were placed under one hour's notice to move in a counter-attack role by day or night. Just before Christmas Day this was relaxed to three hours' notice—which meant that a normal programme was almost possible. Frost settled in good and hard with slight flurries of sleet.

CHRISTMAS 1944

Von Rundstedt's offensive was still gaining ground and transport was moving south fast. Battalion headquarters was on a main road, and it was as much as one's life was worth to dash from the Command Post across to the Orderly Room.

It was generally thought that if Von Rundstedt pushed his nose over the Meuse we should go and push it back again. The Commanding Officer went to have a look at Liège and Huy for assembly areas. An interesting point crops up: for it was hereabouts that the Regiment, then under the command of James, Earl of Barrymore, fought a campaign in 1702 when the fortresses of Huy, Chartreuse and Liège were invested and Venlo and Roermond besieged.

About midday on the 23rd a signal message was received—"Christmas will be celebrated on 25th December"—so, was the one thousand nine hundred and forty-fourth festival of Christmas recognised by the General Staff.

Simultaneously the recce party returned from Tilburg, vastly swollen by a number of short leave parties who had been redirected there. The Quartermaster and the P.R.I. went at speed in every possible direction, everyone had a flood of ideas on how the celebrations should be arranged. So Ops and the Germans took a back seat (bar a parachutist-or-escaped-prisoner scare) and the 'Q' Branch had it all their own way. The result was a credit to the cooks, QM, PRI and amateur decorators. Tinned turkey, pork, vegetables, Christmas pudding, mince pies, fruit, nuts, chocolate, cake, cigars, beer, red wine 'Chateau Naafi'. The Commanding Officer displayed remarkable stamina in accepting the hospitality of all eleven of the battalion's cookhouses between 12.30 and 2 o'clock.

The Herald Angels couldn't have helped harking—at two morning services and at a special carol service in the early evening. Football was played each afternoon, against the Worcestershires, the Duke of Cornwall's and the 'locals'. Two inter-company 'Quiz' competitions were held. Dinner and tea parties were arranged in many cases by platoons who hired cafes for this purpose. Huge Christmas cakes were made up for us by the local baker, and the Anti-Tank platoon engaged the town crier to advertise for girls for their evening dance.

There is no doubt that Christmas was a great success.

This was the last time Padre Richards took a service with us. That he was going was not generally known, but it was perhaps fitting that at both his Communion services (in a loft above a garage, by hurricane-lamp), at both his ordinary services (in a schoolroom) and at the carol service, there should be a greater number of men than I have ever known: which is saying a good deal. He was with us for exactly one year, from January 1st to December 31st, and I feel that any remarks about Christmas 1944 must be coloured by what he did for us then—which was of course no more than he'd done for us always.

On Boxing afternoon we were warned to pack up. We moved before it was light the next morning.

*   *   *

This time we went to Moorveld and Guelle, again near Maastricht, and were billetted (27th December). We were still on call for the Ardennes counter-attack, and in addition one Company at a time had a role as Anti-parachutist Company. The first ten days of 1945 were devoted to reconnaissance for defensive and counter-attack tasks. A complete battalion defensive position was dug at Brunssum, and recce parties went as far south as Eynatten, beyond Aachen. Moorveld was viewed for the defence of Maastricht, and on 8th January a trial convoy run was made to see that the plans would work. Snow began to fall in blizzards.

On the eleventh we were back in the line at Bruggerhof and Geilenkirchen, with two Companies in Hocheid woods. We took over from the Sixth Cameronians and had on our right the Seventeenth United States Cavalry Regiment. A thick blanket of deep, unbroken snow covered the countryside, and the roads up were packed hard to form an icy surface. The tracks of the carriers slithered like toboggans. It was on one such road that the Anti-Tank platoon carrier ran astray carrying with it no less a load than the Platoon Commander, the Doctor, and the new Padre. It ran over a steep bank, turned a complete somersault, and finished on its tracks in the edge of a minefield, whence the uninjured occupants made their way gingerly back on to the road.

Up in the forward areas we found all our old vehicles of November, and the Anti-Tank guns still in working order. The enemy had mined his defences extensively and the mines lay now under a foot of snow. One noticed how strange it was that the deer, and rabbits never went near the mines—in fact there were scarcely any animal footmarks in the snow at all. The woods had that woolly silence that only snow can give, and there was an air of indescribable loneliness.

For sixteen days the battalion lived in the line, among the gloom and the whiteness; they patrolled and cooked, massaged their feet and patrolled again. Those who know their 'Peter Pan' must have felt strangely like the 'Never-Never' boys with their roofed dug outs in the woods, and their little smoking chimneys, and the danger all around of German patrols slinking up in their white snow suits. But here was no Wendy to mother them—so they cooked for themselves, and twice daily they were ordered to remove boots and socks and massage their feet vigorously to prevent frostbite. And every night they patrolled and searched for minefields—and more snow fell, and by day the tracks were level with the surface again. Their water cans froze solid, and they lived on melted snow.

One story speaks for the whole period. It is told by Lieutenant E. F. Larret (Canadian Army) Commanding Seventeen Platoon of "D" Company. The date was 25th January and he had been ordered to take a patrol of his platoon out from the heavily mined cross-roads beyond Bruggerhof to the village of Kraudorf in preparation for a battalion move forward to Nirm on the next day. His chief task was to cover the Engineers who were clearing the minefield and were to beat the roads forward with Flail Tanks. It was during the planning at this cross-roads that Major T. B. Elliott (in temporary command) stepped on a Schu mine and lost a foot. Lieutenant-Colonel Borradaile had been transferred to a Staff appointment at Corps on the twenty-second.

Lieutenant Larret writes:—

"We waited all afternoon but when the Colour-Sergeant appeared with hot supper, which pleased everyone, the inevitable happened—we had to move before we had finished eating.

We made our way down the track where we were met by Major Cox; he was pleased at having got Brennan's platoon into position through the mined area without mishap. He gave me orders to patrol up to the next village—Kraudorf, and to make a firm base for a battalion attack on Nirm—further on. We moved up a sunken side track and the platoon changed into snow suits while I went back to HQ for maps and briefing.

I got my instructions and map, and rejoined the platoon after donning a snow suit seven sizes too large for me. We dumped our packs and collected our five sappers with mine detectors—then I briefed the whole lot in their job and we started out into the darkness.

It was the most unorthodox patrol I ever took out—entirely due to the mass of mines. Imagine five sappers leading and an almost full strength platoon following—all in single file and rather closed up so that everyone could walk in the footmarks of the man ahead.

The worst part was getting around the cross-roads. Ted (Lieutenant Brennan) came back and led us as far around as possible, then we had to bear back towards the main road —axis of our advance. The field was littered with mines and shrapnel—all frozen in so that nothing could be lifted and one had to steer clear of everything. The detectors swept from side to side, and the earphones buzzed continuously. I'm sure the tail man in the patrol could hear the detectors—they buzzed so loud! We worked our way up and down the bank overhanging the road and the sappers couldn't find a way through, so in the end to hurry things up I had to pick a spot and go over. Luck held, and we all got through the one gap without finding a mine.

It seemed hours till we reached a fork in the road and I consulted the map; Sergeant Taylor and I couldn't believe we had reached the correct fork because we were still in sight of the cross-roads. I finally decided—'We'll carry on along the main road'. So, in time we entered the outskirts of a small town. As I couldn't identify it, we proceeded half way along the street into a small courtyard where everyone rested and somebody tripped over a large tin tub which rolled round and round and didn't help my sense of humour at all.

After a short rest we carried on to the far edge of the village where I took a sapper with a detector up a few yards to have a look at a road sign. There it was—in black letters on a yellow background—'NIRM'—the battalion objective for tomorrow.

It had ceased snowing four hours before and here there were stacks of fresh footprints. So Jerry hadn't been gone very long! I had to do something, so I left Sergeant Taylor with HQ on one side of the road and Corporal Caddick and his section on the other to 'hold' the village. I took the remainder of the patrol and began to 'sweep' back to Kraudorf by another direct road. There was no-one in there either, so I set about placing the remaining two sections in position and got the sappers into a barn on some straw where they could rest.

I sent Private Hinton back to Company HQ with our information and the request 'For God's sake—come on up quickly!'—Hinton got back O.K. and Sergeant Penny and I went down to the main road to meet the flail tank Troop who were clearing up the road. Two of the flails were already out of action and there was only one left. I met the Major coming up with a second guide I had sent back, and finally "A" Company took over in Nirm.

It was almost daylight before we were settled in with the platoons in position. The Colour-Sergeant arrived with our breakfast just as we were sorting out a nice cellar for our headquarters. Corporal Millar worked on a stove for his section post with sticks and ropes to see if it was booby trapped for nearly three hours, and just when they had the fire going received orders that the D.C.L.I. would take over from us at ten o'clock. So we never did get our night's sleep."

*   *   *

The same day that the battalion left Nirm Lieutenant-Colonel I. L. Reeves, D.S.O., M.C., arrived to take command. He came to us from the King's Shropshire Light Infantry, after a long period of convalescence in England, for twice already he had been wounded in the campaign.

The rest of January saw us billetted at Schimmert (27th—30th), and at Wortel (31st January to 4th February). These were busy days of resting and refitting. A few more days at Geldrop were all that we were to have for this job, and for Colonel Reeves to get to know his battalion. Our last memory of Geldrop is of a dance attended by three hundred Somersets and not enough girls, of many barrels of beer and not a single tap, of twenty-four glasses to serve the whole assembly.

The period of the winter defensive war was at an end—from Geldrop we moved to the north again for the attack which was to break the Siegfried Line.

Chapter XV

THE REICHSWALD
AND FORST CLEVE

$\mathcal{T}$HE Ardennes offensive had proved itself Hitler's greatest mistake. He had thrown against what he had considered to be the weak link in the Allied line the pick of his mobile reserves—a Panzer Army, and the First S.S. Army. Göring had promised 1,800 planes in continuous support to the German attack—he produced only eight hundred planes in total. The Americans had taken tremendous punishment, it was said their casualties were a hundred thousand, their line had bent but it had not broken. Heavily mauled, von Rundstedt tried to pull out what was left of his panzers, and transfer them to Russia thinking that the Allied offensive must now be severely delayed. Thanks to the R.A.F. it took six weeks for a depleted and much bombed remnant to reach the Russian front.

Field Marshal Montgomery decided that an attack must be re-mounted at once. The Reichswald hinge of the Siegfried line promised the best results, and the Canadian Army attacked through the flooded area from Nijmegen to the Rhine north of Cleve under appalling conditions of snow, floods, and mud, where they had to keep up their supplies by using "Ducks", and often had to bulldoze "Weasels" and other tracked craft through the mud.

On 8th February 30 Corps, under command of First Canadian Army, launched an attack with five divisions, supported by twelve hundred guns. The same night the pivot towns of Cleve and Goch were decimated by an attack from five hundred bombers of the Royal Air Force.

The Seventh Battalion had been very thoroughly briefed in its role both at Geldrop, and in the assembly area at Nijmegen. The working details of the plan were known to the whole battalion by the evening of 8th February. Already at five a.m. the barrage had started which was to prepare the way for the 15th (Scottish) Division to Cleve, and the 53rd (Welsh) Division into the Reichswald forest which flanks Cleve on the west and south sides.

Nijmegen itself was packed with the tightest concentration of armed force which had been seen since the beach-head days, for, though the attack was spoken of as the First Canadian Army, and though the Germans and the public at home believed this to be so, there was concentrated there the bulk of the British Second Army, while elsewhere the Germans who thought they were holding the Maas against the British Second were in many places contained only by American-British Combat Groups.

For 214 Brigade, who were leading 43rd Division, the task was to follow the 53rd Division through the forest tracks (and in this area they would be passing through the northern arm of the Siegfried line), and strike south behind the Line defences to Materborn and Goch. The 5th D.C.L.I. were to lead to the first objective.

At eight-thirty p.m. on February 9th the battalion crossed the start line, and owing to the floods, and the weight of transport on the road, progress was far behind what had been aimed at. The whole battalion was riding on the backs of tanks and carriers in what is euphemistically known as a "quick lift". The road was across the north of the Groesbeek area where they had spent October. "C" Company formed the battalion vanguard.

The column had not travelled far when the German Air Force carried out a short raid on Nijmegen. It was not a heavy raid but it was greeted by a display of anti-aircraft fire such has seldom been seen. The night was sprayed with fountains of glowing tracer shells, till there seemed to be curtains of floating red dots over the whole sky. It made one moment of excitement in a night of unparalleled monotony and discomfort.

It was bitterly cold with spasms of icy rain and driving sleet. There were few hand holds on the cold steel surfaces of the tanks, and there was no room to lie down. There were frequent stops but no official halts, one never knew if a halt would be five minutes or five hours, so that it was only possible now and then to jump down and stamp frozen feet on the road. Slowly the night passed, and with daylight came the problem of feeding a battalion spread out over a stretch of three miles of crowded road. By evening a distance of ten miles had been covered to Kranenburg, and at one a.m. on the eleventh we turned into the Reichswald near Nuttenden at the north-east corner of the forest. Here in the forest rides another bitter night was spent. Materborn should have been cleared by the Division which was mopping up Cleve, but when the D.C.L.I. entered they found it strongly held. It was necessary for them to reform and stage a battalion attack next day. Earthworks, trenches and wire of the Siegfried line cris-crossed the forest and isolated groups of prisoners came in from sectors over-run by the Welsh Division.

Orders were given for the Somersets to cross the start line in Materborn at 4.0 p.m. (11th February) for an attack due south along the Goch road to a bend in the road some four thousand yards away, and for the capture of the village of Hau. "C" Company was still leading with a troop of tanks of the 4th/7th Dragoon Guards, "A" Company was to follow part way and turn left for Hau, "B" Company to draw up on the left of "C", while "D" was in reserve. Artillery was on call after a preliminary fire programme.

The plan received two minor set backs which did not materially alter its result. On the start line we came under fire from pockets of enemy which had not been mopped up. This was not surprising because Materborn and Cleve are practically one town, and the area is thickly interspersed with houses and villas, woods and gardens. The start time was delayed half an hour. Secondly, soon after the start, orders were received that no troops were to be north of a certain line after 5.30 p.m. owing to other plans. This necessitated that Hau should be taken from the south—(i.e.) from "C" Company objective.

"C" Company had been pressing forward during the closing phase of the D.C.L.I. attack, and as soon as the situation seemed reasonably secure they went forward. They advanced quickly for a thousand yards until within four hundred yards of the Goch road where they should turn south. It was their first experience of German refugees—and they felt no pity after the misery which they had seen in France and Holland.

Four roads met at this point—the one from Materborn, the one north to Cleve, the Goch road, and one due East—the road crossing became known as "Tiger Corner". Thirteen platoon was leading at this point, under Lieutenant E. Lawson, with a troop of tanks. An air O.P. had already reported traffic movement there and the Commanding Officer had put the Medium Artillery on to it. Thirteen platoon could see a burning, knocked-out 88 S.P. gun on the cross roads. At the same moment they came under heavy spandau fire, and 88 mm shells from further S.P's started to burst in the trees over their heads—throwing out shrapnel and great mushrooms of black smoke. No-one was injured. The tanks got to work on the spandaus and saturated them with fire from their Besas, while the platoon leapfrogged forward using the houses as cover—the tanks, in order to do their job properly had to spend long periods stationary. Major Durie set his three-inch mortar section to work on the S.P. guns.

Slowly the vanguard group secured the cross roads, but not before the third tank had been hit and set on fire by the German guns, followed later by hits on the leading and second tanks which were able to withdraw.

There was some delay on the cross roads, with the burning tank, the smashed enemy S.P., a Nazi headquarters full of stores, enemy trenches among the gardens, enemy strong points in the houses and the inn. Wireless communications were very difficult, there was trouble in getting in touch with the supporting guns. Colonel Reeves came forward. Sleet storms began again as darkness fell.

A plan was made for artillery "stonks" along the Goch road, and the advance began again—cautious, nerve-racking and exhausting. Platoons passed through each other as farms were searched, prisoners were taken, grouped Bren guns and P.I.A.T.s were used to cover spandaus and houses.

*   *   *

The road was straight for hundreds of yards, and on the verges the only cover was that of the ugly tree trunks at regular intervals. Spandaus seemed to answer every move, spitting lines of red and blueish tracer past them in the darkness. Snow lay in the folds of the stiff gas capes which they were wearing as waterproofs.

They fired two-inch mortar smoke bombs in an endeavour to set houses on fire, but the bombs more often went clean through the roof and out beyond. It was so cold that the covering Bren gunners had to use two fingers to operate the triggers, and gunners were changed at frequent intervals. As each platoon became reserve it replenished its ammunition from the Sergeant-Major's carrier. They found many places where mine holes had been dug, but the mines were still in their crates on the road side; some Tellermines were found ready laid in the grass verges. Commanders and men became so exhausted that they were almost asleep on their feet, and particular mention has been made of Lieutenant Lawson who went around his sections himself firing their Brens and P.I.A.Ts to encourage them and spur them on.

Conditions for the following Companies, if less exhausting, were equally bitter.

It was then that Major Durie decided to take advantage of the Germans' strangely inconsistent habits of alertness and idleness. It was a bold plan which could have led his Company to disaster, but his objective was still a thousand yards away and time was vital. What decided him was the pressure of other troops behind him anxious to get on and deploy to their own attacks, and the need to wake his own men from their fatigue—there comes a time when a man is too tired to be afraid, and any risk is better than that. He gave Fifteen platoon the order to lead straight down the road dealing only with opposition which showed itself from the scattered farms and houses—if there was mopping up, it would be done by the troops following.

It was dark and eerie among the deserted farms; the advance went silently forward, and at 2 a.m. "C" Company was on the bend of the road near the village of Hau. Close on their right were the eastern fringes of the Reichswald, in front and on the left was the smaller Forst Cleve. The road and railway went side-by-side through the narrow gap. The Major went forward with Thirteen and Fifteen platoons to select their positions. Captain G. Wreford and Company Sergeant-Major Evans were left to establish HQ area, with Fourteen platoon in reserve. Somewhere in the Reichswald 53rd (Welsh) Division were still pushing forward; behind "C", "A" Company had come up and turned sharp left towards the village of Hau. There were "Tiger" track marks leading into the Reichswald. "75" Grenades in stacks of three were quickly laid (the seventeen-pounder Shermans were brought up at first light).

Captain Wreford and the Sergeant-Major parted to examine a farm just off the road which promised to make a good headquarters.

I have avoided, as far as possible, any reference to personalities in this book, but because it has some bearing on the story it should be said that Sergeant-Major Evans is thirty-three years old, his height is five foot three, and his weight eight stone eleven pounds.

He approached the farmhouse after searching the outbuildings, and saw a chink of light showing between the shutters; it was not possible to see in, so with the Company runner, Private Hough, as covering party he entered the dark hall with a grenade in one hand and his rifle tucked under his arm. The door of the lighted room was on his right and he pushed it open with his rifle, leaving Hough to cover the passage. The light streamed into his face and there, on the floor, were ten or twelve Germans fast asleep. Seeing them asleep, he put the grenade into his pocket and fired a shot through the ceiling. A piece of chivalry which nearly cost him his life.

They instantly woke and cowered back against the wall, but at the same moment the C.S.M. caught sight of a German officer behind the door, and an automatic levelled at his face at a range of about three feet. He swung left, and both fired together, he from the hip with his rifle. The officer fell—the Sergeant-Major received the pistol blast in his face and the bullet went past his ear—though he wasn't sure that it had at that moment.

The others took courage and started to move; inch for inch, and pound for pound, the odds were probably fifteen to one. At that moment one more Boche appeared from an inner room and made a rush—the C.S.M. shot him in the stomach, and retreated one yard (his longest withdrawal that night) into the passage. He and Hough were now covering the door should a rush be made. He told Hough to go and get a Bren team from Fourteen platoon, but at that moment he heard someone at the back end of the passage, and changed position to cover both ways. In doing so he fell over a bucket. Hough thought the Sergeant-Major had been sabotaged, so he decided to remain covering the passage from the front door. He was still there when Major Durie arrived a few moments later with Private Bond, Bren gunner from Thirteen platoon.

A burst was fired into the room, and they shouted that they were about to toss in some grenades. This brought an answer, in the form of a medical orderly who spoke English, that the Boche had had enough. From the room they took one officer (dead), one wounded, and eight prisoners.

In the lighted room Sergeant-Major Evans asked the Major to examine his face, which was dripping wet. He was relieved to learn that the moisture was only sweat.

Meanwhile, at the back, Captain Wreford had collided in a doorway with another Hun. He was fired at and suffered only a ricochet off his cigarette case.

One of the prisoners, from the 15th Panzer Grenadiers, said that it was ridiculous for the British to penetrate at night, since there were four thousand paratroops in the area, supported by Panther and Tiger tanks.

More incidents during the night disturbed this Company headquarters. Prisoners were coming in at intervals from the Reichswald, dislodged by 53rd Division, and they appeared to have no idea that we had got so far behind them. A brand new German half-track drove up the road and was captured intact by Fourteen platoon. HQ sentries (Privates Bennett and Robinson, the carrier drivers) were attacked by two burly Germans near the out-buildings, and the ensuing rough and tumble caused enough noise and lasted long enough for the Major (with a rifle and bayonet), and Captain Wreford, to reach them from their HQ. As they arrived Private Robinson's opponent broke away and ran; Bennett and his German were locked in a struggle for Bennett's rifle. Major Durie tried to get in with his bayonet, but could not be sure who was who in the dark; Captain Wreford got in a blow to the jaw which knocked the Hun off his balance. This gave the Major a chance to put a shot straight through him. He howled, threw up his hands, and dashed off into the darkness. No doubt he was one of the dead Germans found in the hedge next morning. An anti-tank gun had been captured in position by the roadside, and next morning the whole crew were taken prisoner as they moved up at first light to man it.

Meanwhile "A" Company had turned east for Hau sometime around 1.30 a.m. Major Roberts advanced, on the assumption that it would be held, with Eight platoon (Lieutenant N. E. McKinlay) as vanguard. Their first object was to secure two large farms at the southern end as a base for clearing in a northwards direction.

They found a line of zig-zag trenches, unmanned, covering the whole western side. Here Nine platoon was dropped off with the role of providing covering and cut-off fire across the top of the village in the darkness. The leading platoon reached its first farm and found the door locked. Lieutenant McKinlay made an entry through a window, and was killed instantly from inside; his batman was wounded in the side but got back to the Company Commander. A P.I.A.T. was sent up and the house was surrounded, at the same time the other farm was found empty. Seven platoon set to work on the two village streets and by

3 a.m. the objective was secured though mopping up continued till 4.30. One Captain and twenty other prisoners were taken in the village, and at Lieutenant McKinlay's farm one man was shot on the ground floor, and another Captain and four men were captured upstairs. One of the Captains—a fine Aryan specimen—had in his pocket a photo of himself being decorated by Hitler.

"B" Company moved out on the left of the road while the forward platoons of "C" were getting into position. They met only minor opposition until they reached their objective where they killed three sentries and captured a 75 mm anti-tank gun, a spandau, and fifteen men. Later, while the platoons were digging in, several German contact patrols walked in and were captured. Private Duncan was shot in the side of the head by an officer with a patrol of two men. It was a glancing blow. He grabbed his Sten gun, shot all three, and did not realise till afterwards that he had three bullet holes through his steel helmet. He was later evacuated because of his head wound.

This Company made contact with "C" and "A" and was in position by 4.30 a.m.

At 5.30 after thirteen hours of night fighting, following two nights on the road, the battalion was firmly on its first objectives. Seventy-three prisoners had been taken, and a number more killed.

During that night and all day on the 12th February the forward Companies, particularly "A" and "B", were heavily shelled and mortared. In particular "B" were unfortunate in having ten casualties (one killed and nine wounded)—all in one platoon. Two of their supporting Sherman tanks were also knocked out by 88s, but the one mounting the long seventeen-pounder, it was called "Hellz-a-Poppin", survived all day and, in fact, was still with us at the end of the war.

Twenty-two more prisoners were captured in mopping up operations by "C" Company. At 14.48 hours "B" Company was counter attacked by two companies of infantry supported by three Panther tanks, one of which was destroyed by "Hellz-a-Poppin". At 15.00 hours "A" Company, using Brens, caught a recce patrol of eight enemy on their front, and not one of them escaped alive. At 17.17 hours "A" Company was very suddenly attacked by a force of a weak battalion in number.

Three times, in all, the enemy formed, or launched, a counter attack; three times our outposts passed the word to their Companies, and the Company Commanders to the Commanding Officer. Simultaneously the mortar and gunner O.P's flashed the target area back to their gun positions. The infantry manned their weapons and waited. A distant thunder told that the guns had heard; salvo after salvo screamed overhead, and ripped into the lines of Germans. Great was the slaughter.

In "A" Company Major Roberts had placed his two machine guns (of the 8th Middlesex) with his forward platoons and they caught the enemy in flat, open ground. Before the machine guns and Brens fifty or sixty casualties were mown down, the assault wavered and turned. As they retreated they were caught by the weight of our artillery defensive fire; shells rained down barely five yards apart. The attack was obliterated.

✻   ✻   ✻

During this and the next day it was obvious that the Forst Cleve was full of enemy. It is probable that it was used as a base for each of the counter attacks. Not less than four hundred shells were put down on "A" Company alone on the first day, especially around the church. Company HQ was bombed out twice. Yet the Company suffered only two casualties. Morale remained high and Major Roberts attributes this, in all seriousness, to the quantities of chickens and eggs which gave everyone something new to think about—very different from Holland were these fat, rich, German villages, with their poultry, their hams, and their bottled fruit.

Two prisoners who walked in on the first evening to give themselves up told Major Roberts that the enemy were very anxious to recapture Hau, and that a further counter attack was planned for the following morning. They said that they doubted whether their troops had enough fight in them to make another attempt. They never did.

Prisoner identifications from this front showed that there were opposed to us elements of the following formations. The 19th Parachute Regiment (7th Parachute Division), 156th/104th Panzer Grenadier Regiment, 116th Panzer Division, 16th Parachute Regiment (6th Parachute Division) and 15th Panzer Grenadier Regiment. Prisoners also stated that their support included forty-five 88 mm Self-Propelled guns mounted on Panther chassis, and one Tiger tank battalion of a hundred and ten mixed tanks, plus twenty-five Tigers.

The thirteenth February was "D" Company day. So far they had been concerned only with shellfire from an 88 which fired straight down the road between "C" and "B" and hit their headquarters. They attacked to the edge of the Forst Cleve under cover of mortar smoke. With them went the Commanding Officer and the Adjutant. It was thought that there were enemy there on a reverse slope position. They advanced a thousand yards in thirty-seven minutes, and met no opposition. They searched around and collected eight prisoners before returning to the battalion positions.

Often it is the nameless suffering of helpless animals which leaves a lasting impression of a battlefield. Of horses, and cows maimed by shellfire. Of a little kitten which dashes from a burning cottage with all its fur scorched off. Of a row of cows chained by their halters, and burned to death in their barn. "Hau" was more fortunate.

"Hau" is a magnificent black Alsatian, and the Adjutant found him, chained and terrified, in a burning house. In Captain Clarke's own words:

"Hau was lying in the corner of the farm kitchen, bristling and very frightened, chained to a wardrobe. 'D' Company's platoon was busy clearing the house which was burning furiously. One must always talk to dogs (it doesn't matter what one says—it is the tone of voice they recognise), and the sooner they smell you the better, so I threw him a piece of wood, assured him of my good intentions and, gun in hand, advanced to be bitten. He knew I meant well and contented himself with biting C.S.M. Clarke shortly afterwards."

A few days of Allied rations, and kindness on the part of B.H.Q. staff, soon won him over to our cause, and he is with us to this day.

The remaining days at Hau (half of the 13th, and all day 14th and 15th) grew gradually quieter. The troublesome Cleve forest was contained by artillery and machine gun fire, and harassed by our patrols which worked on its fringes, as well as along the line of the railway. Rocket typhoons raked the enemy supply routes, and three jet-propelled Me.'s were engaged by the Light Ack-Ack over the top of battalion headquarters. Contact was made with 53rd Division, and it was a great comfort for "C" Company to have their right flank secured. Major E. R. H. Harvey with C. S. M. Clarke patrolled into the gap between the two forests. (Armoured cars of the Recce Regiment had been knocked out here.) The terrible "Canadian Carpet"—a multi-barrelled rocket apparatus—was brought into use against the wood. It was the first time we had heard it. "A" Company cleared an area beyond the railway on the fourteenth and took twenty prisoners. This piece was then taken over by a squadron of the Recce Regiment.

Each of these moves was clearing elbow room, and was over ground of desperate importance to the Germans. The Siegfried line now had an eight thousand yard gap at its northern end, with a substantial wedge heading downwards towards Goch.

Chapter XVI

THE GOCH ESCARPMENT

*D*URING this time 129 Brigade had been slowly forcing their way round the northern corner of the Forst Cleve where they were involved in very heavy fighting, and at two o'clock on the morning of 16th February the battalion was given orders for an attack, in conjunction with the 1st Worcestershires, to pass through 129 Brigade and down a second axis towards Goch via the east side of the forest. The route was back past Tiger Corner and then south-east to the start line. It was originally intended that H hour should be 11.00 hours.

It was the most difficult approach march of the campaign. The start line was held by the 5th Wiltshires, and they had already sustained a heavy counter attack in the early morning. In reserve to them on the road was 7th Bn. The Hampshire Regiment, and through both these battalions we had to pass the 1st Worcestershires (who were to attack on the left of the axis), and the 7th Somersets whose role was on the right including the most direct road to Goch.

Both the approach road and the start line were under sustained shellfire, and all four battalions took severe punishment. The Worcestershires had difficulty in getting their own Companies deployed for the attack, and Colonel Reeves personally led our two forward Companies ("A" right, "D" left) to the start line. This was at an angle to the main road, and had been marked with tape to ensure that correct direction was given at the start—a very necessary precaution for a cross-country attack over flat, featureless, country in which all the isolated farms looked identical. The tapes had been laid under fire during the morning by the Intelligence section under the supervision of Major C. Brooke Smith (then Second-in-Command of the battalion).

There was the greatest difficulty in getting the supporting transport, especially the tanks, up to the correct places on the congested road, but the strain of further delay would have been more serious for there is nothing so lowering to morale as delayed orders when under shellfire on a start line. "A" Company on the right were ready and had their tanks. "D" Company were not ready—their tanks had not joined them, and their headquarters was hit by a shell which wounded every member except Captain J. D. Graham, the Company Commander. They were thus without their stretcher bearers and their signallers.

It was in these circumstances that the attack was mounted, and at 3 p.m. (the revised H hour) Colonel Reeves gave the order to advance.

The Right attack · "A" Company

"A" Company had to cover the first four hundred yards cross-country to a farm which marked the point where they would join the Goch road. Early in the advance they lost Corporal Barratt and Private Medhurst, killed by mortar or shellfire, but they secured their first bound without serious fighting, covered by ample artillery and mortar supporting fire.

But one section of Sergeant Chinnock's platoon was held up by heavy mortar and spandau fire. The Sergeant himself led them on a flanking attack and assaulted the house from which the fire was coming. Twice at the first two houses he was struck on the helmet by a bullet—in the second instance he was pulling back one of his wounded men to safety. Later he was knocked unconscious by the blast of a mortar bomb, but within fifteen minutes he rejoined his platoon and again took command.

They were then held up by small arms, and mortar fire all along the houses on the road. Major Roberts called up his tanks (4th/7th Dragoon Guards) and they gave the Company first class support. Each forward section had its own tank which 'brassed up' the houses in turn, first with its 75 mm cannon, and then with its Besa machine guns which generally set the house on fire. Under this cover the infantry cleared the houses, while the seventeen-pounder tanks were kept for flank protection and as a Company reserve.

It was house fighting all the way, and the Company left behind them a trail of burning wrecks. Prisoners were taken in dozens.

The Company secured its objective at about 5 p.m., and during the consolidation Lieutenant R. C. R. Cox with Seven platoon captured three German Regimental Sergeant-Majors together with a number of stragglers and two (American) six wheeled trucks. Their advance gained two thousand five hundred yards and secured three lateral roads.

Later a Typhoon fighter was hit by German Ack-Ack right over the top of the Company and crashed in front of the forward platoons, behind the German positions. Mopping up continued and during the night another American truck tried to crash their cross roads, driven by Germans who were endeavouring to deliver rations to the enemy cut off in the

Forst Cleve. The two occupants were shot by Sergeant Chinnock, and the Company made use of the rations. At two a.m. a file of enemy was reported to be withdrawing from the forest. Seven platoon ambushed them and took fifty prisoners armed with ten machine guns and with rifles. They were commanded by two warrant officers, and for the first time we heard prisoners saying that the war was lost. They said that the troops in the Forst Cleve had not had rations for three days. "A" Company looked sympathetic, and remembered the Packard ration truck.

The Left attack · "D" Company

The order to attack found "D" Company's platoons ready, but still without their tanks—nor did they know at the time that Company HQ had been knocked out. Captain Graham came up on foot but did not say anything about his staff; he himself was slightly wounded in the hand. For "D" Company the attack was all cross-country and through scattered farms—their bounds, as for "A" Company, were the lateral roads. They came up to the first one without much trouble and with Seventeen platoon (Lieutenant E. F. Larret) and Sixteen platoon (Lieutenant G. Shearman) leading in extended order.

On the first bound they paused to get direction, and at once came under the heaviest 'stonking' that they had ever experienced in the open. They went to ground making what use they could of tiny hollows but it was terribly inadequate cover. Captain Graham came up and urged them on, and they advanced in short bounds finding what cover they could. In the words of one of the platoons—"We worked from shell hole to shell hole, and it was almost a question of waiting for the holes to be made—".

The fire was coming from two places, some buildings on the road which was their second bound, and a group of farms out on the left. Had they had their tanks with them, or had the Worcestershires been level with them this flank would not have caused so much trouble. As it was Captain Graham had to detach Eighteen platoon under Lieutenant E. Brennan to deal with the left flank, and to do this they had to cross an anti-tank ditch which was converging from the left and was almost twenty feet deep. Once the platoon got into the ditch they couldn't get out, and it was some time before they emerged (making a ladder with their rifles) and silenced the troublesome farm.

The other two platoons worked forward but just before the road buildings they came under another murderous concentration of mortar bombs mixed with spandau fire. Sergeant Penny crawled up to Lieutenant Larret, and volunteered to try to get back to fetch the tanks. He had only gone five yards on his way when he was hit in the head by a sniper.

At the same time Corporal Caddick was severely wounded and Sergeant Mervyn was killed by a mortar bomb. These N.C.O's were all old friends from service in India, and it is not surprising that the effect on morale was bad; Sixteen platoon, too, had heavy casualties. The converging anti-tank ditch was forcing them gradually on to an ever narrowing front.

It was about this time that they caught sight of Boche running to and fro between the buildings, and they all opened fire; following up with an assault which secured the houses and took twelve prisoners. There were numbers of German dead, killed by our Artillery. The prisoners were sent back at the double without escort, and it was not until they had gone that there were discovered behind the rear outbuildings two large German mortars cocked high for ultra-short range, with their barrels still smoking hot. Had these been found earlier it is doubtful whether the platoons at that moment would have been in the mood for taking prisoners.

While the Platoon Commanders were checking up on casualties Captain Graham came up, and shortly afterwards two tanks were seen approaching from the rear. They were Shermans, but rather than take chances Corporal Osborne tore down white curtains from a house, and flagged them in. They turned out to be from Squadron HQ, and they agreed to support the Company on its final bound.

To the amazement of the Company the next thing that was seen was Captain Graham advancing towards the enemy with a tank on each side of him. At the same time the Colonel arrived in his carrier to announce the success of "A" Company on the right. It is not known how the tanks came to set out with Captain Graham, but the platoons quickly followed suit. The Company Commander, however, held his lead and was on the final objective first with his two tanks. There was very little opposition in this third phase which was fortunate because the Company had taken a severe punishment on phase two. The weakest platoon was Lieutenant Larret's which finished with himself and nine men out of twenty-three, as they started to dig in for the night. The time was now 5.30 p.m.

While Seventeen platoon were digging in, a runner came up from Eighteen to investigate a farm just beyond them on the opposite side of the road (the same lateral road on which "A" Company were already secure). He entered the farm, and emerged from the cellars with one German Officer and fifty-four other prisoners. The officer was a doctor, but the men were armed with one automatic, fifty-one rifles, and another large mortar. Had there been any fight left in them they could have done untold damage as the weary Company was digging in.

They were ordered to shut themselves up in a near-by windmill for the night, but the officer said "Nein, nein, you know how terrible is the German artillery." The Company knew all about the German artillery, and didn't see why the prisoners couldn't face under cover what they themselves had borne in the open. Besides they were too short of men to send back escorts—so the prisoners were bundled into the mill without further ceremony.

Later in the evening a platoon of "C" Company was sent up to reinforce "D", and in the small hours the Fourth Somersets passed through to secure one more lateral road some six hundred yards further forward.

The Seventh battalion had taken four hundred and thirteen prisoners during the day and advanced just under three thousand yards down the second arm of the Siegfried Line.

✻   ✻   ✻

"C" and "B" Companies held the reserve positions during the night 16th/17th February, and "D" Company was re-organised into two platoons next morning. At the same time Captain Graham was evacuated owing to his wounded hand; Lieutenant Larret took command of the Company which became battalion reserve later in the morning.

The attack on the Goch Escarpment was timed for 11.00 hours on a three-company front with "A" again on the right—still working along the road, "B" in the centre, and "C" left. The centre and left Companies each had a number of isolated farms to capture on the way, and the total width of the front was about one thousand six hundred yards. All final objectives were on the escarpment from the point where "A" Company road crossed it on the west, to "C" Company whose role was to cut the Goch-Calcar road where it breasted the escarpment.

The average length of the advance was three thousand yards—it being longest and most complicated on the left. The ground was again even and featureless rising steadily to the escarpment, a ridge some sixty feet high, which dropped steeply on the south side and dominated the pivot town of Goch—three-quarters of a mile beyond.

The Order Group was a hasty one but this time the troops were well deployed, and the tanks were all with their correct Companies.

The Right · "A" Company

Again "A" Company had a running fight from house to house and again the tank co-operation was superb. This time the Squadron Commander himself moved with "A" Company to watch the tactics. The infantry will be the first to admit that the tanks won the day on the right, firing till they were practically out of ammunition. Meanwhile the Company cleared the houses and scoured the zig-zag trenches, and wire barricades which grew thicker at every advance. "A" Company were on their objective in one hour and forty minutes, and although they immediately came under heavy bomb and shellfire they found plenty of German trenches for cover and had no casualties. From their positions on the escarpment they were able to call down our Medium Artillery on troop movements in Goch.

The Centre · "B" Company

"B" Company started their advance with Eleven platoon leading under command of Sergeant Evans. Their route for six hundred yards lay along a line of zig-zag trenches which did not appear to have been manned. Though damaged by shellfire the trenches provided them with continuous cover to their first bound and the leading platoon were able to secure the first objectives without casualties. At this point their route joined a rough track which was to be the axis for Ten and Twelve platoons while Eleven had a number of points to clear up on the right, towards "A" Company. The first house on the track yielded an abandoned ambulance and appeared to have been a first aid post.

From the first group of farms on the right they took twenty prisoners with slight opposition, and continued to work through another line of trenches where fifteen more enemy were captured in a stretch of ground which ran close to "A" Company. Eleven platoon then turned back towards the Company axis and one half of the platoon crossed the open ground covered by the fire of the second half. But when the second half started to cross they were at once engaged by small arms fire from a small copse which had previously been silent. They went to ground and regained the trenches by crawling. A further flanking movement up the trenches brought them another twenty five prisoners before they rejoined the Company.

This is perhaps the best single example of the day of the effect of turning these elaborate defences and working down between them, for this one platoon, little more than twenty strong, had taken three times their own number in prisoners in under an hour on ground which was well known to the enemy.

Meanwhile the remainder of the Company was beating its way up the track and employing the now popular technique of tank-gun fire, incendiary bullets, and infantry section assaults. Not all the houses were defended but the swiftest and least costly method was to treat each house as a strongpoint. At times the resistance was tough, but our concentrated fire won the day. There was a lengthy hold up at one point when Lieutenant J. F. Parrack's Twelve platoon came under heavy spandau fire from the right which pinned his sections in the road ditches. Our tanks moved up on each side of the road, and Private Cooper spotted a German "bazooka" party creeping up on one of the tanks. He shot and killed the man who was aiming the bazooka, but was himself hit by a second German, and received a wound which proved fatal.

A few moments later another tank was hit by a similar weapon, but it was able to carry on. Then later a German fired a rifle grenade from an area from which prisoners were coming in, and this struck a post near Major Harvey, the Company Commander, and wounded him. Major Harvey insisted on continuing the attack, but was later persuaded to go back by his medical orderlies.

At 2.30 p.m. the Company was on the escarpment and was able to report that all intermediate strongpoints had been cleared. The forward platoons were pushed down over the steep ridge into less exposed ground and patrols searched another six hundred yards without meeting further opposition.

The Left · "C" Company

Again the 1st Worcestershires were on the left of Seventh Somersets and the first shock which "C" Company got was when, with Fifteen platoon leading under Captain Wreford, they were greeted by spandau fire from the track junction at which it was thought the Fourth Somersets were holding the line. They sustained casualties at the farm here, and from enemy shelling, but were too close to the enemy to call down our artillery. The name of this hamlet was Imigshof, and a battle developed which lasted for nearly two hours.

The seventeen-pounder tanks were employed against the buildings while an attempt was made by Major Durie to get his Company into the orchard close to the houses. The tank support was excellent, but every infantry movement was met by snipers.

Eventually the farm was captured after every building had been set on fire by the tanks. Sixty prisoners were taken from the cellars at considerable risk to the Company. A German Captain said that they had left their wounded down below and he was ordered to take a party back to get them out. He shrugged his shoulders and refused. Meanwhile the wounded had crawled to the top of the steps, and "C" Company headquarters themselves went into the flames to rescue them.

So, in two hours, an advance of eight hundred yards had been made. Prisoners were sent filing back without escort, while a ten minute artillery barrage was put down on the next hamlet half way to the Calcar road. This was south-east and on the inter-battalion boundary line. At the same time Lieutenant D. N. A. Ford with Fourteen platoon commenced an attack on two separate farms out on the right, covered by the fire of one tank. As they approached they found that the nearer one was held by that Company of the Fourth battalion which they had expected to find at Imigshof, and there were some anxious minutes while an all-Somerset battle was forestalled. Lieutenant Ford's chief difficulty was to stop fire of his enthusiastic tank which was some way in rear. They then went on to capture the other farm which was still held by the enemy.

By this time Lieutenant E. F. Lawson had followed up the barrage with Thirteen platoon and cleared the first two houses on the next bound, and a Company of the Worcestershires had drawn up level with Company HQ, with the intention of going for the same objective. The two Company Commanders conferred and agreed that "C" should go slightly right for a tower which was thought to be an O. P. while the Worcestershires tackled the hamlet and carried on left-handed to the road. Both Companies came under very concentrated shelling at this point.

Germans were coming in from every direction and could be seen walking in with their hands up as far as two or three hundred yards away. In the first two phases "C" Company claimed nearly two hundred prisoners, some of which were evacuated for convenience through the Worcestershires Headquarters.

Fifteen platoon were now pushed through again to attack the tower. They tried to use the cover of orchards but their every movement was obvious in the open ground. The leading tank had two direct hits from an anti-tank gun concealed behind the tower and caught fire. The gun was indicated to the second tank which knocked it out with two shells, but the tanks themselves were nervous about advancing over the open and Fifteen platoon was pinned to the ground by spandau fire.

The attack had now been going on for five hours—the distance covered was sixteen hundred yards.

Major Durie decided to call off the frontal attack and fired a smoke-screen to cover the platoon. Three of their number had been killed and Captain Wreford had already been evacuated wounded at Imigshof. Fifteen platoon wouldn't move. The smoke-screen thinned and drifted away leaving them pinned in the open. Again the Company two-inch mortars fired a smoke-screen from their limited stock of bombs, and this time the platoon got back safely.

The two Commanders conferred again, and it was decided that the Worcestershires should go for the road, followed by "C" Company who would then advance along the road and take their objective from the flank. Ten minutes slow artillery fire was put down on the road and on the tower.

From this east side the tower was finally captured and at its base were many dead Germans, the anti-tank gun was there with its complete crew dead around it. From this cover our own tanks shot the Company in on the last leg of their long attack, with Fourteen platoon leading on the right of the road and Thirteen on the left. Many enemy dead were seen on this stretch, and only a few prisoners were taken in the escarpment positions. The slow artillery fire appeared to have done its work very thoroughly.

"C" Company reported the objectives taken at 5.30 p.m. and among the equipment captured were five 75 mm anti-tank guns. It was found that at least two of the guns had a shell in the breech, ready for firing. There were also machine guns there complete with ammunition. The trenches were in very good order and obviously intended to form part of the permanent defences of the Goch anti-tank ditch. Major Durie attributes the success of the attack to the artillery, to the tank's Besa machine guns, and to the fact that "A" and "B" Companies were already on the escarpment, but it must be recorded that it was the determined manner in which the infantry made use of this support which enabled the escarpment to be taken in one day, and held on such a broad front.

✳   ✳   ✳

The same night was busy with patrols covering the Sappers whose task was to bridge the Goch anti-tank ditch, and with Bren gunners shooting up isolated pockets of enemy which were seen along the front. The Divisional artillery shelled Goch without pause.

At 2 a.m. a Sergeant of 15th (Scottish) Division reported on contact patrol. He said that, thinking the battalion were in Goch, he had approached a factory shouting his identity, and that forty-five Boche had come out and surrendered to him. He had had to march them back to his own battalion before setting out again to find us.

In "C" Company HQ were an old man and a bed-ridden old woman who had chosen to stay on. The old man paced up and down all night cursing Hitler, and it grew so monotonous that at dawn they were both sent away on "Formidable"—the Company jeep.

Morning found local actions taking place at various points. Sergeant Maskell took a patrol from "A" Company early in the day as far as Goch railway station. "D" Company called for volunteers for a Goch patrol—they were Lance-Sergeant Stevens, Private Davison and Private Copeland who had already done one patrol with the Engineers during the night. In the outskirts of the town Davison was wounded but carried on for a while before accepting help, a few moments later Copeland (he had only been back a few days from his first England leave) was killed.

In "C" Company area Lieutenant Lawson's platoon were covering an abandoned German half-track, and each time the Boche approached in an endeavour to move it they were shot up with Brens. Lieutenant Lawson was himself severely wounded in the arm, and though he lost his arm he wrote later to say that he considered that the efficient first aid he received from stretcher-bearer Lance-corporal Barrell had saved his life. He set a splendid example by walking back alone to the Aid Post.

The morning's shelling on our positions was very heavy and sustained, and in the morning mist it was feared that there might be a counter-attack; but nothing came. Our own three-inch mortars kept up a good harassing fire.

At one stage it was thought that the battalion would be ordered to attack Goch itself, but this was cancelled and in its place the 15th (Scottish) Division launched an attack from the Cleve road. In reply to this the Germans shelled the Calcar road heavily around the "C" Company positions. The Scottish attack was covered by most of our own artillery, and all our available Bofors and machine guns were used to thicken up the fire—a process which is called "pepper-potting".

By the evening of 19th February the position on the escarpment had served its purpose. It was left in the hands of "C" Company, who stayed under command of 1st Worcester-shires, for a further twenty-four hours. The remainder of the battalion spent the 20th February in reserve and then went into the line further east at Halvenboom.

Here it was called on to fight only a holding action, though it received much attention from shells, mortars and rockets. Our patrols and snipers operated with considerable success, and we continued to wear the enemy down with three times the volume of fire which they were able to produce.

At 10.30 p.m. on 23rd February the relief of the Seventh Somersets by the First Battalion, Grenadier Guards, began, and by 7.10 a.m. next morning the last members of the Support Company were out of the line.

The best summary of the twin actions of Hau and Goch is in the citation of the award of a Bar to his D.S.O. which was granted to Lieutenant-Colonel I. L. Reeves, D.S.O., M.C., for his command of the Battalion in this action.

"For outstanding personal courage, professional skill and success in the operations between Cleve and Goch in Command of 7th Battalion The Somerset Light Infantry. On February 11th, his battalion was given the task of passing through 5th Battalion The Duke of Cornwall's Light Infantry, which had just captured Materborn, and advancing three thousand yards to Hau. Sleet was falling at the time, and as his battalion formed up for the attack it came under fire from S.P. guns and Spandaus from the Reichswald. Lieutenant-Colonel Reeves personally directed the deployment of his Companies regardless of heavy fire. When the advance reached the cross roads where the roads Materborn—Goch and Cleve—Goch met, Lieutenant-Colonel Réeves found it had been halted by S.P. guns and infantry in the woods close by. On his orders, the opposition was temporarily driven back and the advance south-east continued until all his objectives had been taken.

Later he was ordered to advance from a start line east of the Staatsforst Cleve for about two thousand yards. One road only led up to the area of the start line, which was under exceptionally heavy artillery fire, and this was blocked by the unit ahead. Regardless of risk, he managed to extricate his battalion and lead his two forward Companies personally to the start line so that they could start at H hour. Thanks to his presence the operation was a complete success.

On the following day, when the leading troops of the Brigade had reached a line one thousand yards short of the escarpment commanding Goch, he carried out a further completely successful attack with his battalion, and carried the escarpment. On this occasion he arrived on his objective with his leading Companies and directed personally the mopping up of the objective and its consolidation in the face of very heavy enemy fire.

As a direct result of Lieutenant-Colonel Reeves' leadership, his battalion advanced eight thousand yards and took eight hundred prisoners in these three. battles."

✶   ✶   ✶

The offensive had continued day and night for fifteen days. On to its front it had drawn the last good reserves of the German army in the west—the Sixth, Seventh, and part of the Eight Para Divisions, the 15th Panzer Division, 116th Panzer Grenadier Division, and the Division Panzer Lehr.

The Brigadier has said that the taking of the Goch escarpment was the most decisive battle fought by the Seventh Somersets. In it they lost one officer and twenty-three men killed, and four officers and seventy-two men wounded—three men were reported missing. The Military Cross was awarded to Major L. Roberts and Major D. B. M. Durie, and the Military Medal to Company Sergeant-Major Evans, Sergeant Chinnock, and Private Bond.

The Corps Commander in a subsequent summary of the operation said that he considered that the taking of the Goch escarpment was the Brigade's finest battle and that it came at a time when the success of the whole plan was rather finely balanced. When, two days later, the American Ninth Army attacked across the Roer river it encountered only two infantry divisions. The fate of the German Armies north-west of the Rhine was sealed.

Chapter XVII

THE HOCHWALD AND XANTEN

HERE was still work to be done on the West bank. So far it had been a turning operation through the Reichswald and south to Goch. Now the scope of the attack was enlarged and several fresh Divisions were put into the southward drive towards the Americans and München Gladbach—at the same time a Canadian Corps turned eastwards towards Udem, Keppeln and the Hochwald forest.

The battalion had three days' rest in battered Cleve, during which time much damaged kit was exchanged, and reinforcements arrived to fill the gaps left by the casualties of the previous three weeks.

Cleve was a sorry mess. This historic, and formerly prosperous town, with a population about the size of Taunton, had been composed of large well spaced villas, and thriving local industries centred around an ancient cathedral and a fine old castle.

Then Hitler's engineers made it the northern post of the Siegfried line.

Now it was the worst shambles since Caen. Several thousand bodies were said to be still buried beneath its ruins. Bomb craters and fallen trees were everywhere, bomb craters packed so tight together that the debris from one was piled against the rim of the next in a pathetic heap of rubble, roofs and radiators. There was not an undamaged house anywhere, piles of smashed furniture, clothing, children's books and toys, old photographs and bottled fruit, were spilled in hopeless confusion into gardens from sagging, crazy skeletons of homes.

There were, however, quite enough solid ground floor rooms and cellars, and more than enough mattresses to ensure that all companies were well housed—and the three days provided a very much needed rest. It also provided an opportunity for Colonel Reeves to assemble the battalion for a talk for the first time since his arrival.

On the evening of 27th February positions were taken over in the area between Calcar and Udem on a role of left flank protection to the Canadian operation in the Hochwald forest. It was a bald and unattractive piece of country, very flat with heavy clay soil, and the majority of the farms were severely shot about. The battalion area was Neu Louisendorf, and the gun lines, including some batteries of mediums, were between the forward companies and battalion HQ. A few enemy shells landed in the area on the first night, but subsequently it was a quiet period. Very few were able to get into houses, and platoons lived almost entirely in their straw-lined slit trenches in the large ugly fields. The gunfire in support of the Canadian attack into the Hochwald was almost continuous for several days. Here, as always, the German paratroops were fighting grimly, and it was a period of heavy casualties for the Canadians.

Cold grey days, March wind, and sleet storms marked the last of the winter weather.

On 2nd March the Canadians were well into the forest, and it became necessary to move up on the left again, at the same time another brigade of the 43rd Division had captured Calcar and moved north east towards the Rhine bank. After dark Lieutenant D. N. A. Ford (of "C" Company) with Privates Rougerie and Edwards, patrolled to the villages of Kehrum and Spiershof where the ground dropped to river level between the Hochwald and the Calcar-Xanten road. They reported small enemy posts in the farms on the fringe of the forest. An exchange of grenades with the sentries here had brought them under spandau fire from the direction of Marienbaum on the main road. The enemy appeared to have only small covering parties on this flank.

Next morning, a Sunday, with a light fresh breeze and a feeling in the air that spring was on the way, the battalion moved, but in order to avoid the skyline at the forward edge of this slight plateau the route was north through the edge of Calcar and down the Xanten road. The advance was carried out in tactical formation until Kehrum, where headquarters was established. "D" Company then continued along the road to the edge of Marienbaum, and "C" Company went right to the farm buildings at Spiershof which was half-way between the road and the Hochwald. Both companies penetrated right through the Schlieffen line—the third and final arm of the Siegfried—and established positions beyond. The line was a system of concertina wire, trenches and dug-outs covering a depth which varied from a quarter to three-quarters of a mile. Only on the road was any attempt made to defend it—and here "D" Company had a short struggle to secure their objective.

"C" Company then sent a contact patrol under Lieutenant G. C. G. Hamilton to the forest on the right, where they linked up with the Royal Hamilton Light Infantry (of Canada)—our Canadian sister Regiment, affiliated with the Somerset Light Infantry—and the remaining companies deployed to hold the road; the battalion again settled down to a defensive role moving forward a mile and a half to the village of Marienbaum on 5th March. The screen was extended to the Rhine bank on the 7th, when "D" Company groups pushed out to the left.

The German resistance was still tough, but had been reduced to a pocket around Wesel and Xanten, pressed on the south by the Americans, in the centre by the Guards Armoured and Eleventh Armoured Divisions, at the Hochwald by the Canadians, and at Xanten, where the Fourth Battalion Somerset Light Infantry was largely responsible for clearing the centre of the city.

The Seventh battalion advanced again on the afternoon of 9th March to take up positions on the left of the Fourth, and down to the Rhine bank. The distance from Marienbaum to Xanten was about five miles, the last three being along a straight flat road bordered with trees and under observation from the enemy guns on the high ground beyond the river.

It was a clear afternoon and the continuous stream of tanks and trucks churned hot fume-laden dust in the faces of the marching infantry. Salvoes of shells kept falling around the column, but it was impossible to hear them coming owing to the noise of the traffic. In the circumstances the best plan was to push forward at a good pace, and this was done. Several casualties occurred from shellfire, particularly near the tail of "B" Company where an unlucky shell landed slap on the road. It was with considerable relief that the column forked left at the shell scarred road junction just outside Xanten and moved towards the village of Luttingen and the cover of the Rhine flood banks. Here companies dispersed to positions covering the river. "A" further to the east, "B" on the bund at Luttingen, "C" forward to a group of buildings round a schloss called Scholtenhof, and "D" in reserve at Bn. HQ. The front held was about five thousand yards, and a standing patrol of the carrier platoon filled a gap near Wardt.

Shelling gradually died down towards evening, but an unlucky hit at battalion head-quarters caused a tragedy among the Regimental Police, and men under detention. Head-quarters was in a group of buildings on the Xanten side of Luttingen. RSM Knight had ordered slit trenches to be dug as was normal for the defence and protection of battalion headquarters. Shells were coming over occasionally, particularly as vehicles on the road could be seen from the far bank. Colonel Reeves had just told the RSM to put up a notice board on the road "Dust means shells—Shells mean death—Go Slow!" when a batch of shells fell around the headquarters.

The Sergeant-Major ran across with the Provost Sergeant to find that a heavy shell had struck a tree immediately above the slit trenches occupied by battalion prisoners. Two men under arrest were killed, as well as the Guard Commander, Lance-corporal Munday, and another member of the guard. One prisoner, and a third member of the guard were severely wounded.

Immediate aid was rendered by the Medical Officer who was in the building at the time, but one of the wounded died of shock very soon afterwards.

For four nights standing patrols were maintained by all Companies on the Rhine bank, and by day the patrols withdrew to their Company areas. "C" Company had a lucky escape next afternoon, when a heavy long range gun (estimated by our gunners to be a 155 m.m.) scored a hit on a large tree a few feet from the wall of their schloss. Four or five shells from this gun had already hit either the garden or the outbuildings, and there had been a considerable lull before this last one arrived. At the time all the Company officers were together in a room off the main hall, and about twenty men of the Company were drawing their tea ration from the cooks in the hall. The shell brought the twenty inch-tree down on the roof, and filled the room above the hall with shrapnel. The Company sustained no casualties, but it was decided that it could probably do exactly the same job from a safe position behind the flood banks, and this became the main company area later in the night.

Various incidents were reported from the bank patrols who called artillery concentrations down on one or two of the huge Rhine barges which were still attempting to move. There were amusing and tense moments while Bren gunners trained their sights on small parties of Germans who came down to the waters edge and stood talking, or climbed into reconnaissance boats, but only one party attempted to cross and this was met by a hail of bullets in mid-stream.

During those three days a large number of officers and men shared in the night patrols on the river bank. The sentry, as he lay silent just below the skyline of the flood banks, was not alone. Above him the tall leafless poplars stirred noiselessly in the cold air; the wide smooth river gurgled against the shallow mud flats, dimly lit by distant roving searchlights. Occasional noises on the other side called his searching eyes, now here, now there.

Lonely shells whined overhead from East or West, sudden batteries of shells tore the air in a quick burst of hate. He shivered as the March night rustled the damp grass in which he lay. Round about him were the memories of those who had fallen in the dusty fields of far away Normandy, in the clear September days of Holland, the gloomy woods of Geilenkirchen, and the tortured mud of Goch—those men, some of whom he had never known, who had won with him this foothold on the Rhine.

The battalion had been in the line, or on the flank of the line, for twenty eight days since the first Reichswald attack, with a rest period of only two and a half days at Cleve. There was bound to be a lull now while formations were regrouped and equipment brought up for the Rhine crossing. On 13th March they were relieved by 52nd (Lowland) Division, and returned over the Dutch border in preparation for the final battle.

FROM THE Rhine TO THE Elbe

Chapter XVIII

T H E   F I N A L   P L A N

ON 13th March the Battalion pulled out of the line for the last time: from the time that the Rhine was crossed there would be no more rest, no more line perhaps, until the German Army was smashed and unconditional surrender signed.

To the advance parties which were sent back to Afferden on the banks of the Maas in Holland the prospect was not cheerful. It was a cold grey day and the deserted village street was swirling with little eddies of dust and straw in the March wind. Very recently this had been the battlefield of the troops which had advanced southwards clearing the east bank of the Maas, and before that it had contained the Boche positions covering the river during the winter. There was not a house with an undamaged roof, not a house from which some doors had not been removed to make roofs for German dug-outs: the flat, sour countryside was strewn with German wire and unlocated mines, and into the hundred or so habitable farms and houses had to go at least two battalions and Brigade headquarters.

The Battalion arrived next evening two hours before dark. Each Company numbering about 120 men had four, or at the most five, houses into which it had to squeeze. There was the alternative of two-man bivouac tents, but that was a doubtful blessing should the weather turn worse.

Gloom was universal—here was a "rest area" in which there was very little space to rest, and a Dutch village with no friendly Dutch people.

Into the houses disappeared the seven hundred men and out through the broken windows came the dusty straw, broken boxes, empty tins, and other unmentionable filth left by the retreating Germans. By nightfall the rooms were cleared, the floors swept, the windows patched up, and doors improvised. Fires had destroyed the junk outside the windows and stoves had been made for the rooms—everyone was under cover, and the tents were not needed.

Even so, it was a comfort to be out of sound of the guns and out of range of shells: that we were also out of range of German eggs, chickens and farm produce made some people question the general benefit of rest areas.

For ten days a routine of training and recreation was carried out: assault boat crossings on the River Maas, bridging exercises with kapok floats, field firing on open heather country with all Company weapons, road runs and football matches, cinema and ENSA shows in a canvas marquee. Regimental Sergeant Major Knight supervised the fattening of the mess geese, and in the evenings they could be seen being exercised, each with a string lead round its leg, and led by any unfortunate "defaulters" who happened to be serving punishment at the time.

From here for the last time short-leave parties went off to Brussels and the Medical Officer sharpened his inoculation needles—some say he didn't sharpen them—and took a fresh stab at everyone he considered might be the least bit susceptible to typhoid, typhus or tetanus. New weapons arrived, flame throwing carriers named "Wasps", of which a section were allotted to the Carrier platoon, were demonstrated to the whole battalion, and as many as possible went to see the "Kangaroos" (Ram tanks with turrets removed) adapted as armoured troop carriers, whose motto *"Fundit Armatos"* proclaimed them as the 1945 offspring of the Trojan horse.

Throughout the period the weather was perfect, and many will remember the training days on the dry heather country, "shirt sleeve" order was worn again, the swirling dust penetrated through every gap in the broken windows, and the spring evenings were filled with a red-gold light, as the setting sun caught the myriad particles in the dust laden air.

On 22nd March Colonel Reeves held an Order Group at which he commenced with the general plan for the crossing of the Rhine. The intention of Field Marshal Montgomery was quite simple—*"21st Army Group will now cross the Rhine and will penetrate to an unlimited depth"*. Details of the plan were made clear to all officers and NCOs and on the next day the Colonel explained it to each company of men in turn. Four Army Corps were to be used on our sector, and in addition an Airborne Corps was to drop behind the woods across the river from Xanten to secure that part of the bridgehead. Each Corps was allotted roads leading parallel across the North German plain, and each Division would be limited to one road with one Brigade in the lead. There would be no rest by day or night until the German Army surrendered. Rest would be taken on the route through the principle of having only one Brigade "up" in each Division.

It was estimated that from seven to ten days would see a period of hard fighting before a break-out could be made, and that the forming of a sufficient bridgehead would take three days. The 43rd Division on 30 Corps Sector was to cross behind 51st (Highland) Division, and make the break-out. When they were successful the Guards Armoured Division would make the break-through and lead as the spearhead into North Germany. As events turned out the timings were almost perfect, and it is doubtful whether in all history an operation has gone more according to plan.

At nine p.m. to the minute on Friday 23rd March the Black Watch, carried on amphibious "Buffalo" tanks—"Schwim panzers" the Germans called them—slid into the river, and a few minutes later the first British troops were on the east bank of the Rhine.

Saturday 24th March dawned as a cloudless day—to the waiting troops in the rear areas it was not known yet whether the crossing had been made.

At breakfast in England from the coast of Kent right round to Norfolk the excitement spread as wave after wave of heavy planes, Dakotas, Stirlings, Halifaxes, Lancasters, Fortresses and Liberators, with their attendant trains of gliders began to sweep out over the sea towards the British Army. Here was a sight they had not seen since Arnhem day. A little red headed boy ran out to the door shouting "Look Mummy, planes". The ground crews who had sent them off to Caen and Eindhoven, Nijmegen and Bastogne crossed their fingers for them, anxious eyes and anxious hearts followed them out on every part of the coast. The great British Taxpayer had one of those rare glimpses of the results of his stupendous labours. Where were they going this time? And would there be the same tense waiting for the ground forces to reach their Airborne spearhead?

At nine-fifteen the hundred thousand waiting troops in the forward concentration area saw the airborne bus service arrive in perfect order from a clear sky, and the parachute boys went down.

The flocks of Dakotas circled away northwards, and were followed at once by the first waves of glider-towing bombers running in low. For an hour and a half the steady flow went on. As far as the ground forces could see it was a perfect drop, no sign was seen of the German air force—the flak opposition was slight.

The Seventh Battalion now knew that they would not be needed till Monday. A church service was held in the village school, and those who could not get into the crowded hall stood in groups in the sunshine outside the glassless windows. The battalion band led the hymn—

"Guide me, Oh Thou Great Redeemer"

and the Padre offered the prayer of Sir Francis Drake at Cadiz (1587).

> *"O Lord God, when thou givest to thy servants to*
> *endeavour any great matter, grant us also to know*
> *that it is not the beginning, but the continuing*
> *of the same, until it is thoroughly finished, which*
> *yieldeth the true glory: through Him that for the*
> *finishing of thy work laid down His life".*

At the end of the service came the battalion hymn—

"He who would valiant be, 'gainst all disaster".

After the service, a celebration of Holy Communion was held.

The Brigade Commander ordered that the remainder of the day should be treated as a Sunday, but he ordered that each man should re-sharpen his own bayonet as a symbolic reminder that a hard struggle with evil, desperate, men still lay ahead.

Chapter XIX

THE RHINE

THE Prime Minister of England had already sailed up and down the Rhine and landed on its farther bank when the battalion moved off to the bank assembly area on the afternoon of 26th March. The news cheered everyone and no one could grudge him the risks he took in this, his own special hour of triumph.

As we moved through this sandy, wooded country between the two rivers the great work done by the supply build-up columns during the previous ten days was evident everywhere. Enormous dumps of ammunition and explosives lined the routes: there were stacks of shells of every type from 20 m.m. to the 7.2 inch heavies. At one point only about twelve miles from the Rhine a full scale fighter aerodrome was operating. Flights of Typhoons were continually taking off and returning from the bridgehead, and one great uncamouflaged silver Flying Fortress stood alone at the edge of the field. Speculation ran on whose this single heavy machine might be—perhaps Churchill's, or the Field Marshal's, or Eisenhower's?

Nearer the river bank the road began to pass through the gunlines, and it was possible to see something of the hundreds of guns which had been 'softening' the east bank ever since the fall of Xanten twenty days ago. During the four days covering the assault period a tremendous concentration of guns had been plastering every enemy post and every known gun position—no words can describe the inferno of noise which broke out each time a specific target was called for: the snap-snap-snap of the Bofors, the 'plomp' noise of the massed 25-pounders, the tearing crash of the mediums, and the deeper note of the heavies. The work of the gunners and the details of their grouping will, no doubt, be described in many books: from the infantry viewpoint the speed, the accuracy and the enormous concentration of guns which was achieved in Normandy, at the Reichswald, and again on the Rhine, was an inspiring and most comforting thing. No praise can ever be too high for the Royal Artillery and for the close support for which the Infantry never called in vain.

For communications the Royal Corps of Signals had ploughed in nine hundred miles of telephone cable in the 30 Corps marshalling area alone.

The marching troops de-bussed at the assembly area near Marienbaum, and the Fighting and A Transport Echelons were grouped separately for their own crossing areas.

It was now 6 p.m. and it seemed unlikely that a crossing would take place before the early hours of the morning. Companies were spread in company groups in an open field and sections were ordered to dig themselves shallow trenches and fetch straw from a farm to get some rest. One of the transport columns was near-by and greatcoats were unpacked for a little extra warmth.

The settling in had scarcely started when a violent thunderstorm broke, rolling up heavy ominous clouds over the landscape and splitting the gloom with vivid streaks of lightning. Gun flashes and thunder, lightning and cordite, rivalled each other in a display of venom for twenty minutes—most of the troops and all the strawed trenches were drenched, but the dusty atmosphere was freshened and the evening remained reasonably warm.

The moon came up, and we lay down on our straw and pulled our coats over us to sleep. But the night was too beautiful and the occasion too special for sleep to come. There was the dome of the sky to watch, with pale watery clouds scudding across the moon: or the fringe of tall poplars against the Monty moonlight from the searchlights back in the Hochwald: or the other lights on the river bank sweeping the areas where sapper units were extending or maintaining the bridges, and lighting the roads eastwards towards Munster. And sneaking spotter planes which caused all our Bofors to lift skywards, spraying fountains of glowing tracer which seemed to glide upwards like myriads of tiny red bubbles floating in a blue bowl. One four-engined bomber was caught high up in a cone of thirty searchlights and chased across the sky by a barrage of heavy Ack-Ack, looking for all the world like a lonely moth.

We must have dozed off eventually because at quarter to midnight the sentries went round shouting that we were to move in fifteen minutes, in single file in the order A, B, C, D Companies with five yards spacing between each man.

It was over seven miles to the crossing point, and everyone was wearing super-heavy order. This included battle equipment, pack, steel helmet, 100 rounds of ammunition, rifle, filled water bottle, haversack rations for breakfast, 24-hour emergency ration pack, a tin of self heating soup, extra tea and compressed-fuel cooking tablets, a pick or shovel pushed through the belt and two or three grenades. In addition each platoon carried its normal scale of weapons, magazines and bombs. Before dawn about eleven miles were covered— not in itself any great distance, but under the weight and discomfort of the heavy load, and over loose broken roads, quite a wearing experience.

THE RHINE   4 A.M. 27th MARCH

The files moved slowly forward in silence, keeping their distance and halting occasionally to allow clearance of troops in front. Branch roads led off at different places, and dimly lit signs pointed to Waterloo Bridge, London Bridge, Westminster Bridge and 'Buffalo columns turn right'. The guns kept up a desultory harassing fire on to the opposite bank, but not a single enemy shell interfered with the march.

The head of the column moved down on to Lambeth Bridge a few minutes before four o'clock, and four minutes later the leading platoon was marching up the stone causeway towards Rees. The bridge was firm and straight across the fast grey river, and it was hard to visualise the struggles of the sappers who had built it not many hours before under the most difficult conditions of mud, current, and enemy fire. As we crossed a column of about ninety dirty, weary, Herrenvolk passed us going west—'marching against England'.

Looking back from the causeway the scene was almost like a Peter Scott painting—the background fan of searchlights outlining a frieze of tall leafless poplars, the wide smooth stream reflecting a path of rippling moonlight, the firm hard line of the criss-cross bridge-work low on the water, and the endless file of silent, patient, steel-helmeted silhouettes.

Somewhere after five o'clock the marching troops came to the dispersal area at Esserden where the transport had already arrived, and greatcoats were again handed out. Shallow trenches were dug in the clay of a dewy stubble field and a couple of hours' sleep was snatched before the business of shaving and cooking breakfast on a hexamine tablet need be faced.

At eleven o'clock Colonel Reeves issued orders for our task of pushing through the leading brigade on a two battalion front with the object of clearing a ridge over which ran a partly constructed autobahn. The bridgehead was now something over five miles deep on 30 Corps sector and was continuous, and in some places much deeper, on the whole Army front. The period of the bridgehead was over—the time for the break-out had come.

Chapter XX

BREAK OUT

E advanced again just before mid-day and, after four miles, passed through the forward battalion of the Wiltshires (Commanded by Lieutenant-Colonel Brind of the Somerset Light Infantry) in the shattered village of Millingen. The lie of the ground was that the Divisional axis of advance was crossed at right angles by a partly constructed autobahn running along a low sandy ridge. Strong enemy trenches were located along the back of the ridge on either side of the huge concrete ramps prepared for a "fly-over" bridge. The village of Vehlingen lay about two hundred yards back from the crossing.

The story of the attack is best told in the battle reports of the leading companies.

Battle report of "A" Company

"A" Company were right forward company of the battalion attack, and crossed the start line at 1400 hours. Almost at once they were halted to allow our artillery to move forward. At this point there was slight enemy mortar fire.

As the artillery lifted the Company moved forward till they reached a farm five hundred yards from the start line, where they encountered very heavy spandau fire from a ridge two hundred yards to the front. At this juncture the Company had two platoons forward (Numbers: Seven and Eight) and one in reserve. The enemy positions were such that they commanded a view of the whole front, and despite the heavy artillery, mortar and tank fire brought down on the enemy positions, both "A" and "B" (on the left of "A" Company) were still held up by MG fire from the enemy.

Eventually Eight platoon under Lieutenant A. T. Smith was organised as fire platoon, firing from positions just forward of the farm, whilst Seven platoon under Lieutenant R. C. R. Cox, pushed forward in a left flanking movement. Seven platoon moved into "B" Company area and advanced along the left of the road leading to the Autobahn. Assisted by fire from the support tanks of the 4th/7th Dragoon Guards and "B" Company, the platoon reached a trench system on the Autobahn itself. The enemy positions on the right having become silent, Eight platoon was also able to move forward by the same route as far as the Autobahn.

Meanwhile Seven platoon had advanced a further two hundred yards into the houses on the right hand side of the road leading through the village of Vehlingen. Under cover of their fire Eight platoon advanced to some farm buildings level with Seven platoon and about two hundred yards to their right. During this phase some eight or nine Germans were captured by Seven platoon and Eight platoon in the houses. Advancing through dug in German positions Eight platoon found four dead Germans, and finally reached their objective without further opposition.

Nine platoon under Lieutenant F. K. Wheeler M.M., meanwhile had been heavily shelled in the original farm five hundred yards from the start line and had one killed (Private Clarke), and six wounded. They then moved up through a strip of wood on the right of Eight platoon, and remained there until withdrawn by the Company Commander, to a position in the houses at the beginning of the village.

The Company eventually reorganised on the objective after four and a half hours' heavy fighting, and "B" Company moved in on the left some time later.

Throughout the operation excellent artillery and mortar support was afforded. The accurate artillery support was largely due to the efficient co-operation of Captain Bridges RA, who was Forward Observation Officer with the Company.

The Company took twenty prisoners, its own casualties being one killed and nine wounded.

Battle report of "B" Company

The battalion came up under enemy shellfire and formed up on the start line by 1400 hours. The artillery fire plan then started, but was obviously in the wrong place, and the Companies were unable to advance more than a few hundred yards. All efforts to get it lifted were of no avail. At 1430 hours it lifted and tanks and infantry advanced. Eleven platoon were astride the main road, Ten platoon were on the left and Twelve platoon in reserve. The ground was very boggy and a small stream intersected the advance so that the tanks were confined to the road.

The two forward platoons went forward quickly and very soon after a couple of bursts of spandau fire Ten platoon captured a farm house and collected eight badly scared prisoners, with a couple of machine guns and a "bazooka".

They then swung left towards the Autobahn, which was a long low ridge of sand and earth running across the front, with a couple of hundred yards of dead smooth green fields between the captured farm house and the ridge which we had called our first bound.

As they advanced across the fields they came under heavy spandau fire and one man was killed (Private Kellock): the rest were split, and the platoon commander (Lieutenant G. Eastop) withdrew into the farm house, while his platoon sergeant (Sergeant Evans) was driven into another group of farm buildings well on the left.

At this moment enemy machine gun fire opened up along the Autobahn ridge. "A" Company on our right were obviously held up, and Eleven platoon on the road itself were pinned to the ground in a ditch. One man was wounded, and Lance-corporal Hemmings evacuated him very gallantly. The tanks tried to come up, but two were bogged in the stream and the rest were confined to the actual road causeway and could not locate the enemy, nor give much assistance.

Then followed a very tiring period of trying to find the exact spot from which the fire was coming. Eventually a post to the left of some great concrete road erections was located and we directed heavy fire on to it from our own weapons and from the tanks. Soon up came a surrender flag and after a lot of yelling and waving, we induced some twenty Huns to come and give themselves up: several were wounded.

Taking advantage of this, Corporal Comm of Eleven platoon crawled forward under the still very heavy enfilade fire and got into the concrete block with his section, and was then able to clear a whole sector of the rabbit warren of trenches dug into the back of the Autobahn. The rest of Eleven platoon were sent up to exploit this.

Corporal Comm received an immediate award of the D.C.M. for this action—the citation reads—"He at once brought accurate fire to bear on the enemy; himself got the wounded back, continued to neutralise the opposition, and indicated the positions to the supporting tanks.

Under the tanks' fire this N.C.O. then led his section forward under a hail of criss-crossing enemy bullets. Then by bold and clever use of ground he crawled right up to the enemy defences and got to close quarters. Thirty Boche gave themselves up; several dead were counted.

This brave and skilful advance under exceptionally heavy fire at once enabled the flanking platoons to advance and close with the enemy.

Corporal Comm's gallantry, initiative and leadership without doubt turned the whole enemy defence line."

An 88 suddenly opened up and got two direct hits on Ten platoon's house, wounding many of the Hun prisoners and unfortunately wounding Lieutenant G. Eastop and several of his men in the same building. The whole area was still being sprayed with machine gun fire and casualties kept on occurring both in Company headquarters and in the rear platoon. We got the mediums to fire on the village from which the 88 was firing.

We were now securely ensconsed in the enemy defence line and turned our attention to exploiting it. Any advance was, however, barred by another post on the far side of the Autobahn, which sent bullets flying over our heads in the concrete blocks.

I got the Observation Officer up, and we plastered all the known positions for some time. This they continued to do all the afternoon.

"A" Company were by this time crawling up our line of advance and were able to push platoons through the gap we had made on to their own objective, which was now turned by our successful advance. They advanced up into the village.

The Commanding Officer came up and I asked him for 'Wasps' to tackle this obstinate post. He went away, promising help. Meanwhile we got two tanks and a section under Corporal Sedgwick to attack. All went well at first and both tanks and men advanced safely. The men got right up under the bank of the position and were about to assault when a bazooka was fired at the tanks. They immediately withdrew. Corporal Sedgwick was killed, two men were wounded and the rest had to scramble back. It was a costly failure.

Twelve platoon were now sent round the rear to advance up the left and get into the left hand end of our objective.

Meanwhile the Commanding Officer, with the 'Wasp' Officer, had come up but he was unfortunately wounded by the very gun that was holding us up. This delayed matters a lot, and it was not till Major C. Brooke Smith came up that we got the 'Wasps' sent up to us, and were able to make an excellent plan.

Again, however, we were delayed, this time by another battalion on the left, who put down a terrific smoke screen on us and covered the area with machine gun fire from their Kangaroos. All movement had to cease whilst this was in progress.

The dusk fell, and we called off the 'Wasp' attack, advancing under cover of darkness to our objective just short of the Vehlingen windmill. There were no incidents and the move up went smoothly. We took up good positions within the village.

Whilst digging in enemy mortaring started. We had bad luck with a direct hit on Twelve platoon headquarters. Lieutenant G. F. Parrack was wounded, two men killed (Lance-corporal Conaty and Private Martin), and two men wounded. It was a nasty blow, coming at the end of the operation. We had no further incidents that night and next day 'C' and 'D' Companies passed through.

The whole operation lasted seven hours after a night march with little or no sleep. Two officers were wounded (one died of wounds), five men were killed and fourteen men were wounded. We counted five enemy dead in their trenches next day and took about thirty prisoners. The enemy posts were manned by Parachute troops, but the really troublesome post was manned by S.S. and the dead were all S.S."

* * *

Meanwhile "C" and "D" Companies were lying up in the ditches and small houses some four hundred yards to the rear. There they had to wait for about four hours under intermittent shelling and a small amount of sniping, until required for the battalion plan. It was a trying period, especially as it was difficult to "read" the battle up forward, and the ditches were unpleasantly shallow and damp—there was also the disadvantage that the road was lined with trees, and treeburst shells had long been an unpopular feature.

It was with deep regret that Colonel Reeves, who had done so much for the battalion, and set such a fine example of personal bravery since his arrival in January, was seen riding back on a stretcher bearers' jeep with a wound in his left shoulder. Sergeant Martin, too, Pioneer Sergeant of many battles, and a founder-member of the battalion, went past, wounded in the back by shrapnel.

Just before dark the reserve Companies were ordered forward and as soon as they started to move the leading platoon came under fire from unlocated machine guns on the left. Smoke was put down and covering fire from the supporting tanks. Private Hood, a P.I.A.T. man was wounded in the shoulder, and as he fell was most unfortunate in having his foot, and his P.I.A.T., crushed by one of our own tanks. They continued to move in bounds until reaching the small stream already mentioned. Here there was another pause while "B" Company cleared their objective. Several farms in the area were now blazing, and the night was fully dark, heavy shellfire was falling on both sides of the road, and there were no ditches in which to disperse.

RSM. Knight showed a complete disregard of the enemy's fire at this time—to him it was obviously not as heavy as a Guardsman had a right to expect. He moved up and down the centre of the road several times, organising ammunition supplies and the evacuation of prisoners. He provided one valuable piece of comic relief when he chased a batch of Boche prisoners, who were not moving fast enough, back down the road at the double.

After fifty minutes the way was open and "C" Company moved out on to the left rear of "B", with "D" on the autobahn behind "A", where they had to start digging like beavers under occasional shellfire. Small arms fire was still coming from the left but it was thought better not to return it, thus indicating that the ground was held—double sentries were posted, and permission was given at midnight to use the self heating soup emergency ration, as no food had been able to get up since breakfast. Shelling continued throughout the night, and a particularly heavy gun appeared to have the range of the area, scoring one or two direct hits on the concrete ramps between the two Companies.

At first light the rear Companies set about cleaning up the Autobahn entrenchment area. The positions were very strong, and well constructed—each was capable of containing a company and could have held off a battalion. Prisoners who had laid low during the night now started coming in from the outlying positions. On the side through which "B" Company had fought "C" Company took a further thirty prisoners before breakfast. "D" Company took a similar number in the same period. Large quantities of weapons including plenty of ammunition for the spandaus, and crates of grenades were found still in the trenches.

Later in the morning "C" and "D" Companies passed through with orders to exploit up to one thousand two hundred yards on the left and right of the axis respectively. In each case the operation consisted of clearing groups of inter-supporting farms, and the order was for speed. Prisoners were taken in almost every farm, but there was no attempt to fire. The operation was completed on each side of the road in under an hour ("D" Company having started some time before "C"). Platoons were then told to clear the flanks, and platoons of "C" and "D" Companies searched their way forward through the large woods covering Anholt—in this area they maintained standing patrols for the next two days.

Another Brigade was now ordered to pass through and capture Anholt; in twenty-four hours the Vehlingen Autobahn had been a battlefield and become a back area. The total of enemy prisoners was one hundred and forty six—all S.S. and Paratroops. On the 27th the distance of the advance was seven hundred yards, on the 28th two and a half miles. This was without doubt the beginning of the break out—the next time the battalion moved it covered twelve miles. The bridgehead had been a closely contained perimeter based on a bridge, now the bridge was a powerful jet ready to send flames fanning far and wide into Germany.

Chapter XXI

EASTER BELLS
AND ORANGE RIBBONS

I wish I could say that Easter Sunday 1st April was a brilliant spring day, but it wasn't, it was dull and grey. I wish I could claim that the Battalion led the drive into Northern Holland, but in fact it was in the third Brigade on the line of march. Nevertheless, neither the day nor the one thousand two hundred vehicles which had passed before prevented the sturdy Hollanders from their determination to greet the "Tommies". For all the reinforcements who had joined since the winter battles, this was a first taste of liberating and a very emotional experience it was.

The Guards Armoured Division had broken out two days before from the Anholt area, and the 43rd Division had moved over the Dutch border the previous night. Now we were acting as left flank protection to the Guards in a left handed sweep northwards towards the Twenthe Canal at Hengelo. This drive was to cut across all the direct communications from Germany into the Zuyder Zee area—the V2 rocket supply lines being not the least important. Behind us the Canadian Army was turning due west for Arnhem, Utrecht and Zutphen.

Our own leading battalions were riding in Kangaroos and all the remainder in troop-carrying lorries. Any resistance was to be tackled at once by the spearheads, and the column was to keep going—each battalion had under command a squadron of tanks from the 8th Armoured Brigade in addition to its normal supporting arms.

From early morning till long after dark, with only a short interlude during morning church, the roads, villages and towns were lined and packed with waving, cheering people. Old men in peaked blue caps with knobbly sticks and twisted pipes, old women with close fitting bonnets of linen or lace, girls and children with orange ribbons, orange bows, orange flowers, young men with long shovels filling in the pot-holes and tank ruts with turf from the roadsides as each vehicle passed, and everyone shouting "Hello Tommie" and not forgetting also to shout for chocolate, and "Cigarette for Papa".

The column which they saw was impressive even to those who had followed the Army across Europe. To those who only yesterday had seen the battered, retreating lorries and horse-drawn limbers of the Germans it must have seemed irresistible.

First a spearhead screen of small and large armoured cars, then a squadron of tanks with long menacing guns, each with its Commander standing upright in the turret, then twenty or thirty armoured kangaroos carrying the vanguard companies of Infantry. Next, another squadron of tanks, the remainder of the Infantry, a platoon of mortars, a troop or a battery of anti-tank guns, more armoured cars, more tanks, a command group with waving radio aerials and clouds of noisy despatch riders, a regiment of Artillery with bouncing limbers and a score of ammunition trucks, more Infantry riding in open-sided troop-carrying lorries with Bren guns mounted on the roof and rifles pointing from the sides.

A slight gap, perhaps due to some obstacle in the road—then a battery of light Ack-Ack, flame-throwing Churchills, more Infantry, more tanks, more Bren carriers, a regiment of Medium Artillery—long barrelled guns—with sixty or seventy attendant ammunition waggons, Engineers, trucks full of Bailey bridges, tanks carrying scissors and sledge bridges, Military Government flying squads, ambulances, mobile dressing stations, cooks, catering advisers, tanks, infantry, guns—as far as the eye could see and as long as the people cared to wait, came the endless columns through the small, inadequate by-roads of Holland.

At every halt the trucks were covered with swarms of children: burned-out German lorries and smashed guns became more frequent on the roadsides. People said "The Mof (Hun) went yesterday: he went at midnight: he went at eight o'clock this morning, pulling his trucks with horses—he has no benzine". It was the same at Aalten, Lichtenvoorde, Ruurlo, and when we pulled into Neede at dusk where the streets were full of tired, happy people.

It became known that the bridges on the Twenthe Canal were blown and that the enemy were holding the North bank. An advance on foot was ordered and began at ten p.m.

Diepenheim, 5 miles north on the canal bank, was reached in the small hours, and the battalion took up a position covering the canal and guarding the road from Lochem on the Westward side. Dinner (that is, dinner for the previous day) was served at four a.m. The distance covered during the advance was between 35 and 40 miles. At Diepenheim a large German Signals Headquarters with valuable equipment was captured intact. Local people said that the Germans had left the previous night, very drunk and demoralized. They had been prevented in their attempt to burn down the lovely manor house in which the HQ was housed.

Two or three days were spent covering the area from Lochem to Hengelo while bridges were built and the towns of Hengelo and Enschede were cleared. The people did everything they could to house in their small villages the enormous influx of soldiers. The Guards then pushed on to the German border and April 5th found 43rd Division in Nordhorn, with the Guards and 3rd Division striking for the Dortmund-Ems Canal. A total arc of about 70 miles had been swept through Holland, which was now left to the Canadians as one of their main areas.

At the frontier post the change of atmosphere was striking. There were the last groups of Hollanders offering hands full of eggs and waving goodbye: the last cigarettes and sweets were tossed from the vehicles, waves and V-signs were exchanged. Two flag masts stood fifty yards apart: on the one to the West flew the flag of the Netherlands—the one on the East was bare.

At Nordhorn we were back in Germany among a subservient and beaten people.

Chapter XXII

JELLALABAD BRIDGE AND HASELÜNNE

EANWHILE to the south things were happening fast. Almost a week previously the Remagen bridgehead on the American front had suddenly broken, and the U.S. First and Third Armies were racing each other down the autobahns into central Germany. Cassel had fallen, and Heidelberg; the Ninth Army was in Münster and Hannover; British troops were through Osnabrück and half way to the Elbe. Hitler had lost a third of Germany in seven days.

Without detracting in any way from these achievements it may be said that for some time the Germans had regarded the 30th as the break through Corps. The original Corps had come all the way from El Alamein. A prisoner confirmed this view when he said "Thirty Corps like this—" making with his hands and fingers a symbol of an arrowhead—and the northern front was opposed most resolutely by what was left of the Sixth and Seventh Para Divisions, 15th Panzer Division, 116 Panzer Grenadiers and the Gross Deutschland Division Clever use was made of the innumerable canals and waterways, and demolitions were encountered at every bridge and stream. It was later estimated by General Horrocks that from Normandy to Bremen his engineers had constructed sixteen and a half miles of Bailey bridging—enough bridging to carry a forty ton load from Hyde Park Corner to Epsom Grandstand!

On April 7th the Battalion again took the lead, passing through the Guards and 3rd Divisions on the Dortmund Ems Canal at Lingen, and advancing on Haselünne.

The advance guard was a strong one comprising a regiment of tanks (13/18 Hussars), a motor battalion (12th Kings Royal Rifle Corps) and the 7th Bn Somerset L.I. The vanguard Company was "C" riding in Kangaroos and supported by two troops of Sherman tanks, and a motor platoon K.R.R.C.

A swift advance of about seven miles was made straight down the road towards Bremen. Just short of Bawinkel was a very strong road block of heavy felled trees interlaced and covered by another built up block of timber, earth and rocks. This was typical of the type of obstacle which now became a daily feature—normally very well constructed and sometimes booby-trapped and mined.

The trees used were long, straight, pines but the troops, as they climbed over them or levered them apart, applied to them names which will not be found in any book of horticulture, or arboriculture. Names which, in truth, you will not find in any book of culture at all. This one was partially cleared by the battalion pioneers using a Kangaroo, but it proved too much and was eventually blasted away by a "Petard" firing Churchill, and swept up by a "Sherdozer" (Sherman tank mounting a bulldozer in front).

The remainder of the battalion closed forward, and passed through on foot to occupy positions just west of the village: "B" Company patrolled into the village.

Early on April 8th a squadron of armoured cars was sent in to occupy the village followed by "D" Company and a troop of the 13/18th Hussars. The village was captured after a scrap with a few enemy, and the Company went on to take a small wood to the north-east.

The main road now lay through dense pine forests for several miles, and it appeared certain that the bridge over the river HAZE would be blown. The whole advance guard was ordered to make a wide flanking movement to the left through the extensive, but less dense, state forest of Engelbertswald with "A" and "D" Companies riding in Kangaroos. The brigade plan was to capture the smaller bridge at Hamm while the 5th D.C.L.I. pushed along the main road making their advance as obvious as possible.

The drive through the Engelbertswald over bumpy sandy tracks was a complete success and the defenders of the bridge were caught sunbathing at Bückelte and were shot up; however the bridge itself was blown and covered by spandaus from the farther bank.

A reconnaissance was carried out and Colonel Brooke Smith decided to make an assault crossing in the evening, slightly to the east. The infantry companies had come up on foot to an assembly position. Battalion headquarters· moved into Bückelte village.

Captain J. A. H. Clarke (the Adjutant) writes—

"What I mainly remember about the battle of Bückelte–Hamm was that it was a very hot, fine day. We had had a troublesome time along that road with demolitions and road blocks. Now we had to take to the woods again. The bridge at Haselünne was blown and the D.C.L.I. was to engage the Germans' attention from the front while we and the Worcestershire Regiment made a wide detour to seize the bridge at Bückelte.

Off we went, Kangaroos, Tanks, TCVs, appendages of every sort, 'D' Company in front, through this thick-wooded country along a straight track with many intersections. Frequent halts while forward recce was made. Flank recce? None. We got out of our vehicles: I personally went to sleep in the sun. Even the wireless dozed. The track became looser and narrower—a fine sand surface for Tanks and TCVs! So we motored into Bückelte which was a charming village in the sunshine—daffodils, forsythia, tulips, jonquils, fat farms and blossom. The bridge was blown, of course: a dozen sunbathing Germans were captured. But it was a peaceful summery scene. Our snipers went ferreting round for any trouble there might be: Battalion HQ and all their conglomeration of vehicles settled in, and the Germans seemed oddly remote.

The wood we'd come through had plenty of skulking Huns in it who tried to ambush a Gunner Line Recce party later in the day.

River crossing with boats. It was 4 o'clock. We were to cross an hour and a half before dark. It was like any exercise in England. Still no signs or sounds of the enemy. We could see the river. I had to find out how deep it was, how strong the current was, what the banks were like. Brigade wanted to know. RE officers appeared and sat in the garden or on the front door steps of our HQ. Tea and bread and butter was being got ready in the kitchen.

'Go and find a place to off-load the boats—I don't want them seen or heard.'

'O.Group at five.'

At five o'clock 29 people sat on the front door steps in the sun. Facing them the Commanding Officer at a table. Orders—just as if it were a cloth model exercise. The eventual bridge was to be built at the original demolished one's site and we would cross at a loop in the river about half a mile away from it.

The sun was hot and people digested the orders and chewed grass. We had tea.

The RSM went off to sign a route for the Worcestershire's approach by night, to cross over the bridge when it was built. The REs said 'four hours after Hamm is captured'. Our sandy track had long since become hopeless. The Pioneers (in an hour) made and painted twelve large signs 'TO JELLALABAD BRIDGE' for it was April 8th—(Possibly the first time a bridge had been christened so long before its birth). The signs went up, lamps were got.

Headquarters' food arrived and was being served out in a barn adjoining Battalion HQ, when a heavy shell landed five yards from the queue. Fortunately the 'HQ' Cooks truck and the Officers Mess truck took the damage—three tyres, two windscreens and a carburettor. Two men were scratched. The officers mess canary died from shock.''

The Brigadier was delighted with the place selected by the Commanding Officer for the assault. It was not the point at which he had rather intimated it could be done. It was, in fact, around a bend, and was a less obvious place, but he later attributed the success of the operation, and the surprise it achieved to the C.O's choice of ground.

Captain J. W. Baden was appointed "beach master" to control the loading and return of boats and at 8.15 p.m. they were off.

"A" Company was the first across in assault boats. The crossing was not observed, and companies filed into a small wood on the opposite bank in quick succession. So swiftly, in fact, that they had to go to ground and lie up while the fire plan ran its pre-arranged course. They had also been covered by diversionary noises and smoke on the flanks supplied by our three-inch mortars, and the heavy mortars and machine guns of the Middlesex Regiment.

When the Companies were across the attack on Hamm began with considerable artillery support. "A" Company led the way, but were held up by several well sited machine guns and sustained several casualties as dark fell. "B" Company went straight to their objective, the destroyed bridge and seized the bridging site.

"A" Company were still unable to get on immediately west of Hamm, between the bridge and the village, so "D" and "C" Companies made a wide detour to the north and seized the village from that direction. All opposition ceased immediately, and the defenders were taken prisoner. Lieutenant E. Brennan's platoon pulled out a number of young Nazis who were hastily changing into civilian clothes. Consolidation was quickly completed, and by 0130 hours on 9th April Hamm was firmly in our hands. Work was started by the REs on a Class 9 bridge immediately.

✳   ✳   ✳

Meanwhile the Adjutant, at rear headquarters—

"Through the night things looked up. The wireless never stopped, officers of every size and persuasion came. Colonel Hope Thomson M.C. of 1st Battalion The Worcestershire Regiment, RE officers from the C.R.E. downwards: Tank officers, Brigade liaison officers. The bridge took longer than was planned owing to bad approaches, but at 0800 hrs the battalion headquarters transport crossed, then 'F' Echelon in blocks, by arrangement with 1st Worcestershires. By 10 o'clock the battalion was complete in Hamm. A double helping of bacon and eggs, and the German prisoners blacked all Battalion headquarters' boots.

'O' Group at 11 a.m.,—the Worcestershires had gone straight for Haselünne and we were to follow and pass through when they had a portion of the town. We moved at 1.30 p.m. Another summer day. We passed through the Worcestershires in Haselünne after an approach march of some two miles. One or two shells were coming over. Battalion headquarters halted in a narrow street. Seven or eight big shells came over, landed just where we were. Two pioneer jeeps written off, but no pioneers—the Worcestershires were unlucky in their R.A.P. and some of our men were wounded.

Street clearing went on methodically according to plan, though one company took a wrong turning. The code word report lines were 'VICTORY', 'PEACE' and 'FREEDOM', and this company had 'FREEDOM' before 'PEACE'—(We had had Matthew, Mark, Luke and John the day before and Lieutenant-Colonel Reeves would never deviate from Pip, Squeak and Wilfred. The battalion pipped and squeaked all down the Siegfried Line in February).

'Find a battalion headquarters.'

We found the Hitler Youth Training School Headquarters—a vast barracks with about five hundred rooms, laundry, classrooms, physics labs and stuffed birds, beasts and fish, and appendices in glass jars. The RSM and three men of the Pioneer Platoon having done a little house-clearing, battalion headquarters established itself.

It was still warm and sunny. The companies were soon all in position and Haselünne was captured.

Shellfire continued all day and during the night.

It was our first experience of a fairly large town and we were soon beset with problems. 'We've found two factories full of raw alcohol'—civilians—curfews—interesting looking documents in the command post. A huge Nazi standard which is now in the regimental museum at Taunton—an engine at the railway station—a post office—some displaced persons. Two more gin factories.

'A' Echelon joined us in Haselünne that night (quick work!), Military Government and a Field Security Section were early arrivals that afternoon. The D.C.L.I. passed through to the next village over a new Hase bridge the next morning. 'JELLALABAD BRIDGE' took the rest of Brigade and its 'A' Echelon over the Hase and was then dismantled.

We drink Haselünner Edelkorn—a ginny substance (via N.A.A.F.I. at four marks a bottle)—to this day."

That afternoon, at battalion headquarters, Private Huggins was struck in the chest by a piece of shrapnel. He did not, as film heroes do, plunge his hand into his bosom and bring it out dripping blood; he started methodically from the outside. He looked down and saw a rent in his breast pocket. He opened the button and pulled out his soldier's Pay Book—torn like his blouse. He drew out a steel shaving mirror—gashed beyond further use as a mirror. He reached once more (there wasn't much left to reach for now), and there— buried in his last bar of chocolate—was the splinter which didn't have his number.

∗   ∗   ∗

One lesson which had been, by now, very thoroughly learned was that of keeping the cooks trucks well forward. The value of a hot meal or a fresh cup of tea is beyond price, and the Company Quartermaster-Sergeants and cooks gladly took the added risks to ensure that these should be available.

Of course, in some battles there had not been room to have the cooks up, but in England it had always been said that one could not have them up because they had a "soft" vehicle. Why it was any softer than a similar truck carrying ammunition, or why "soft" by day, but not at night (when it had to come up anyway)—no one ever explained. That conception, however, had always necessitated serving dinner, the last meal of the day, after dark, and breakfast before dawn, which, in the summer months, was a gastronomic feat of the highest order—leaving about one and a half hours in between for the night's sleep.

However that may be—the cooks went into Haselünne, and all the other German towns that fell, as close as was operationally possible behind the battalion.

This action was typical of the opposition on the left flank throughout the advance. The German policy of fighting a minor delaying action in every village and town was costing them very dearly without making any appreciable difference to the outcome of the war. In Haselünne they lost twenty or thirty killed, and sixty or more prisoners. (We, too, lost a dozen casualties, fortunately some of them quite minor wounds). The covering barrage of artillery and mortars from the battalion held up on the main road did probably over a million pounds' worth of damage to this prosperous country town, and the delay caused amounted to less than eighteen hours. Along the whole of the way from the Rhine to Bremen the route was scarred with burned out farms, smashed bridges and cratered roads. As the Brigade Commander remarked it made one despair for the sanity of the human race—here was one group of men going back along a perfectly good road blowing holes, and another group of men pursuing and filling them up. He said "Besides the hole doesn't stand a chance—it only lasts an hour or two—how man has the nerve to look an honest horse in the face, I don't know."

However Hitler's decision to fight on was serving one very useful purpose—it was bringing the horrors of war in an unforgettable manner to the country districts which would never have felt them had there been an earlier surrender.

Chapter XXIII

FORST CLOPPENBURG

WHILE the battalion rested at Haselünne—where good billets were enjoyed, and where battalion headquarters was most sumptuously housed in its Hitler Youth head-quarters—the other two Brigades of the Division had made good progress along "Heart" route, by which the axis was known. The Divisional Recce Regiment at the same time searched huge areas of ground between "Heart" route and the next Divisional axis to the south. Herzlake, Loningen, and Lastrup were captured, and 214 Brigade was then called forward to a concentration area just short of Cloppenburg, twenty-five miles to the East.

The town itself was cleared the same night (13th April) in an all night action by part of 130 Brigade, and by the 5th D.C.L.I., as the leading battalion of 214. It had previously been heavily bombed, and many of the houses were still burning.

Of that dark and confused night I have very clear memories, and I quote them not because they are in themselves outstanding, but because they are typical of so many entries into enemy towns. I was, at the time, detached from the battalion to Brigade HQ as Liaison Officer.

I had just rolled up in my blankets at 2 a.m., after a three hour watch on the command wireless set. It seemed that I had scarcely rolled over when I found myself being shaken by the shoulder. The tall figure bending over me was strangely remote as I struggled to collect my senses. "The Brigadier wants you in the Command Post." The time was a few minutes short of four o'clock.

I pulled on my jacket, and fastened my belt as I groped my way across the farmyard— passing the word for my imperturbable Cornish batman to stand by with the jeep.

The Brigadier was waiting—wearing his khaki shirt, open at the neck, and pyjama trousers. I felt keenly for him, as I took my orders from this man of whom I had heard much in the battalion—of how he never spared himself in making the best possible plans for his troops, of how many owed their lives to his wise planning. This morning he was anxious. "I have been out of touch with the D.C.L.I. for three hours, they have not come up on the air since 0130 hours. They should be in this area (indicating the map). You must find Colonel Taylor and tell him etc. ... etc. ... I want an exact report of his progress when you return."

I memorised the map for there was still fighting in the town, and snipers were about. To use a torch would be foolish. One mile straight down the main road, then a left hand bend and a level crossing. Turn right and there would be houses on both sides. Shops, perhaps. Four hundred yards and then a wider section, it seemed like a market place; turn left here and over a bridged stream, a quarter of a mile, built up all the way, and then another market place. Enemy very near here, turn left. Curve right once, then slightly left, and there should be a church in front. Probably I should find some Duke of Cornwall's sentries there.

We set off down the darkened, tree-lined, road in the unlighted jeep with the setting moon low behind us. Over the level crossing and into the first row of shops. I had my pistol in one hand and Tresidder's Sten gun in the other. I don't know whether I was more scared of snipers, or of the enormous bomb craters in the road. Shattered buildings flanked the road, outlined against fires, and burning timbers. The jeep climbed over sprawling bricks, and piles of crunching glass. Past the first market place and over the bridge.

Not a sign of human life anywhere, the street seemed much too long; shots in the distance echoing between the buildings, but none at us. No, the street should not be as long as this. Where was the second market place? Had we come too far? Should I turn back and start again? Just as I was convinced that we were lost, we came upon the silent silhouette of a tank and another beyond. A whole squadron of 13th/18th Hussars waiting in file to move up with the dawn. Comforting sight!

We threaded our way up the line of tanks, and found the D.C.L.I. headquarters—all tired, but quite safe and firmly on their objectives. Information and orders exchanged with Colonel Taylor over a big cup of tea, and back we went, more boldly now, to Brigade.

Next morning the 1st Worcestershires passed through, and at 3 p.m. we followed them to the south-west corner of another heavily wooded area, Forst Cloppenburg, where their leading troops were already well into the forest. The battalion was given the task of searching the thick woods to a depth of two thousand yards on each side of the axis. For the night 14th/15th April they held a stretch of some three thousand yards of road facing north and south—the Support Company was used to help hold these wide fronts.

Out beyond the forest was an important cross roads where, it was later discovered, the Germans had a stragglers collecting point. The south-north road was a main line of retreat from the central front towards Wilhelmshaven, and, in addition, just beyond the cross roads was an important aerodrome and Luftwaffe base.

On this cross roads they were collecting their own forces and reforming them into battle groups. One such group, about three hundred strong, threw in a fierce counter attack at Neu Lethe, where the Worcestershires had a bridgehead over a cratered bridge and stream, at dawn on 16th April. The attack was "seen off" most thoroughly by the Worcestershires and their supporting tanks, who inflicted casualties to the extent of forty killed, forty or fifty seriously wounded, and fifty to sixty prisoners, but once again the frontal advance seemed likely to be slow going. Seventh Somersets were now ordered to carry out a wide clearing movement to the north, through the forest, and to get in a position for a combined advance to the Ahlhorn cross roads level with the Worcestershires.

As in the case of the Haselünne attack the forest was an enormous tract of pine and spruce, closely planted, covering an area of twelve to sixteen square miles. The only available routes were along sandy tracks, and rides; there were occasional clearings and isolated farms and lodges. Two small bridges were found to be blown and it was impossible to get any vehicle up; the battalion, therefore, carried out the attack without transport, or its own supporting arms. "D" Company was sent forward to clear the start line, about which nothing was known.

Another difficulty of control which had made itself felt on several occasions was that in these wide forest areas wireless communication was often masked or distorted, in addition to being overlapped by several British and Allied "nets" and frequently jammed by Luftwaffe, or civilian, transmissions. On this occasion "D" Company could pick up nothing but a brass band!

On the way to the start line they dealt with one blown bridge by pushing a farm cart into the water which enabled three-quarters of the Company to get across dryshod. The start line was found clear—the only cottage was flying the now ubiquitous German flag—a white one.

The Brigade operation was divided into three phases in which the first involved the battalion in a deep searching task due eastwards, and well north of the road, to a line which would turn the flank of the enemy facing the Worcestershires on the axis. In phase II the Worcestershires were to move forward level with the Somersets' new positions, and in phase III a combined frontal attack would secure the Ahlhorn cross roads, and the road to Oldenburg and Wilhelmshaven.

The Somersets started phase I with "C" and "B" Companies forward, ("C" being on the right). The artillery laid down block concentrations lifting in front of the advance, and all available light AA guns, mortars, MMGs and tanks kept up a steady "pepper potting" from the back areas. "C" Company followed the barrage closely, and took their objective which was round a quarry; they took a small number of prisoners. "B" Company followed the concentration in a similar manner until they came to a large open clearing about eight hundred yards short of their objective. The tanks had now caught up with them and "D" Company was close behind. A left flank advance was planned by Major Bickford (Worcestershires), who was temporarily serving with the battalion. "D" Company took up positions as fire company, and two platoons led by a troop of tanks did the attack which was completely successful. About ten prisoners were taken in the objective. The Sergeant-Major said "It was the only time in the whole campaign when I saw everything work exactly as in 'Battle Drill'."

Meanwhile "A" Company, following "C" to the objective, spotted some Boche to the right and turned to attack them; seven prisoners were taken.

The whole phase was accomplished very swiftly and without serious incident, and shortly afterwards the Worcestershires moved up unopposed. On the battalion objective "A" Company had taken over a chicken pen for their prisoners, together with some more handed over by "C" Company—to ensure that there was no nonsense the prisoners were made to lie face downwards in the pen. Presently a stray prisoner, a late arrival, came in and was ordered to join the others. Here then, before his eyes, was the evidence of what he had so often been told, here were German prisoners shot face downwards in the mud. Sweat poured down his face as he dropped to his knees, begging for mercy. It was a tense moment, until one of his compatriots told him to shut up and lie down like any other good German.

At another point a number of enemy opened up on Eight platoon from a sandpit. A shooting match started and they were finally induced to surrender—they consisted, to everyones' surprise, of five senior N.C.Os (one wounded), three Corporals and only one Private. A senior Warrant Officer remarked that our fire had been extremely accurate. The chicken coop now contained twenty-seven residents.

The tanks of 13th/18th Hussars were close up when phase III started at 5.30 p.m. with "A" and "D" Companies forward. Artillery support was used again, and generous use was made of smoke on our exposed flank. Thirty-five prisoners, including two immaculate and polite Luftwaffe officers, fell to "A" Company, who got astride the cross roads in quick time, and another twelve were brought in by Seven platoon who pushed up the north road to link with "D" Company; a bulldozer was also captured. Suddenly thirty enemy were seen coming up the road from the south. The tanks engaged them, and Lieutenant

F. K. Wheeler M.M., took a fighting patrol out to meet them, but they did not give up and Lance-corporal Dodd was wounded in the shoulder. He later died of wounds. The Gunner O.P. then turned his Field Regiment on to them to the tune of two hundred and forty rounds, and they were rapidly dispersed.

On the cross roads itself Sergeant H. Carroll of Seven Platoon was checking over the buildings when he found a telephone exchange, half of which had been wrecked. On the switchboard of the undamaged half were two sockets labelled Bremen, one of which was plugged in. He put in the other lead, and heard a female voice talking, so he summoned up the majority of his German vocabulary, and said "Wer da, bitte?" (Who's there, please) and received the answer "Hier ist Bremen".

Realizing that this was a matter for the Royal Corps of Signals, or the Intelligence Branch, a message was passed back to Brigade. During the evening a voice came up on the line, several times, saying "Luftwaffe, Bremen", but the line went dead before any effective use could be made of it.

"D" Company on the left had had misgivings about their start line, as the open country was being swept by spandau fire. This, for some unknown reason, ceased as Sixteen and Eighteen platoons moved forward. First class tank support was given the whole way to the objective by 13th/18th Hussars. A number of enemy were shot, and prisoners taken. The road was secured for the loss of two wounded and one case of battle exhaustion—the casualties being caused on the road by an S.P. gun to the north. In fact, all resistance now appeared to be on the north flank where a number of S.P. guns were located during the next two days. The battalion now focussed its attention on holding the cross roads and the north flank, where some miles north and to the rear, the Canadians were coming up for an attack on Oldenburg.

On 16th April Company Sergeant-Major D. Clarke led a patrol well beyond our forward posts, and discovered recent track marks made by several heavy armoured vehicles. He also found stacks of enemy shells near the track marks, and freshly dug trenches; an enemy, who was seen crossing the track lower down, was shot. Next morning, at first light, he led an ambush patrol back to the scene, with orders to waylay the enemy and destroy any tracked vehicles which might return.

As dawn broke, the enemy did not return; but the dead body had been removed during the night. Not satisfied, they advanced into the woods, and came under fire at short range from some buildings. They returned the fire and prepared to attack. This brought them under further fire from the left, so CSM Clarke skilfully withdrew his patrol under covering fire from the Brens, and was able to give the location, by wireless, and that of trucks and motor-cycles which were heard, to a Gunner officer who had followed the patrol.

The patrol had attempted considerably more than the task set for it, and the withdrawal was carried out without loss. As they withdrew a heavy "stonk" from the medium guns came down on the targets they had given.

On 17th April, with the battalion extending its hold to the northward, Lance-sergeant B. Hinnells, in charge of the Sniper section, led two daring and highly successful patrols to the village of Sage, which was on a cross roads on the direct road north to Oldenburg. On the first, in daylight, with two men he penetrated one thousand eight hundred yards into the forest and located a self-propelled gun. He sent one man back with the map reference to call down medium artillery fire, and with the other man reached a small copse a further one thousand yards forward, where they surprised sixty Germans and shot the sentry. He found that Sage was strongly held and on his report it was heavily bombarded.

At 9.30 p.m. he went out again with his patrol from "B" Company lines, and moved in total darkness to some houses four hundred yards beyond our forward positions. He could find no sign of the enemy either there or in the woods close by, but had to dispatch a troublesome barking dog which was giving away his movements. He then decided to move one thousand yards due east along a winding sandy track to meet the main road south of Sage. He found and examined no less than seven road blocks built of fallen trees, in the final stretch of road leading into the village; the road was bounded on both sides by wide water ditches, but he could find no apparent sign of mines. He also found a large crater which had completely removed one sector of the road.

His next plan was to make a two thousand yard sweep through the smaller plantations to the east and strike the side road into Sage from that direction. There was an eerie silence about the star-lit darkness, and each man's heart sounded to him "like a beating drum" until the outskirts of the village were reached, where several burning farms filled the night air with hissing sparks and the crash of falling timbers.

A telephone cable was found and it was decided to follow it in the hope of coming to a Nazi Headquarters. This was done simply by using the cable as a guide line running free through one hand, but it led them into deep marshy country, where they got soaked with mud and slime, and emerged closer than they would have wished to an enemy post, making a great deal of noise in their wet clothes.

Here they were able to hear the sound of tank engines warming up, and much shouting and swearing in German.

Lance-sergeant Hinnells decided that his position would not be much worse if he moved forward, so he led his patrol "crawling like snakes through the grass" to a hedge only a few feet from the tanks. They counted thirteen or fourteen tanks and self-propelled guns, and watched the crews standing around them, and preparing to move. He reckoned that they were being given orders to withdraw, and half an hour later was able to confirm this as they moved off heading for Oldenburg. The patrol then searched every sound building (three-quarters were on fire from the afternoon shelling)—"the torches of burning timbers throwing weird shadows as we flitted from wall to wall. We found that the enemy had completely gone, and there was no abandoned equipment; so, after signing the visitors book in the church, we passed into the woods on the west side again. We found a group of about thirty or forty Germans sleeping, and guarded by a sentry who was smoking—the remainder of this large wood was empty. We had now been out nearly five hours and were very tired and wet, so we returned to battalion headquarters via 'D' Company forward posts. Here the alarm was raised, and we were challenged for the only time that night."

The patrol returned at 3 a. m. after five and a half hours of hard and anxious work. The distance covered (by the map) was ten thousand five hundred yards outside the battalion forward line. Sergeant Hinnells received the Military Medal for this patrol as did C.S.M. Clarke for his patrol of the previous day.

The kit bags now came up for the first time since the Rhine crossing, and we were able to get at our clean clothes, and other personal comforts, though still living in the woods, holding an extended line, and engaged on active patrols.

Chapter XXIV

BREMEN

HE stage was now set for the attack on Bremen. The German forces had been split into three areas, one based on Oldenburg, Wilhelmshaven and Emden which was being pressed back by the Canadian Army; one based on Bremen and the Bremerhaven peninsula; and one already being squeezed by the Corps on the British right flank from Hamburg back to the Baltic.

For the Bremen attack two Divisions were already in Delmenhorst and would have the task of clearing the suburbs south of the river Weser, after which the whole of their artillery would be available to cover the city. The main part of the town lies along the north bank for a distance of nine miles and is nowhere wider than two miles. For this task the 52nd (Lowland) Division were passed over the Weser well to the south with the object of clearing the waterfront and industrial areas. 53rd (Welsh) Division crossed next and went North East to cross the Bremen–Hamburg autobahn, and 43rd (Wessex) Division was to clear the area between the two, cut the autobahn, and turn back due West to work on the right of 52nd Division, clearing the residential areas, the garrison "flak" sites, and the central park.

While this regrouping was going on the Seventh battalion moved by march route, in shirt sleeve order, to Visbek, where it rested for three days (April 20th–22nd). It was here that Jack Grant (Captain Quartermaster) was most unfortunately involved in a jeep accident which necessitated his return to hospital in England. He had served the Regiment faithfully for twenty-seven years and throughout the campaign from the Normandy landing had been a tower of strength in the "Q" branch. It was very largely due to his efforts that the supply position in the battalion, both before embarkation, and through all the fighting, had been a model of efficiency. His many friends heard later from England, with deep regret, that his soldiering days might be over, and that he was permanently placed in medical category "D".

The battalion moved forward forty miles by a southern route on the afternoon of the 22nd April, harboured one night near the Weser, and crossed by the Verden bridge next morning. During the long drive forward, along roads lined with apple trees laden with blossom, it was noticeable how much less war damage had been done. Here and there burnt out farms showed traces of battle, but nowhere were the craters and blown bridges on anything approaching the same scale as in the North.

From Verden the route ran north to Langwedel, and the battalion was given its task of clearing an area to the North, four miles deep and a mile and a half wide—the right flank being a road built-up the whole way with small houses, and miniature farms; and the base line at the northern end the Reichsautobahn.

Two stories should here be told from Bremen itself. As soon as the south bank was cleared the artillery had been switched to firing surrender leaflets into the city. The people were told of their hopeless position. They were told that unless they surrendered their town would be decimated, and that they had no idea what destruction would shower upon them. When the city was later captured it was evident that the citizens had had a pretty good idea for some months!

The story was told that, a few days before the attack, wealthy industrialists had given a reception for the General commanding the garrison. In conversation it was suggested that as a General it seemed likely that he would shortly be out of a job. He agreed, gloomily, that this was very probable. "Of course" they said, "we could offer you a directorship in one of our great factories, but then, if this rumour of a fight to the death is true there won't be any factories to direct, Herr General!" The Commander's reply is not recorded, but the city was not surrendered.

Then later, at Achim, the 52nd Division captured the railway station and found that the telephone to the stationmaster of Bremen was still connected. An expert linguist from Corps was put on the line and the stationmaster was told that his town was outflanked and that the RAF were on their way at that moment. Five minutes later the line went dead. Five hundred Lancasters of Bomber Command had arrived just in time for tea.

These final battles of April from Haselünne onwards would not have been classed as a battle of the Normandy or Goch standards. But as resistance became more spasmodic, so the scope of the operations became more ambitious, and the ground covered was many times greater.

The infantryman, still carrying much of his heavy equipment, was driven hard over great distances. On foot he combed the areas (whether woods or gardens), and searched endless houses—any of which might prove to be an enemy strong point. To him it seemed that the higher commanders had no understanding of his problems, or sympathy for his tired, aching feet. The commanders, on the other hand, knew that only by hitting the enemy hard, and hitting him all the time, could a mentality of complete surrender be imposed. They were anxious, too, that the very minimum of lives should be lost, for they could see that it was only a matter of days before the end. The striking of a correct balance between speed, and a minimum of losses, placed a severe mental strain upon them.

But the Brigadier knew very well how much he could ask of his infantry. On one occasion he was being pressed from above to make more speed and two battalions were already committed in wide street-clearing operations. Three Order Groups were held between 6 p.m. and 1.00 a.m. and still Division was pressing for information. After the last he exclaimed with some asperity—"Really, you know, when I plant a row of shallots I don't dig them up every ten minutes to see how they are growing."

Starting time for the Seventh battalion's operation was 0030 hours on 24th April. The country was flat and intersected by dykes and peat cuttings; there was a very large number of small residential farmsteads and the sandy tracks were, in some places, mined.

The roads to be cleared were in the form of a square capital letter H, with an additional road across the top. The start line for all companies was at the foot of the left hand road.

It was planned for "B" Company to lead up the first road and across the top, "C" Company would follow and secure a sector just above the top right hand corner, to prevent a counter attack and act as a cut-off. Next "A" Company would clear the right hand road back from the top, and this was the road which contained houses all the way. "A" Company were to get as far as the cross-bar, a sandy track; and from there to the bottom corner, ending in a small stream and bridge, was allotted to "D" Company.

"B" Company covered four thousand yards in clear moonlight, moving with two platoons forward, fanning well out each side of the road, which proved to be on a slight embankment. Captain H. P. Norgate regulated the pace so that neither platoon over-ran any unsearched house on the opposite side of the road. It was tedious and exhausting work.

Mid-way across the top road the leading sections came under fire, and soon afterwards both platoons were checked by rifle and "Bazooka" fire (infantry rocket projectors). An immediate attempt to carry out a flanking movement was also halted—both here, and on the road, a number of casualties were suffered.

At this stage a 20 m.m. calibre gun started firing down the road and the noise of a tank was heard. Eleven platoon was sent round to outflank the enemy positions. Soon their Bren guns were heard in action, and a runner confirmed success and said the enemy were trying to tow away an 88 m.m. gun with what appeared to be a small French tank. Twelve platoon were dispatched as a further cut-off and the 88 was captured. The tank got away, but a number of prisoners was taken.

The advance continued, and the Company objective was finally taken at 5.30 a.m. "C" Company then passed through, and secured the top corner without much trouble.

"A" Company now turned south, and found that small belts of fir trees separated the houses on their road. Soon a party of about thirty enemy engaged Eight platoon on the left of the road. Captain J. M. Taylor (Commanding the Company) ordered up his "Wasp" section, and they raced forward spouting flame. The effect was immediate, and the Boche fled in disorder. The advance continued with Platoons supporting each other forward, searching houses as they went. A number of Riegel mines was discovered on the road and lifted by the pioneers. Captain Taylor showed untiring energy and enthusiasm in leading his Company from bound to bound, and the objective was secured at 7.30 a.m.

"D" Company had intended to cut across the centre track and meet "A" at their objective. Instead, however, they followed the other Companies the whole way round, and this was fortunate for later in the day an M.O., temporarily attached to the battalion, used that track and was killed when his car struck an unlocated mine. "D" Company now advanced through "A", and cleared the remaining bottom left corner of the objective, removing road blocks and mines en route.

The whole operation had lasted ten hours, and had resulted in a good haul of prisoners, but there was not yet to be any rest. "D" Company were pulled back, very tired, and sent to pass beyond "C" with the object of reaching the autobahn—still two miles away.

In the hurry to get on it was thought that the first bound (about half way) could be achieved by one platoon. Lieutenant G. Shearman, with Sixteen platoon was sent to do this. Again there were plenty of houses to be cleared, but they progressed well until a pronounced zig-zag in the road. Here spandaus and snipers gave them a nasty knock, killing three of the platoon and wounding four. Major N. H. J. Cox at once committed his other two platoons, and a troop of A.V.R.E's (Sappers' Churchills equipped as road-block busters) very sportingly offered to go in in front of the infantry, acting as tanks. They did so, and the pocket was mopped up with swift success.

Captain Taylor came up again with "A" Company, and, having seen the type of opposition to expect, decided not to advance "leading with his chin". Platoons provided mutual support until just short of the Autobahn, and met no opposition. Artillery was used on likely targets to discourage any enemy from holding on. It was now 6 p.m.

As they approached the Autobahn the leading platoon was pinned by heavy rifle and automatic fire, in the open. The next platoon dived for buildings, and covered them until they were able to reach an abandoned searchlight site, with suitable fire positions and cover. The third platoon wriggled forward to a farm on the other side of the road and started shooting it out with an enemy farm four hundred yards away.

The enemy won this round, setting fire to Seven platoon's farm first. This, however, only spurred them on, and they succeeded in getting first a section, and then the whole platoon into the ditch on the north side of the vital road.

After some delay, artillery was called down on the remaining enemy holding a blown bridge, and Nine platoon assaulted behind the flame throwers just before 8 o'clock. This was too much for the Boche who got out as fast as he could. Prisoners stated that the position had been held by about forty men.

A very grimy and weary Company was now firmly astride the Autobahn. No Company had had any rest for about twenty-four hours. Prisoners taken by, or as a result of the battalion action, amounted to well over a hundred. Captain J. M. Taylor received the Military Cross.

*　　*　　*

The whole operation, including that of the other battalions, lasted about thirty-six hours, during which strong patrols went well north of the Autobahn with Sappers who blew some of the bridges on the flank, leading into their positions from the marshes. For this task Major J. S. Wood took "C" Company, the same night, with a platoon of engineers, two trucks loaded with explosives, and two flame throwing "Wasps" two miles across the Autobahn to the series of bridges leading into Ottersberg. A reconnaissance by a flying O.P. had reported that the bridges were still intact. The Company moved off at 1.30 a.m., and was ordered to be back again before first light. Major Wood found that, in fact, there were a series of bridges over streams and dykes, one of which the Germans had partly demolished. With the advice of the Sapper Officer the nearest whole bridge was selected, and an hour and a half was allowed for the preparations. When the work was nearly completed Fourteen platoon were left as local protection for the engineers, while the Company started to withdraw. Ten minutes later the Sappers gave the word to pull back, and the charge was touched off, leaving a very satisfactory sixty-foot gap—a very sound piece of work, in limited time, by the Engineers.

When this flank was secured, the Brigade turned in towards Bremen, and the Somersets (in reserve) followed up as far as the suburbs. A task had been allotted to them, but great progress had been made through the dock areas by 52nd Division, and 43rd Division was able to clear the remainder of the city without calling up the battalion.

129 Brigade fought as far as the central park where a stiff fight was put up by the S.S. General and a band of fanatical enemy, and civil supporters in the concrete S.S. Headquarters in the Burgher Park. These were finally burned out by flame-throwing Churchill tanks (Crocodiles) in a night attack on 26th April, and 214 Brigade passed through to clear from the park down to the main submarine yards, from the railway station to the blown bridge at the north western end (the road to Bremerhaven), and the extensive Ack-Ack sites between the top side of the town and the marshes. This was accomplished in a further twenty-four hours fighting by the Worcestershires and the Duke of Cornwall's Light Infantry.

Bremen itself was a shambles of tangled tram wires, cratered gas mains, and fallen buildings. Open sewers gaped at many places, the devastation of the factories and docks was indescribable. At many places the leading troops had to drive their way through mountains of rubble, searching for the road with armoured bulldozers.

The civil population were living in concrete shelters, and dug-outs in the railway embankments. Fortunately the German emergency wells, sunk at intervals throughout the city, had prevented a water famine, but the population was a dazed and crippled wreck of a human community, sacrificed to the pride and stupidity of the Nazi party.

At the house of a prosperous shipbuilder a copy of "Mein Kampf" was found by 214 Brigade. It was pasted carefully in the centre of a large round coffee table, and on the open fly leaf the Brigadier left this advice—

"This illuminating volume is left to you by courtesy of the British Liberating Army. If you can believe it, you can believe anything. It is left in the hope that you will study its follies in the years that are to come."

When the Bremerhaven bridge was found to be blown, the plan to "bounce" it with a dash by the Seventh Somersets was called off since it would have involved extensive bridging operations and the deployment of the necessary guns in support, among the ruins of the narrow city, was found to be extremely complicated. Instead 43rd Division handed the whole of Bremen to 52nd Division, and pulled out East again for another wide right hook into the peninsula, through the centre route where the Highland, Guards, and Welsh Divisions had already driven a good bulge towards Bremerhaven, Cuxhaven, and Hamburg.

Chapter XXV

" S   W   A   N   N   I   N   G "

THE centre route ran north through Ottersburg where the Sappers had carefully rebuilt the bridge, blown by "C" Company with so much zeal only four nights previously.

The whole Division was rumbling forward nose-to-tail on a pitifully inadequate road, with the object of getting the greatest possible force up to Bremervorde in the shortest time. It was reminiscent of the drive through Holland, but without the orderly spacing, and with the sides of the road sliding away into troughs of liquid mud under the weight of the tremendous column. Rain set in as soon as the advance started and continued in a steady downpour throughout the afternoon and night.

The convoy rolled by during the whole afternoon; the drenched crews of open tanks and vehicles looking only slightly more miserable than the infantry under the doubtful canvas hoods of their T.C.V's. Tank commanders brightened the scene a little, sheltering under gaycoloured women's umbrellas which swayed, dripping, above their turrets. Sodden mascots flapped limply against the bonnets of the trucks. Everyone was wondering when, if ever, the German would realise that it was no use going on.

At Quelkhorn, after several miles, 214 Brigade was switched off to the left to clean up a vast area of bog and marshes which stretched along the left flank of the route—from which artillery and Nebelwerfer were causing considerable trouble at the head of the column.

It was now seven p.m., and the Somersets were faced with a fair road running off westward for some fifteen thousand yards, flanked by woods of straggling pine trees, and intersected by innumerable dykes and ditches. The map showed bogs on the sides of the road at many points; and a stream beyond which a good south-north road (running up from Bremen) was shown at a distance of about seven thousand yards from the start line.

Orders were received to secure the stream crossing and road junction during the night—starting at once.

The expression "swanning" was originally coined in the desert to describe the action of tanks cruising to an fro over the rolling landscape of the forward areas. Anyone who has seen the graceful movement of British cruiser tanks travelling cross-country will realise its aptness. In these last days of the war it acquired a much broader meaning and was used frequently by the Infantry. It did not mean, when they applied it to themselves, that their cross-country efforts were either graceful or effortless, but rather that they were setting off into an area of unspecified size with no hard and fast boundaries and little accurate information, "seeking"—like the devil—"whom they might devour".

Indeed, they felt on this occasion not so much like swans, as ugly ducklings.

Already, three times, the battalion had carried out these wide searching operations on foot—at Haselünne, Forst Cloppenburg, and the Bremen autobahn, and this one only differed in that it covered more ditches and fewer tracks, more mud and less sand, more birch trees and fewer pines, and was followed by a number of six and twelve barrelled moaning-minnies of uncanny accuracy.

Wherefore, I shall not again recount the actions of each Company in detail, but tell only the incidents which coloured, or darkened, this final action of the war.

The advance was confined mainly to the road with Company groups moving out on to the flanks wherever there was a side road, or the going was suitable. The side roads were found to be mined in many places, and booby traps of vast size were being used as a last resource by the Germans.

Though the Somersets were fortunate in not running across any of these, several neighbouring units had severe losses on such traps as thousand-pounder aerial bombs (so low had the Luftwaffe fallen) buried in the verges and linked with ordinary road mines. The same technique was used to create havoc with buried sea mines. In some cases they were found to have been detonated by a ratchet device which appears to have sunk one notch each time a vehicle passed over it, and thus did not blow up until one or two hundred vehicles had crossed. In this way the second battalion on the main axis had a jeep and a carrier blasted to fragments. Two days later our own Battery of the 179th Field Regiment ran over a sea mine, which caused the loss of two "Quads" and their complete gun's crews.

Resistance took the form of small groups armed with spandaus, and intense fire from Nebelwerfer which appeared to be working on a pre-arranged plan to coincide with the speed of our advance. Certainly they were very well handled, and it is probable that they were being fired by the instructors of the Nebelwerfer School which is known to have existed north of Bremen.

Our own 179th Field Regiment together with a battery of Mediums gave us support whenever called for, and we were continually passing back compass bearings of the firing positions, but the moaning minnies were not silenced.

Major Durie has said that he considered these rockets were the most concentrated since Normandy, and he recalls his disgust when, at one very close salvo, he bit the dust so literally that when he stood up he found he had a mouth full of sand. Private L. C. Hart, of his Company, was killed during this advance, and Corporal S. E. Shiers of "S" Company. They were the last members of the battalion to be killed in action. There were again a number of casualties wounded.

Seven thousand yards was the depth of the advance made during that night by 5 a.m. Any further progress by the road was ruled out by two large craters. Tanks and Self-Propelled guns could not leave the roads because of the ten-foot deep ditches, and those that did attempt to do so, sank with something resembling a sigh, waist deep in the black bog. For all we know they may be there yet.

Battalion HQ transport bogged itself, at various angles, in an attempt to circumvent the craters, and the infantry companies spread out some way beyond. "A" and "D" Companies starting at 3 a.m., got platoons up to, and over the stream, and "D" was prepared to lay a protective minefield, but when two parties of Germans drove up and surrendered in rather nice cars the minefield was not laid.

The trouble started at daylight when every movement brought down mortar and rocket salvos and the difficulty of feeding the forward platoons was acute.

A further four thousand yards was explored during the day, as well as the woods on either side. The bridge over the stream was gone, and the cross roads had disappeared into one of the largest craters yet seen. Several Sapper officers and Recce parties came forward and viewed the hole with obvious disfavour, and it was finally ordered that the crater would not be filled. The Somersets were told to get under cover and get some rest—this they gladly did! Battalion headquarters found for itself an immense hunting lodge in a clearing of the woods.

Early next morning the advance was resumed over the Worcestershires bridge on the right and the final four thousand yards (plus some extra distance for the detour) was covered swiftly by infantry and carrier groups. Here the country was much more open and the roads were long and straight.

The village of Worpswede was occupied soon after mid-day without further resistance. It stood on a pretty little wooded hill with a church on the crest. The whole place had a most English appearance, and a hundred foot hill was a feature we had not seen for many months.

Worpswede was an artist colony, and was remarkable for the number of its inhabitants who wanted to inform against each other. The village schoolmaster who, someone said, was training their little boys to be Hitler youth; the matron of a sanatorium who was alleged to be a "Werewolf" and who turned out to be an aged Baroness who had spent over twenty years as a nurse; an old man of some seventy years who (also said to be a "Werewolf") turned to the crowd and said "Tell them I am not a Werewolf", and all the crowd yelled delightedly—"Yes, you are a Werewolf."

It was a trying time for the Intelligence Officer (Lieutenant R. A. Wollheim), the Netherlands Liaison Officer (Lieutenant O. J. E. M. Lutkie) and the Military Government Officer, but practically all of it was found to boil down to local jealousy.

On the report of a local saboteur, Lance-sergeant Ingram (in charge of the Pioneer platoon) took a jeep and a couple of men two miles beyond the village to examine some aerial bombs. As a precaution he also took with him the saboteur.

It was late evening as they approached down a straight road, and as they arrived they saw two Boche on the road about three hundred yards ahead. These men at once made off cross-country.

On the road he found a place where a bomb was obviously buried, and leading into the ground a fuse which was already smouldering. He considered that the men would have allowed themselves a safety margin to get away, so he seized the fuse firmly in both hands and pulled.

About five feet of it came out of the ground. They then set out to round up the two enemy and caught them near a farm. Sergeant Ingram tried to persuade these two to dig the bomb up, but, by signs, they indicated that it was much too big, so he returned to head-quarters just before dark.

In the morning he was given a squad of six prisoners with a jeep and a truck to return and get the bomb out. Some two dozen enemy had occupied the position during the night and were armed with automatics and bazookas. Seeing the prisoners they at once gave them-selves up together with their officer. The bomb, and another one further along, was then uncovered sufficiently for Sergeant Ingram to remove the detonators and primary charges, both were thousand pounders; after taping off the areas he returned to his Company with his twenty-four new prisoners, and his six old ones.

By the end of the second day the prison cage at Brigade had been filled and emptied several times. Batches of prisoners were giving themselves up—many of them said they had heard the war was ended. Their communications were in chaos. Convalescent homes and hospitals were being left behind with their patients and their staff. Such petrol as the Germans still had was reserved for their guns and Nebelwerfer, and it is significant that none of these was left to be captured. Farther to the north, another Division of the Corps over-ran a concentration camp of the Belsen variety at Sandborstel.

After a day and a night at Worpswede we moved back on to the main axis, and took over the villages of Wester-, Oster-, and Kirchtimke, captured a day or two previously by the Guards. Here the roads were thronged with liberated prisoners from Westertimke camp—mainly merchant marine. We were greeted by bearded British sailors, Lascars, Indians, Negroes, as well as a smattering of French airmen, Polish cavalry, and soldiers of all the Allied powers.

Plans, maps, and aerial photographs were distributed at once. It seemed that Bremerhaven, and Cuxhaven, containing units of the German fleet and the crack Atlantic liner Europa, must be the end of the road for the Somersets, unless they were called upon to liberate the North Sea.

Chapter XXVI

WHICH TAKES A PEEP
BEHIND THE SCENES

IN a line battalion there are some four hundred and sixty "bayonets". That is, there is when at full strength, that number of troops armed with rifles, Stens, or Brens who carry out an assault. In the Support Company there are a hundred and eighty men who form the Assault Pioneer Platoon, the (Bren Gun) Carrier Platoon, the Anti-Tank Platoon and the (Three-inch) Mortar Platoon. In this Company are all the heavy weapons, and the tracked vehicles—the driver mechanics, gun fitters, range takers, and gun crews; and because they work in sections and detachments, often in support of different Rifle Companies, each sub-unit is commanded by a Sergeant.

The remainder of the battalion is administered by a nebulous body known as Head-quarter Company. It is this Company which comprises Battalion Headquarters, planning maps and Intelligence, Transport, Communications, Administration, Police and Supplies. It is manned entirely by men from the battalion, with the exception of the R.E.M.E. fitters, the Ordnance Corps boot-repairers, and the Catering Corps cooks. But as a Company in action—it is never seen.

F O O D

"There will be a hot meal on reaching the objective"—How often that was heard at the end of a Commander's orders for an attack. How often a Second-in-Command and a Quartermaster-Sergeant wore a puzzled frown, and wondered how it was going to get there. For between him and the forward troops there would be a river or an anti-tank ditch, a mine-field, a forest, or a bog. And almost certainly there would be darkness; but get there it must, and he must find a way.

The Colour-Sergeants in their 15-cwt trucks are the men who get it there. The driver drives, the Colour-Sergeant finds the way, but often he has no map and he only knows the rough direction. If he goes too far he will be captured, but he knows his men are up there in front somewhere, tired out from a difficult attack and exhausted by the strain of battle. So he will get it there, come what may, because he knows that a hot drink and a hot meal are vital to them. And because he knows many of the men up there too, and with him will go the Mail which will be eagerly read when daylight comes.

In the Normandy days it was different. We lived on "COMPO" then. The Colour-Sergeant drove up as near to the front line as he could, maybe in a carrier, dumped the boxes in platoon lots, and went away. Company HQ then sorted it out in the dark and got it to each platoon with their precious cans of drinking water.

The Platoon Commander issued it by throwing the tins from slit trench to slit trench and each pair of men cooked for themselves on their "Tommy" cookers in the bottom of a trench. But no-one ever really stopped cooking. There was always the odd mess-tin of "compo" tea being "brewed up" by the careful soldier who had saved some. Battles were won, or lost, on the packets of tea saved for a crucial moment. Nobody ever left the slit trenches for food, it was far too dangerous. It was every man for himself at the bottom of his hole.

Sometimes in a reserve position platoons cooked centrally; for this an old biscuit tin or camp kettle was used. Platoons used to mark them, but they still stole one another's; the loss of a biscuit tin was liable to sour a man's temper for days. Little things loomed large.

If it is true that Napoleon's Army marched on its stomach, then surely ours did on its „Compo". Packed in neat tins of every size there were biscuits, margarine, tea, and jam; sausage or bacon, steak, or spam, or steak-and-kidney pudding; treacle duff, and Christmas pudding. It was the same should the day be rainy and cold, or if it was eaten under a blazing August sun. It was superbly good, but because we were British we grumbled sometimes that there was not included the orange and tomato juice which the Americans had. That was before we captured German rations and had a taste of their, so called, tinned pork.

Then, during the winter, the food was cooked back in some field or farm by the cooks and Colour-Sergeants. It was put up in hot boxes, and carried forward in trucks or carriers. From Company headquarters it had to be man-handled forward to platoons in the hours of darkness, and the boxes had to be returned before daylight to be taken back to the cooking area to start all over again. In German territory the cooks would sometimes kill a pig, and if a move was in the air, it would be killed, dressed and quartered within an hour. At these times the 15-cwt truck looked like a travelling Smithfield market—with sides of pork and rows of poultry swinging from its roof supports—blood and feathers falling on the caps of the smiling cooks.

With the speed of the advance beyond the Rhine it was often vital to come to a decision quickly so that the food should be cooked neither too near nor too far away from the place where it was anticipated the advance would be held up. The advance was by day and by night—the food truck must not get so far forward that it was shot up, nor so far back that the food should arrive cold. If the food did not arrive at the right time the troops might lose their drive through sheer exhaustion.

At this time a cooking echelon was formed and it travelled at the back of the fighting vehicles—but not too far back. The advance would continue all day. A hot meal would be due fairly soon, but an attack was going in over a stream and a bridge was to be made.

Right! "Cooks stop and cook here, the food will cross the bridge immediately it is built."

The Cooks and Colour-Sergeants waited all night; at dawn the bridge was made, and over they went. Or again; "We are attacking that village some seven miles on. Maybe we will be there by midnight. Cooks get cracking in these houses"—opening the door—"in here"—they back out hurriedly; a corpse in a coffin is in the kitchen.

The truck is swung into place in the yard. The driver has been at the wheel all day, but he is an assistant cook now. He has picked up a sack of potatoes a few miles back—there are never enough to satisfy the Company. All he has to do now is to peel potatoes for a hundred men—its too easy!

Cooks pile out from their seats on compo-boxes, grimy and choked with dust. Their eyes and their teeth show white against their faces. Soon the petrol burners are roaring, throwing a four-foot jet of blue flame. The Colour-Sergeant bustles around opening cans, someone else fills the six-gallon dixies, another is cutting up bread and cake for tomorrow's haversack ration.

They stir the thick stew thoughtfully with a long spoon, as dusk falls.

Later guides come back, the red-hot sections of the fire plates are kicked apart, and soused on the ground with cold water till they are cool enough to handle.

The trucks creep steadily forward without lights—through the night. "Monty Moonlight" is provided by far away searchlights to help them. It used to be said, "Moonlight will be provided by Montgomery, and God, in that order".

The guide says that the Company has reached its first objective: well, they shall be fed before they go forward again. And so they were, but there was a booby trapped road block beyond, and the further Companies did not get their supper before dawn.

The Cooks and the Colour-Sergeants had striven, but the Boche had won.

SIGNALS

"The Commanding Officer wants to talk to Baker Company." But he can't because the interference on the radio is too great. "That's all right, Sir", someone reports, "the line party has just come up, you can get Baker on the Charlie line." The time is an hour before dawn.

Suddenly a light comes on the exchange and the bell rings, the exchange operator plugs in and hears the tired voice of the IC line party reporting "line to Baker through". A sigh of relief goes through headquarters, and the Commanding Officer is connected up. The relief is universal because it is approaching dawn—time for counter attacks—when communications are more vital than ever, and also because it indicates that the line party is safe.

When a battalion is attacking communications are maintained by wireless. There are two signallers with each rifle company who have to carry and operate a wireless set weighing 36-lbs. and must follow the Company Commander wherever he goes so that any time he wishes to speak to the Commanding Officer, or the Commanding Officer to him, he need only turn round and put on the ear phones. These signallers have an unenviable job, having to cross ditches, barbed wire, and stone walls encumbered by their set and a waving, fragile 10-ft. aerial. Because of ear phones they cannot hear the whistle of a shell or mortar, and must rely on the reactions of those around them. To man a wireless or telephone alternately for twenty-four hours of the day requires endurance, intelligence and guts. None of the signallers who started out with Companies finished the campaign with those Companies: a few were transferred to BHQ, the others either killed or wounded. Reinforcements filled their places. A signaller on one occasion operated a set for forty-eight hours alone, during which time his Company attacked, dug in, and was counter attacked.

The Mortars and Carriers, and the Commanding Officer, each have their sets and operators, and these operators usually ride in carriers. The master set is at BHQ and the operators there have to take a note of all messages passed, and keep the Adjutant informed of all that is going on so that he, in turn, on his higher powered set may tell Brigade.

For the British Liberation Army campaign wireless was more reliable than ever before, but even so it was subject to all kinds of climatic, geographical and other conditions. For instance on a wet day it may not be possible to contact another set because that set is in the middle of a wood. Interference from some of the thousands of wireless sets in the Army comes and goes. One minute speech might be loud and clear, but just as a Commander wishes to speak urgently a morse station will come up and drown all speech. Enemy stations also try to "jamb" the air and once they start the only remedy is to change frequency, which is a difficult procedure when Company operators may at that moment be moving across an open field under machine gun and rifle fire. An officer under the stress of action may become irritable when saying "Get me the C.O. on the set straight away", if he is told that interference is too bad, and that he must wait a few minutes. When tempers are frayed it is the operator who must keep calm, adjust his dials, and try again.

On reaching an objective the signals' first job is to establish an "office" and get lines laid to the forward Companies. An objective is most often reached when darkness has fallen, or is falling, and the men who form the line parties have been following up the advance all day receiving their fair share of shelling and mortaring. They know that by the time they return "Grub" will have been up and theirs will be cold, and that they will also have to dig their slit trenches. The route is pointed out to the IC party and if possible he is taken along it by the Signal Officer in a jeep. Time is the important factor, because interference on wireless is always greatest during the hours of darkness. When the task is completed in the early hours it does not always mean that these men may then have food, and sleep till daylight. Shelling and mortaring may have broken the line even before they have returned.

In Hocheid Wood line parties were out day and night for three days laying and repairing broken cable until at the end of that time line had to be abandoned, the intense enemy shell-fire proving too great. At Geilenkirchen four men worked twenty-four hours on a line four miles long and during that time it was possible to speak to the Company for only an hour, so soon was the line broken. When line is laid on the ground tanks and tracked vehicles play havoc with it. Sometimes at daylight it is found to be under enemy observation, but when cable is broken it has to be repaired. The line party must crawl, running the cable through their hands as they crawl to find the break. Enemy patrols have been known to come across our lines and cut them, lying in wait to ambush the line party as they come out for repairs.

Apart from wireless and telephone, runners and despatch riders play important parts in battalion communications. When all else fails, the runner will get there, or die. If he dies another must take his place. Whenever the Commanding Officer leaves battalion head-quarters he is accompanied by two D.Rs on motor cycles; their protection is slight from any kind of enemy action. There have been occasions when the Commanding Officer and his wireless operator in the carrier have been with the leading section in an attack and the D.Rs have been there on their motor bikes, unable to hear the shells or bullets owing to the noise made by their machines. They have ridden over roads, tracks and fields, which have been deep in mud or covered in ice. They have been coated inches thick in summer dust, and drenched to the skin by autumn rain,

The signal office never sleeps: except for two periods of fourteen days out of the line it has been on duty from the time of landing until "cease fire". Clustered round their "borrowed" stove, and sustained by a never failing bucket of hot, sweet tea the "Sigs" have held the threads together.

The battalion has known that when the operator has said "Wilco" the message will go through.

SOME HEADQUARTERS

"Headquarters" is a magic word in the Army which embraces everything from the darkened slit-trench where a section issues its ammunition and divides up its rations by the light of a dimmed torch, to the castle which is the nerve-centre of an Army Group.

After we had learned that strong buildings and cellars are reasonably safe, platoons always had a house when they could. Indeed, in the latter days, they got so particular that an HQ was scarcely reckoned to have the modern conveniences unless it included a chicken run and a well stocked garden. From Captain J. A. H. Clarke I have these thoughts on— "Battalion Headquarters I have known."

"It is a long way back from Nazi Englehardt's house in Bevensen to the holes in the ground, the cellars, the farms, kitchens, villas and yet more farms that Battalion Headquarters has occupied.

We moved about a hundred times in ten months. This is no ordered account of wanderings or work, but a haphazard patchwork of things and places which for many reasons remain in my memory—from October 1944 when I joined Battalion Headquarters from Charlie Company.

Siting a Battalion Headquarters depends on much. Living, sleeping, working and eating space for Commanding Officer and staff: signal office, Intelligence office, Gunner Command Post, R.S.M., signallers, snipers, police, batmen, runners, drivers; usually the R.A.P.—upon which the Doctor always had very decided views and would snap up, regardless, what one had earmarked for Command Post. Moving in, probably in the dark and the rain: moving out at short notice. Perhaps twice a day. Often just one miserable farm to fit the whole contraption in.

Of course we had comfort when we could. For luxury I remember the Hitlerjugend Headquarters at Haselünne, a preposterous barracks with hundreds of rooms, busts (cheerfully dispatched by Major Whitehead and the snipers), shellholes, and propaganda against England. Then 'Collaboration Cottage' at Hengelo in Holland whose owners had been put in gaol just before we arrived. Full of good, rich stuff. The hunting-lodge on the way to Worpswede which was just like a Metro-Goldwyn-Mayer set with chandeliers, too much "olde oake" and wrought ironwork. (Of course neither water, light nor heat worked.) The nouveau-riche merchant's house at Nordhorn with its stocks of looted furniture and paintings and the cringing owners who 'had always hated the Nazis'. The Putney Hill mansion at Marienbaum where there was a Steinway grand in one bedroom and the Intelligence Section had in theirs a bed which Queen Bess would have envied.

For gloom I remember, of course, the winter and that succession of cellars round Groesbeek; the long nights and the precarious supply of mantles for the one Tilley lamp. The unspeakable cellar at Hocheid (adjoining a burnt-out house and full of soot, smuts and questionable smells) for four days, though I know what it was like in the wood itself. Xanten's miserable cottage where the big shell landed on the doorstep and killed Lance-corporal Munday and three others. The squalid farm at Hau where cooking, sleeping, working and eating went on in two rooms by Command Post, signals, intelligence and visitors. The famous 'get a day's rest' in February when six officers, lived, ate, slept (sic—it was in a gun lines), worked and conferred in one room with no windows. And even that by the kindness of the Grenadier Guards.

The hole in the ground at Mook where everything collapsed after forty-eight hours' rain. The hole at Niederheide where nothing whatever could get up on wheels. Dorset Wood's square dugout into which we slid covered with mud. One particular night I remember was en route to Goch when the Command Post was in a cellar almost filled with coal and bottled fruit. The Commanding Officer and I sat up all night with the wireless shouting, eating bottle after bottle of cherries with a spoon. The R.S.M. reported at two in the morning and fresh batches of prisoners kept on coming in. In the bog near Bremen, having found a detour round a blown bridge, Battalion Headquarters moved off at 5 a.m. It then spent from 5.20 a.m. till 6.40 p.m. stuck fast in a water-meadow in a sleet storm. Lance-corporal Heard found eight hundred eggs (marked "Holland", of course) in a nearby grocer's shop and he and Private Morby fed all comers that day.

In all these circumstances Commanding Officers have planned actions, given orders, held conferences, and discussed the future, immediate or remote. 'Send for the Buglers' (from England) was, I think, decided upon on the Vehlingen Autobahn.

Our routine was always the same—one seldom knew how long the stay was going to be. The signallers' line-parties would go out, the Intelligence would produce overlays, traces, fresh maps, the Police get the signs and lamps ready and soon "Wyvern 67" would sprout from nearby road-junctions and hedges. The snipers always went ferreting after odd

Huns and no-one could ever beat Private Holdaway to the egg boxes and hen-runs. D.Rs from Brigade, a wad of letters, Captain Catford from "A" Echelon would be early on the spot, with the mail, the water-cart, the rum, the papers and usually another wad of official letters. Then the officers from the gunners, the Middlesex, the Sappers, the Recce: the Brigadier, or Commanding Officers of other Battalions.

At last, just two things. I once said to the R.S.M., on the escarpment at Goch—"Can you get that stinking place in some sort of shape in half an hour? I can keep the C.O. away that long." Of course he could—in twenty-five minutes. And without being mawkish I repeat, in tribute to the men of Battalion Headquarters, what our Doctor said to me just before he left us for the last time—"I shall miss the Battalion Headquarters smile."

MOTOR TRANSPORT

Much had been said already of the transport and its drivers. Of the jeep drivers who did the reconnaissances with their Company Commanders and carried the stretcher cases out of battle, and of the drivers of the cooks trucks. One more jeep story should be told—it concerns "Formidable" the "C" Company jeep which came right through the campaign driven by Private Bell. It was the only original company jeep to survive and its normal place in battle was with main Company HQ waiting for stretcher cases. The story is short, but for a few glorious minutes "Formidable" led "C" Company in the Oosterhout attack, travelling in front of the tanks until it was hauled back into a more modest place by an anxious Company Commander.

Then there were the Company ammunition carriers and trucks, the wireless trucks and office truck of battalion headquarters, and the three-tonners who plied between the battalion and the supply points with their daily loads of ammunition and rations. Sometimes these supply points were seventy or a hundred miles behind the line and the roads were crammed with vehicles engaged on the same task.

On Mont Pincon we captured a 1940 model six-wheeler Morris which must have been taken by the Germans in the first battle of France. We adopted it, and because it was fitted with a winch it salvaged for us many a ditched truck of more modern make. It is with us still.

On the Island the battalion supplies had to run daily the gauntlet of shellfire on Nijmegen bridge.

Throughout all the campaign that most precious vehicle, the water truck, continued to keep the forward troops supplied, driven by Private Parsons (who earned the Commander-in-Chief's Certificate for Good Service), and accompanied by Private Holland, the water duties man. The water truck covered a distance of 19,000 miles.

The fitters carried out a host of running repairs in the field ranging to jobs as large as changing a propeller shaft or a cylinder head. By far the biggest proportion of losses was in tyres torn by shrapnel, and often their first thought was to dig a trench to save their reserve tyres—for anything left above ground at Chateau de Fontaine or Hocheid Woods had very little chance of survival. Two hundred and seventy five new tyres were supplied in ten months.

The most eloquent account of the work of the transport is in the figures themselves—the battalion's established vehicle strength being just over a hundred (including thirty-eight tracked carriers) at any one time.

Vehicles lost through enemy action totalled—Motor cycles 25, Jeeps 3, 15-cwts. 5, Carriers Universal 21, and condemned as no longer serviceable—Motor cycles 3, Jeeps 2, Utility car 1, Carriers or Lloyds tractors 15.

"Crock" cards received by the fitters ranged from "Recoverable from a bomb crater", through "Bogged down, impossible to recover" (Hocheid Woods), to "Burnt out—total loss", and the fitters installed seventy-two new engines during the course of the advance.

Finally the total amount of petrol used was in the region of a hundred thousand gallons, and the aggregate vehicle mileage run seven hundred and fifty-nine thousand miles. For those who love statistics this is equal to a journey from Taunton to London every week-end for 97 years.

"*WE, THE ORDERLY ROOM*"

"There is little that can be said by present members of the Orderly Room Staff of the hectic period immediately before, and immediately after, landing in Normandy. The present members have come from various 'channels'—Reinforcements, M.T. and Company Offices. We have but heard tales from our predecessors who landed as Orderly Room clerks with the battalion, and who plied their trade in the very forward areas at Hill 100 and Chateau de Fontaine. Our predecessors have departed, wounded or unnerved, to England or to L. of C. duties.

Our own Orderly Room experiences date from about 20th July 1944 onwards, in Normandy, to the end of the campaign.

Unlike our predecessors we have worked little in the very forward areas, although various Orderly Room clerks have trundled little boxes and satchels over Mont Pincon, and on the immortal 'Island'. Our main Orderly Room was, after our arrival, in 'B' Echelon, and remained so until the drive to Nijmegen, when we travelled with 'A' Echelon. This was, thereafter, our most favoured home.

Memories of the Normandy days centre mainly around our revered truck, solid and trustworthy, but rather better suited to a more static age. Throughout the campaign the Orderly Room staff fought a losing battle to secure a replacement. Adjutants were subjected to orations on the virtues of more modern vehicles. The M.T.O. was subjected to the same propaganda. How successful the staff were, can be judged from the fact that on VE Day the old truck was still with us. This campaign, having been lost, a more subtle approach was tried. 'A trailer' it was said, 'would solve all problems.' This battle was won, on VE minus One, following a great fight with 'S' Company. On VE Day the hardly-won trailer had to be abandoned. It was not destined to travel the path of the conquerors.

Normandy—dust, devastation, scorching sun, dead cattle, and the rich orchards—a never ending succession of orchards, stretching from Bayeux to the Seine. Invariably we worked in an orchard, under the tented sides of the truck, which was our office and our home. Here we were the first to welcome the new 'A' Company, who arrived en bloc from the Staffords. We have been proud of being the first to welcome them to our Regiment. Here we heard the glad news of battles won, and new advances. Here, too, we heard the inevitable sad news which accompanies battles, lost or won. Yes, we lost many of our friends in Normandy.

And so on to the Seine, a rest at Vernon, and then the exhilarating run to Belgium, through the battlefields of the last war—through a wildly cheering Brussels, Louvain, and on to Diest. At St. Pol our truck headed a 'lost' column and safely brought it to Seclin, in spite of a dreadful moment when we nearly headed for Dunkirk, then still in German hands. All this without the aid of maps; but this is an idle boast, for France is superbly signed.

The night drive to Nijmegen will be forgotten by few who took part in it—the first view of flat Holland, the first sound of the clogs in Eindhoven, the vehicles still burning just off the road. And then there was the cheery Dutch family who welcomed us at first light in Veghel, to be overrun again by the Boche within almost a matter of hours. But although we were cut off, we were with good friends in Nijmegen. We made our beds on the tram lines, and then dragged them into a comforting ditch, where we were lulled to sleep by the big guns and sporadic machine gun fire away in the distance, but seemingly on all sides. And then on to the Island, over the famous Railway Bridge, which was broken in half on our return. We made good friends on the Island—the wife of the stationmaster at Zetten-Andelst Railway Station made superb coffee, and existence was made pleasant by many pears from the Zetten Fruit Farm, and unpleasant by several sharp air raids.

Later we came south, to the Brunssum and Geilenkirchen area. By this time it was late autumn, and we decided (with necessary authority) to live like civilised people in houses. The houses of Holland were warm and comfortable: those just over the border, in Teveren were windowless, cold and draughty. More often than not the upper rooms were missing. That was Germany.

It had been planned to spend Christmas at Tilburg, in Holland. Instead we spent it in Belgium, at Bilsen. At this time the Ardennes offensive was in full swing. In spite of this we mad British occupied our time mainly in compilation of the first Leave Roster—'real' leave—U.K. Privilege Leave, of which we had dreamed so long.

Another spell around Geilenkirchen—this time we set up our paper machine at Grotenrath—in a bare cold room, heated by a little contrivance loaned to us by 'HQ' Cooks. In our spare moments we grappled with such academic problems as these—'If a Battalion is allowed 40 Sergeants and we have 42, what is to be done?' 'Why have we only 25 Driver Mechanics in the battalion when we should have 45?' The figures, of course, are fictitious.

Before our wondering eyes we saw card indexes evolve and thin files become thick ones. We produced complicated Move Orders at dead of night under the eagle eye of the Adjutant, made furtive trips to neighbouring units with problems that defied solution. To redress the balance, other units came to us with similar problems. We were called upon to send Field Messages on such matters of grave import as the daily closing and opening of the Maastricht Bridges. We paraded Reinforcements and took details of their prowess in Signalling, Stretcher Bearing, and all the other specialised duties which are done by the infantryman.

We typed citations with a good heart, knowing inwardly that of the many brave deeds performed, only a few would be rewarded as we should have wished. To some of us fell the duty of writing the words 'Killed in Action' on the index cards of our friends.

Above all, we packed and unpacked, packed and unpacked. The War of Movement was a nightmare in some respects. Fortunately there were practical souls among us— one even who could make a cup of tea in the back of the truck on the move. We acquired a blow lamp for this purpose. Unpromising billets became little palaces—or so they seemed, then.

From Grotenrath we reached Nijmegen again—this was the start of the Operation which was to clear the Boche from the Rhineland. At last light we saw the battalion leave. The following day we left Nijmegen ourselves, or to be more truthful we set out to leave it.

We did not get far—the floods were against us. Our 'A' Echelon convoy halted—for three days. During this time we had very little news of the battalion. At last it was possible for 'A' Echelon to move up—and our Sergeant Clerk decided to send the Orderly Room truck and staff back to 'B' Echelon and to go up to Materborn himself with 'A' Echelon. Then came the oft-heard remark 'A' Echelon moves at midnight, the Orderly Room truck will accompany it. At 'B' Echelon the staff had just congratulated themselves at completing unpacking before dark. Alas for plans—they packed again, and all went to Materborn.

Later, after the crossing of the Rhine, moving became a daily affair, and it was almost impossible to work. And so we were given a free hand, to move where we wished, on condition that we arrived back at the battalion with all outstanding work completed. This we did, even at one period getting some forty miles behind 'B' Echelon. But the next day we excelled ourselves—spending a portion of the day with each Echelon—at Hengelo, Lingen, and Haselünne.

When VE Day came it found us with our trailer—and ready to tackle new problems that only peace can bring—Drafts to other theatres, Postal Voting, and above all, Release to Civilian Life.

We have seen much of War from our vantage point. We have seen how all branches of our battalion worked as one team, and how each job done by each man, however unimportant it seemed, aided our common effort. We have seen homeless refugees, ruined villages, brave deeds, joy and sorrow. We shall take all these memories with us into civil life, resolved to do all we can to prevent other such tragedies.

We have been proud to serve our battalion, which we know has proved itself the very cream of the British Liberation Army. Most of us can remember the bad old days when we had little or no transport, and leather equipment. We were not all armed. From that small beginning our battalion has grown. The columns which threaded their way through the leafy lanes of Kent have thundered along the great German roads to Victory."

*   *   *

And who are these "We" who have served so patiently behind the scenes, in tents and orchards, shattered houses and cold, damp hovels. Who have set up their desks and typewriters in draughty cellars, and typed our records, and made our leave arrangements by the light of a stinking oil lamp. Who have moved their office more times than they can count, who worked long into the night on movement orders to ensure that plans should run smoothly, and sub-units move in their appointed time and place.

In June 1945, they work in a sunny office, with bowls of pinks and delphiniums upon their desks. Unapproachable? They will greet you with an Old World courtesy, if you ever get past "Hau"—Captain Clarke's large Alsatian who always lies across the threshold.

First, Colour-Sergeant Hoare, producing from his records detail for the accurate completion of this book, working with Sergeant-Major Milton (at Brussels, Second Echelon) on release groups; training for an Athletics meeting. Corporal Newell, half-back in the battalion football side; Lance-corporal Hack, footballer, battalion cricketer, and typist for the manuscript of this story; Lance-corporal Holland, who brought his ancient waggon, somehow or other, right across Europe.

Of them the Adjutant writes—

"The Orderly Room has one Commander-in-Chief's Certificate of meritorious service to its credit. A meagre return for their work, their wit and their willingness. I know what I and the battalion really owe to them."

Chapter XXVII

LAW AND ORDER

WE were regrouping at the village called Ostertimke when the surrender news came through. It was a village full of allied prisoners. At the time, plans were being made for an attack on Bremerhaven and Cuxhaven, and the leading British troops had already secured the bridge at Bremervorde which was the key to the peninsula. The BBC news was received some minutes before it became official over the command wireless links—the German Armies in the Netherlands, Denmark, Norway and North-West Germany had surrendered unconditionally.

There was no wild celebration—not even much visible excitement. A slight pause, in most places, while people slowly realised what had happened, and then a quiet feeling of tremendous relief. Men who for months had walked with danger, who had risen each day not knowing whether they would be there to see the day's end, just thought to themselves "So its all over! Now I know that sooner, or later, I shall see my home again."

Men visited each other, or friends in other platoons, feeling vaguely that someone ought to celebrate, but mostly they just talked. The released prisoners of war showed more enthusiasm— they had good cause to, for, after five or more years in Germany, they were being flown to England at a rate of some two thousand a day. They cheered and sang and fired rockets and parachute flares into the air. Our own Ack-Ack put up a display of tracer and shells for a short while.

The surrender was timed to take effect from 8 a.m. 5th May, but an unofficial truce was already in force. Europe went to bed for the first time in almost six years, knowing that organised murder had ceased.

*   *   *

Reconnaissance was started at once of those areas in the British Zone which had been passed over, or not reached during the battle. A tremendous amount of hard work had to be done immediately. On 8th May 214 Brigade moved to that part of Hanover Province between Uelzen and the Elbe bend east of Lüneburg where Field Marshal Montgomery had his advanced Headquarters.

The day of the move forward was the first of the two days enjoyed as a holiday in England. It was a brilliant summer day, and the greater portion of the drive was along the great Bremen—Hamburg autobahn and main roads scarcely damaged by war.

The astonishing spectacle everywhere was the German Army. In groups of two, or three, or six, with only such parts of their uniform and equipment as they cared to take, the German Army was walking home. With them went an occasional woman or girl: sometimes a "Blitz-maiden" (German ATS): sometimes just a girl friend or camp follower, living with them in the woods, and tramping with them the weary road to somewhere. There were hundreds of thousands of them. Few can have known whether the places they hoped to reach would still be there, few even hoped that they would go far before being rounded up—they just trudged on, dirty, unshaven, and with down-cast eyes: the remnants of a proud army, the shadows of a great people deceived by their leaders and their own false values.

At Barskamp in the Kreis of Lüneburg began several days of hectic work. First of all, every itinerant German soldier was arrested, disarmed, and sent to a prison cage. Then huge tracts of woodland and farm had to be searched for enemy factories, ammunition dumps, oil, petrol, and secret Headquarters. Next searches were made for S.S. in hiding, for German troops who had changed into civilian clothes, and for hidden arms.

This discomfiture of the Germans delighted the liberated slave workers who seized on the opportunity to loot and prey upon their former masters, to help themselves to horses, carts and bicycles, and to set off on the roads. Since this was not on the programme, since the roads must be kept free, and because there was also no food if they once started roaming, they were all rounded up and taken to Displaced Persons collecting points, whence Military Government gradually made arrangements for their evacuation. For Russians, Poles and Eastern Europeans, national settlements were formed until plans could be made for their return.

A separate book could be written about the pathos and the comedy of the early days of occupation—about taking expectant mothers to hospital in army trucks from the slave camps, about a camp of ten thousand Prisoners of War guarded by one Company from Somerset, about the ten Chinamen who had enough luggage to fill three three-ton trucks, about a French or Belgian girl who, having become the mistress of a German officer, now found herself without a home and without a State, about Russian farm workers distilling gut-rot Vodka from sugar-beet, and about the Chief Girl Guide of Lithuania who gave the Intelligence Officer a Girl Guide salute.

But that is not the story of the campaign.

The Seventh Battalion settled down to govern and police the Landkreis of Uelzen, an area about half the size of Dorset. They tackled the job well as they had done every task they had been given. Headquarters and all Companies were established at Bevensen—a pretty cobbled village on the banks of the river Ilmenau.

Billets were reasonably good, and on the whole more comfort was enjoyed than in England. No contact with civilians was permitted so they were thrown on their own resources for amusement and recreation. A cinema and a bathing-lido were taken over, and a pub was re-opened and named "The Willing Horse": on the banks of the Elbe the XIII Club was opened—a country club at a farm where a 72-hrs. break from Army routine and discipline could be enjoyed by two officers and twelve men at a time.

Here in Hanover the march of the Seventh Somersets was ended. It had carried them over eight hundred miles, and cost them in killed, wounded, and missing over eleven hundred casualties—one and a half times the total strength of the Battalion.

It is their proud record that they always took their objectives, and that they never failed to hold their ground.

As Hazlitt wrote in the year of Napoleon's death:—

> *"I think the reason why the British are the bravest nation on Earth is that the thought of blood, or a delight in cruelty, is not the chief excitement with them.*
>
> *Where it is, there is necessarily a reaction: for though it may add to one's eagerness and savage ferocity in inflicting wounds it does not enable one to endure them with greater patience.*
>
> *The British are led to the attack or sustain it equally well because they fight as they box, not out of malice but to show courage.*
>
> *This is the only manhood that will stand the test."*

ROLL of HONOUR

OFFICERS

Lieutenant Donald Francis BEAN MC	Cauville 12th August 1944	Died of Wounds
Major Edward Jeffrey BRUFORD TD	Chateau de Fontaine 13th July 1944	Killed in Action
Lieutenant John HOWARTH	Chateau de Fontaine 12th July 1944	Killed in Action
2/Lieutenant John Herbert William HILL	Les Hameaux 9th August 1944	Killed in Action
Lieutenant H. M. JONES	Verson 8th July 1944	Killed in Action
2/Lieutenant Arthur KEELEY	Les Hameaux 9th August 1944	Died of Wounds
Lieut.-Colonel Geoffrey Charles Phillip LANCE DSO	Chateau de Fontaine 10th July 1944	Killed in Action
Lieutenant Geoffrey Lionel MACEY	Hill 100 29th June 1944	Died of Wounds
Lieutenant L. O. O'BRIEN	Foret de Vernon 27th August 1944	Died of Wounds
Captain Bernard PEARSE	Cauville 12th August 1944	Killed in Action
Lieutenant Archibald Charles Alvin WHITE	Fontaine Etoupefour 7th July 1944	Killed in Action
2/Lieutenant Anthony Charles GREEN	Zetten 27th September 1944	Killed in Action
2/Lieutenant Frank George GOWER	Elst 23rd September 1944	Killed in Action
Major Sydney Charles Wayman YOUNG MC	Oosterhout 22nd September 1944	Died of Wounds
Lieutenant W. A. R. BRYANT	Hocheid Woods 22nd November 1944	Killed in Action
Lieutenant Nigel Edwin McKINLAY	Hau 12th February 1945	Killed in Action
Lieutenant John Frederick PARRACK	Vehlingen Autobahn 27th March 1945	Died of Wounds

Private Norman Frederick ABBOTT	River Noireau 17th August 1944	Killed in Action
Sergeant Horace John ACREMAN	River Noireau 16th August 1944	Died of Wounds
Private William Henry ALCOCK	River Noireau 15th August 1944	Died of Wounds
Private Sydney ALDRIDGE	Chateau de Fontaine 10th July 1944	Killed in Action
Corporal Thomas Billings ANDERSON	Verson 8th July 1944	Killed in Action
Sergeant Francis Richard ARMSBY	Chateau de Fontaine 17th July 1944	Killed in Action
Private Robert Sydney BAKER	Verson 2nd July 1944	Killed in Action
Private Ernest BARKER	Chateau de Fontaine 13th July 1944	Killed in Action
Sergeant Charles Frank BARNES	Chateau de Fontaine 13th July 1944	Killed in Action
Private William Henry BARNES	Les Hameaux 9th August 1944	Killed in Action
Private Eric William BARTON	Cheux 29th June 1944	Killed in Action
Private William John BLATCHER	Mont Pincon 7th August 1944	Killed in Action
Corporal Charles BREWER	Plessis Grimoult 9th August 1944	Killed in Action
Private Albert BRISENDEN	Hill 112 21st July 1944	Killed in Action
Lance-Sergeant George Francis BUCKNER	Plessis Grimoult 10th August 1944	Killed in Action
Private Bernard BUTLER	Chateau de Fontaine 10th July 1944	Killed in Action
Lance-corporal Charles Edward CHAPMAN	Tourville 3rd July 1944	Killed in Action
Private Charles CHAPPELL	Chateau de Fontaine 13th July 1944	Died of Wounds
Private Walter David CHILDS	Verson 8th July 1944	Killed in Action
Private William George CHIVERS	Mont Pincon 8th August 1944	Died of Wounds
Private Leslie Thomas COLLINS	Hill 112 17th July 1944	Killed in Action
Private Frederick COOPER	River Noireau 17th August 1944	Killed in Action
Lance-corporal Leonard COOPER	Mont Pincon 10th August 1944	Died of Wounds
Private Ernest COPSON	Hill 112 17th July 1944	Killed in Action
Lance-corporal Jack Charles COTTRELL	Hill 100 29th June 1944	Killed in Action
Lance-corporal Richard Bryan Ralph CUMMINS	Cauville 12th August 1944	Killed in Action
Private Leslie DAVIES	Les Hameaux 9th August 1944	Died of Wounds
Private Richard DAVIES	Chateau de Fontaine 11th July 1944	Killed in Action
Private Hedley Gordon DEAN	Mont Pincon 9th August 1944	Killed in Action
Private Cecil Frederick DEADMAN	Mont Pincon 16th August 1944	Died of Wounds
Private Augustus DELANEY	Mont Pincon 9th August 1944	Killed in Action
Private Leslie DENNIS	St. Pierre du Fresne 1st August 1944	Died of Wounds
Private Arthur Lyn DUCKHAM	Chateau de Fontaine 13th July 1944	Killed in Action
Corporal Henry George ECKLEY	Mont Pincon 9th August 1944	Died of Wounds
Private Thompson EVERS	Verson 9th July 1944	Killed in Action
Corporal George Samuel John EASTER	Les Hameaux 9th August 1944	Died of Wounds
Private Alfred FOSTER	Hill 100 29th June 1944	Killed in Action
Private Alfred Roy GATES	Les Hameaux 10th August 1944	Died of Wounds
Private Ronald GIFFORD	Chateau de Fontaine 13th July 1944	Killed in Action

Private Hector GRAHAM	River Noireau 16th August 1944	Killed in Action
Private William John GULLICK	Mont Pincon 9th August 1944	Died of Wounds
Private John James GULLIVER	Miebord 13th July 1944	Killed in Action
Private Hedley HART	Mont Pincon 9th August 1944	Killed in Action
Private Edward George HARVEY	Tourville 2nd July 1944	Died of Wounds
Private Ivor William HELLIER	Miebord 14th July 1944	Died of Wounds
Private Harry HOLLAND	Hill 100 29th June 1944	Killed in Action
Private John Gilbert HUMPHREYS	Mont Pincon 9th August 1944	Killed in Action
Private Herbert Benjamin HUTCHINGS	St. Pierre du Fresne 1st August 1944	Killed in Action
Private George Lennard JOHNSON	Verson 9th July 1944	Killed in Action
Sergeant Henry JONES	Hill 112 25th July 1944	Died of Wounds
Private Patrick George KEARNEY	Chateau de Fontaine 10th July 1944	Killed in Action
Private George Edward KIRBY	St. Pierre du Fresne 1st August 1944	Killed in Action
Corporal Leonard Walter William KNAPP	Chateau de Fontaine 13th July 1944	Died of Wounds
Private William Charles LAKE	St. Pierre du Fresne 1st August 1944	Killed in Action
Private Henry LATHAM	Verson 8th July 1944	Killed in Action
Sergeant James Frederick LONG	Hill 100 29th June 1944	Killed in Action
Private Robert Edward LOWE	River Noireau 18th August 1944	Died of Wounds
Corporal James Henry Long McCLERNON	Cauville 12th August 1944	Killed in Action
Private Robert John McHIGGINS	Plessis Grimoult 10th August 1944	Killed in Action
Corporal Peter Yates MACEY	Hill 112 21st July 1944	Killed in Action
Private Arthur Lennard MADDOX	Verson 9th July 1944	Killed in Action
Private Wilfred MALE	Mont Pincon 9th August 1944	Killed in Action
Lance-Sergeant Alexander John MARTIN	Mont Pincon 7th August 1944	Killed in Action
Sergeant Leonard Henry MASSEY	Vernon sur Seine 27th August 1944	Killed in Action
Lance-corporal Francis Norman MICHELL	Chateau de Fontaine 13th July 1944	Killed in Action
Private Kenneth William MILLINGTON	Vernon sur Seine 27th August 1944	Killed in Action
Lance-corporal Hugh Roy MINTEY	Hill 100 30th June 1944	Died of Wounds
Private Henry Robert MOLLISON	Hill 100 29th June 1944	Killed in Action
Corporal Patrick NEARY	Cahan 16th August 1944	Killed in Action
Private Arthur Frederick NEWMAN	Chateau de Fontaine 10th July 1944	Killed in Action
Private Leslie Thomas NOBLE	Caumont 30th July 1944	Killed in Action
Lance-corporal Lionel James NORRIS	Mont Pincon 9th August 1944	Killed in Action
Private Ronald OLDFIELD	Mont Pincon 7th August 1944	Killed in Action
Private Ronald Henry Reginald OLIVER	St. Pierre du Fresne 1st August 1944	Killed in Action
Corporal William Reginald PADFIELD	Hill 112 21st July 1944	Killed in Action
Private Albert Edward PALMER	Verson 9th July 1944	Killed in Action
Private William Edward PARRY	St. Pierre du Fresne 1st August 1944	Killed in Action
Lance-corporal Frank PEARSON	Mont Pincon 7th August 1944	Died of Wounds
Private John Alfred George PERRY	St. Pierre du Fresne 3rd August 1944	Killed in Action
Private Stanley POCOCK	Cauville 12th August 1944	Killed in Action

Private William George PRICE	Tourville 29th June 1944	Died of Wounds
Corporal John Edward PRITCHARD	Mont Pincon 9th August 1944	Killed in Action
Private Henry Frederick PURSER	River Noireau 16th August 1944	Killed in Action
Corporal Robert Henry PURVIS	Verson 9th July 1944	Killed in Action
Private Robert Henry RANSON	Mont Pincon 7th August 1944	Died of Wounds
Lance-corporal Arthur Robert Moyes REILLY	Mont Pincon 7th August 1944	Killed in Action
Private George William RICHENS	Tourville 30th June 1944	Died of Wounds
Lance-corporal Raymond Morgan RUSSELL	Vernon sur Seine 27th August 1944	Killed in Action
Private Paul Roy Herbert John SELWOOD	Chateau de Fontaine 10th July 1944	Killed in Action
Lance-corporal Arthur Henry SHELSHER	Mont Pincon 9th August 1944	Killed in Action
Private Robert Arthur Fitzroy SHEWRING	Mont Pincon 9th August 1944	Killed in Action
Corporal Arthur Alexander SMITH	Chateau de Fontaine 10th July 1944	Killed in Action
Private Philip Ernest William SMITH	St. Pierre du Fresne 1st August 1944	Killed in Action
Lance-corporal William SMITHERS	Chateau de Fontaine 13th July 1944	Died of Wounds
Private Jack SOUTHWELL	Caumont 30th July 1944	Killed in Action
Private Douglas Walter STRIDE	Tourville 4th July 1944	Died of Wounds
Private Ronald SWETMAN	Chateau de Fontaine 13th July 1944	Died of Wounds
Private Leslie Thomas Charles TEMPLE	Hill 100 29th June 1944	Killed in Action
Private Arthur Albert THOMPSON	Hill 112 21st July 1944	Killed in Action
Corporal Herbert James VINCENT	Vernon sur Seine 27th August 1944	Killed in Action
Private Alfred Charles WHITEHORN	Mont Pincon 9th August 1944	Killed in Action
Private Reginald John WILTON	Mont Pincon 9th August 1944	Killed in Action
Private Leonard WOOF	Mont Pincon 9th August 1944	Killed in Action
Corporal John WOOLDRIDGE	Chateau de Fontaine 13th July 1944	Killed in Action

* * *

Private Samuel GARDNER	Vernon sur Seine 6th September 1944	Accidentally Killed

BELGIUM AND HOLLAND

Private William John BARRALL	Groesbeek 26th October 1944	Killed in Action
Private Arthur George BEACH	Zetten 29th September 1944	Died of Wounds
Private James BULLEN	Zetten 28th September 1944	Killed in Action
Private V. S. C. BUTCHER	Elst 25th September 1944	Killed in Action
Private John James CLARKE	Elst 23rd September 1944	Killed in Action
Private Thomas William DUNLOP	Zetten 2nd October 1944	Killed in Action
Private Frederick William DUTFIELD	Zetten 28th September 1944	Killed in Action
Private Sydney William Charles DYSTER	Elst 25th September 1944	Killed in Action
Private Charles Stewart FOSTER	Elst 23rd September 1944	Killed in Action
Corporal Joseph GIBLIN	Zetten 27th September 1944	Killed in Action

Private William George HADLEY	Zetten 28th September 1944	Killed in Action
Private Richard LANCASTER	Elst 25th September 1944	Died of Wounds
Private Francis O'SHAUGHNESSY	Elst 25th September 1944	Killed in Action
Private Ronald Harry PENNICK	Elst 25th September 1944	Killed in Action
Corporal Frederick Henry PICTON	Albert Canal 19th September 1944	Died of Wounds
Private Stanley Francis James SAUNDERS	Albert Canal 19th September 1944	Killed in Action
Private Henry James SETTER	Oosterhout 24th September 1944	Died of Wounds
Private Bertram SIBLEY	Elst 25th September 1944	Died of Wounds
Lance-corporal Benjamin David SOUTHIAN	Groesbeek 27th October 1944	Died of Wounds
Company Sergeant-Major Thomas John TRINDER	Elst 25th September 1944	Killed in Action
Private Harold James VINCENT	Oosterhout 22nd September 1944	Died of Wounds
Lance-corporal Harry John WHITFIELD	Elst 25th September 1944	Killed in Action
Pte. Charles Arthur Harry George Albert WILLIAMS	Zetten 27th September 1944	Killed in Action
Private Cecil Charles WARNER	Groesbeek 7th November 1944	Died of Wounds

GERMANY

Corporal William Allen ALLAN	Hocheid Woods 20th November 1944	Died of Wounds
Private Arthur Charles ANDREWS	Goch Escarpment 17th February 1945	Killed in Action
Private Ronald David ANDREWS	Bremen Autobahn 24th April 1945	Killed in Action
Corporal Claude Francis BARRATT	Goch Escarpment 16th February 1945	Killed in Action
Lance-Sergeant Edmund Howard BATES	Hocheid Woods 22nd November 1944	Killed in Action
Corporal Walter BIGGS	Niederheide 18th November 1944	Killed in Action
Corporal Cecil Arthur BIRD	Hocheid Woods 21st November 1944	Died of Wounds
Private Arthur Derek BRADBURY	Niederheide 25th November 1944	Died of Wounds
Private John BROWN	Goch Escarpment 17th February 1945	Killed in Action
Private Allan BURY	Niederheide 19th November 1944	Killed in Action
Corporal John Richard CADDICK	Goch Escarpment 17th February 1945	Died of Wounds
Private Dennis CLARKE	Vehlingen Autobahn 28th March 1945	Killed in Action
Corporal Victor COEVORDEN	Hocheid Woods 22nd November 1944 Died 31st January 1945	Died of Wounds
Private Kenneth Lawrence COLLINS	Hocheid 20th November 1944	Died of Wounds
Lance-corporal Andrew Patrick CONATY	Vehlingen Autobahn 27th March 1945	Killed in Action
Private Thomas John COOPER	Goch Escarpment 17th February 1945	Killed in Action
Private George COPELAND	Goch Escarpment 18th February 1945	Killed in Action
Private Frank CRAFT	Hau 12th February 1945	Killed in Action
Private Charles DEAN	Xanten 13th March 1945	Died of Wounds
Lance-corporal George DODD	Ahlhorn Cross-roads 16th April 1945	Died of Wounds
Corporal Arthur DYSON	Goch Escarpment 16th February 1945	Killed in Action
Private Thomas EDGE	Hocheid 22nd November 1944	Killed in Action

Lance-corporal Ronald James FAIRWEATHER	Goch Escarpment 17th February 1945	Died of Wounds
Private Victor Arthur GILBERT	Haselünne Approach 9th April 1945	Died of Wounds
Private Arthur James Haydon GILL	Hocheid Woods 23rd November 1944	Killed in Action
Lance-corporal Ernest HADLEY	Xanten 15th March 1945	Died of Wounds
Corporal Bertram George HARRIS	Goch Escarpment 17th February 1945	Killed in Action
Private Charles HARRISON	Xanten 9th March 1945	Killed in Action
Private Leonard Charles HART	After Bremen 29th April 1945	Killed in Action
Private William Dennis HARTLEY	Goch Escarpment 17th February 1945	Killed in Action
Private John HEMINGWAY	Hocheid Woods 21st November 1944	Killed in Action
Private John Victor HEWITT	Niederheide 18th November 1944	Killed in Action
Private Victor Thomas HILLS	Rischden Woods 16th December 1944	Died of Wounds
Private Kenneth Ivor HOBBS	Xanten 9th March 1945	Killed in Action
Private Francis Charles HODGE	Goch Escarpment 16th February 1945 Died 10th March 1945	Died of Wounds
Corporal J. P. HUGHES	Xanten 9th March 1945	Killed in Action
Private Basil Alfred KELLOCK	Vehlingen Autobahn 27th March 1945	Killed in Action
Lance-corporal William Arthur LEA	Hocheid Woods 23rd November 1944	Died of Wounds
Private Charles LITTEN	Goch Escarpment 16th February 1945	Killed in Action
Lance-corporal Percy LONGSHAW	Forst Cleve 16th February 1945	Killed in Action
Private John Edward MACKIN	Vehlingen Autobahn 27th March 1945	Killed in Action
Lance-corporal William James Lawrence MARTIN	Hocheid Woods 20th November 1944	Killed in Action
Private William Archibald MAY	Hocheid Woods 22nd November 1944	Killed in Action
Private George Edward Thomas MEDHURST	Goch Escarpment 16th February 1945	Killed in Action
Private Arthur MEER	Bremen Autobahn 24th April 1945	Killed in Action
Private Richard Saunderson MELLOR	Vehlingen Autobahn 29th March 1945	Died of Wounds
Lance-Sergeant Michael MERVYN	Goch Escarpment 16th February 1945	Killed in Action
Private Thomas Mallows MORLEY	Hocheid Woods 23rd November 1944	Died of Wounds
Private William Harry MORSE	Hocheid Woods 22nd November 1944	Killed in Action
Lance-corporal Alfred George Charles MUNDAY	Xanten 10th March 1945	Died of Wounds
Private E. MURPHY	Goch Escarpment 17th February 1945	Killed in Action
Corporal Kenneth Walter NICHOLS	Niederheide 20th November 1944	Died of Wounds
Private Ronald George PARSONS	Hau 13th February 1945	Died of Wounds
Private William PEGRAM	Xanten 9th March 1945	Killed in Action
Lance-Sergeant Reginald PENNY	Goch Escarpment 16th February 1945	Killed in Action
Private Francis John PERKINS	Bremen Autobahn 24th April 1945	Killed in Action
Private Harold PLANT	Hocheid Woods 22nd November 1944	Killed in Action
Private Leonard Harold POTTER	Cleve 27th February 1945	Killed in Action
Lance-corporal John RAVEN	Bremen Autobahn 24th April 1945	Killed in Action
Private Horace William Charles RAYNER	Hocheid Woods 23rd November 1944	Killed in Action
Private Courtney William Edward RICHARDSON	Ahlhorn Cross-roads 15th April 1945	Died of Wounds
Corporal Ralph ROBERTS	Bremen Autobahn 24th April 1945	Killed in Action

Private Philip Raymond RUMMING   Goch Escarpment 17th February 1945   Killed in Action
Private Ronald Walter SADD   Xanten 9th March 1945   Died of Wounds
Private F. SAGE   Kehrum 4th March 1945   Killed in Action
Private Reginald Alfred SCALES   Niederheide 19th November 1944   Died of Wounds
Corporal John Thomas SEDGWICK   Vehlingen Autobahn 27th March 1945   Killed in Action
Private Joseph SHAW   Hocheid Woods 22nd November 1944   Killed in Action
Corporal Stanley Edwin SHIERS   After Bremen 30th April 1945   Died of Wounds
Private Charles Courtney SKELTON   Niederheide 18th November 1944   Killed in Action
Private William Donald SMITH   Hau 12th February 1945   Killed in Action
Private Jack SPURR   Niederheide 19th November 1944   Killed in Action
Private Richard STEVENS   Kehrum 4th March 1945   Killed in Action
Private Arthur Ernest STYANCE   Hocheid Woods 23rd November 1944   Killed in Action
Private Lewis SWIRES   Goch Escarpment 18th February 1945   Died of Wounds
Private Edgar Montague TOWNSEND   Hau 12th February 1945   Killed in Action
Private William TRAVIS   Niederheide 23rd November 1944   Killed in Action
Corporal Raymond Reginald TURNER   Vehlingen Autobahn 27th March 1945   Killed in Action
Private James William Harold UNITT   Goch Escarpment 17th February 1945   Died of Wounds
Private Bisby WARD   Niederheide 19th November 1944   Killed in Action
Private Griffith John WILLIAMS   Hau 11th February 1945   Killed in Action
Lance-corporal John Edward WILLIAMS   Geilenkirchen 23rd January 1945   Killed in Action
Private Kenneth Leslie WINFIELD   Goch Escarpment 16th February 1945   Killed in Action
Lance-corporal Arthur WOOD   Hocheid Woods 19th November 1944   Died of Wounds
Private Romeo Antonio David ZANELLOTTI   Hocheid Woods 22nd November 1944   Killed in Action

ARMY CATERING CORPS

Private Arthur Kenneth HITCHENS   Chateau de Fontaine 10th July 1944   Killed in Action

*   *   *

M I S S I N G

FATE NOT KNOWN ON 1st AUGUST 1945

Private Herbert BEASLEY	Niederheide 19th November 1944
Corporal Albert DOLPHIN	Groesbeek 11th October 1944
Private William James HOLMSTEAD	Mont Pincon 7th August 1944
Private Clarence Stanley JENKINS	Groesbeek 10th October 1944
Private Arthur LAW	Niederheide 18th November 1944
Private Daniel PRITCHARD	Mont Pincon 7th August 1944

In memory of those who gave their lives, and of those who served, the re-endowed Carillon of St. Mary's Church, Taunton, will play each day in perpetuity the tune of the 7th Battalion Hymn

> *"He who would valiant be—'gainst all disaster;*
> *Let him, in constancy, follow the Master.*
> *There's no discouragement shall make him once relent,*
> *His first avowed intent—to be a Pilgrim."*

COMMANDERS 1944 - 1945

CORPS COMMANDER

Lieutenant-General B. G. HORROCKS, CB, DSO, MC

43rd (WESSEX) DIVISION

Major-General G. I. THOMAS, CB, DSO, MC

214 INFANTRY BRIGADE

Brigadier H. ESSAME, DSO, MC

*   *   *

COMMANDING OFFICERS

Lieutenant-Colonel R. G. P. BESLEY, TD	Emb to 3rd July 44	(SOM LI)	Wounded
Lieutenant-Colonel G. C. P. LANCE, DSO	4th to 10th July 44	(SOM LI)	Killed
Major E. J. BRUFORD, TD	11th to 13th July 44	(SOM LI)	Killed
Lieutenant-Colonel J. W. NICOL, DSO	14th July to 8th Sept 44	(OXF & BUCKS)	Posted HQ 30 Corps
Lieutenant-Colonel H. A. BORRADAILE	9th Sept 44 to 21st Jan 45	(DEVON)	Posted HQ 30 Corps
Lieut.-Colonel I. L. REEVES, DSO & Bar, MC	22nd Jan to 27th March 45	(KSLI)	Wounded
Lieutenant-Colonel C. BROOKE SMITH	28th March 45 to end of Campaign	(KSLI)	

SECONDS-IN-COMMAND

Major E. J. BRUFORD, TD	Emb to 10th July 44	(SOM LI)	Assumed Command
Major S. C. W. YOUNG, MC	11th to 20th July 44	(SOM LI)	Acting
Major T. B. ELLIOTT	21st July 44 to 25th Jan 45	(FORESTERS)	Wounded
Major C. BROOKE SMITH	5th Feb to 27th March 45	(KSLI)	Assumed Command
Major K. J. WHITEHEAD, MC	28th March 1945 to end of Campaign	(SOM LI)	

ADJUTANTS

Captain A. F. SCANNALL	Emb to 10th July 44	(DCLI)	Wounded
Captain W. H. GOUDIE, MC	11th July to 23rd Sept 44	(SOM LI)	Wounded
Captain J. W. BADEN	24th Sept to 14th Oct 44	(E. SURREY)	
Captain J. A. H. CLARKE	15th Oct 44 to end of Campaign	(SOM LI)	

OFFICERS WHO SERVED WITH THE BATTALION DURING THE CAMPAIGN

Captain R. ALLDEN	From 17th July to 12th August 1944	Wounded
Captain J. W. BADEN	From 17th July onwards	
Captain V. S. BAILY	From Embarkation to 9th August 1944	Wounded
Major C. L. G. BAKER	From Embarkation to 7th August 1944	Wounded
Lieutenant D. F. BEAN, MC	From Embarkation to 7th August 1944	Died of Wounds
Lieutenant-Colonel R. G. P. BESLEY, TD	From Embarkation to 3rd July 1944	Wounded
Major J. BICKFORD	From 28th February to 16th April 1945	Posted 1 Worc R
Lieutenant-Colonel H. A. BORRADAILE	From 8th September to 21st January 1945	Posted HQ 30 Corps
Captain D. J. BOUGHTON	From 21st March 1945 onwards	
Lieutenant W. BRADLEY	From Embarkation to 3rd July 1944	Wounded
Lieutenant E. BRENNAN	From 11th November 1944 onwards	
Lieutenant-Colonel C. BROOKE SMITH	From 5th February 1945 onwards	
Lieutenant J. G. BROWN	From 26th April 1945 onwards	
Major E. J. BRUFORD, TD	From Embarkation to 13th July 1944	Killed in Action
Lieutenant W. A. R. BRYANT	From 11th November to 22nd November 1944	Killed in Action
Major W. J. CHALMERS. *Croix de Guerre*	From Embarkation to 10th August 1944	Posted 214 Bde
Captain H. J. R. CATFORD	From 12th August 1944 onwards	
Captain J. A. H. CLARKE	From 14th August 1944 onwards	
Lieutenant W. A. COLBERT	From 16th December to 26th Decbr 1944	Hospital
Major N. H. J. COX	From 16th September 1944 onwards	
Lieutenant R. C. R. COX	From 6th February 1945 onwards	
Lieutenant A. DORAN	From 6th September to 23rd September 1944	Wounded
Major D. B. M. DURIE, MC. *Croix de Guerre*	From 17th July 1944 onwards	
Lieutenant G. EASTOP	From 10th December 1944 onwards	
Lieutenant R. K. H. ECOB	From 23rd July to 9th August 1944	Wounded
Captain H. C. EDMONDS	From 1st September to 5th November 1944	Posted
Major T. B. ELLIOTT	From 21st July 1944 to 25th January 1945	Wounded
Lieutenant P. A. EVES, MC	From Embarkation to 22th November 1944	Hospital
Lieutenant P. J. FAGG	From 21st August to 27th August 1944	Prisoner of War
Lieutenant D. N. A. FORD	From 9th October 1944 onwards	
Captain J. F. FRIPP	From 19th August 1944 onwards	
Captain J. P. FRUIN	From September to November 1944	R.Netherlands Army
Major W. J. GILMORE	From 14th August to 27th August 1944	Prisoner of War
Captain W. H. GOUDIE, MC	From Embarkation to 23rd September 1944	Wounded
2nd/Lieutenant F. G. GOWER	From 19th September to 23rd September 1944	Killed in Action
Captain J. D. GRAHAM	From 30th Octbr 1944 to 17th February 1945	Wounded
Captain (QM) J. W. GRANT	From Embarkation to 22nd April 1945	Accidentally injured

2nd/Lieutenant L. M. GREENWOOD	From 21st July to 1st August 1944	Wounded
2nd/Lieutenant A. G. GREEN	From 31st August to 27th September 1944	Killed in Action
Lieutenant R. S. HAMILTON	From 8th September 1944 to 18th February 1945	Hospital
Lieutenant G. C. G. HAMILTON	From 18th February 1945 onwards	
Major E. R. H. HARVEY	From 17th July 1944 to 17th February 1945	Wounded
Captain W. A. HAYBALL	From Embarkation onwards	
Captain B. G. HEBDITCH	From 9th October to 22nd November 1944	Wounded
Captain W. D. C. HEDGES	From Embarkation to 30th June 1944	Wounded
2nd/Lieutenant J. H. W. HILL	From 21st July to 9th August 1944	Killed in Action
Lieutenant J. HOWARTH	From Embarkation to 12th July 1944	Killed in Action
Captain G. J. JAMES	From 21st February 1945 onwards	
Lieutenant W. L. JENKIN	From 17th April to 24th April 1945	Wounded
Lieutenant B. F. JONES	From 15th April 1945 onwards	
Lieutenant H. M. JONES	From Embarkation to 8th July 1944	Killed in Action
2nd/Lieutenant A. KEELEY	From 21st July to 9th August 1944	Died of Wounds
Captain M. LAMB	From 6th September to 11th December 1944	Posted
Lieutenant-Colonel G. C. P. LANCE, DSO	From 4th July to 10th July 1944	Killed in Action
Lieutenant E. F. LARRET	From Embarkation to 9th August 1944 and 22nd January 1945 onwards	Wounded
Captain A. LAWS	From Embarkation to 16th August 1944	Wounded
Lieutenant E. F. LAWSON	From 11th November 1944 to 19th February 1945	Wounded
Lieutenant D. E. LE BOUTILLIER	From 15th April 1945 onwards	
Lieutenant R. W. T. LOVE, MM	From 2nd October to 22nd November 1944 Commissioned direct from ranks, served since Embarkation	Wounded
Lieutenant O. J. E. M. LUTKIE	From 20th December 1944 onwards Royal Netherlands Army	
Lieutenant N. E. McKINLAY	From 2nd November 1944 to 12th February 1945	Killed in Action
Lieutenant G. L. MACEY	From Embarkation to 29th June 1944	Died of Wounds
Captain H. E. S. MARSHALL, R. A. M. C.	From Embarkation onwards (RMO)	
Lieutenant L. T. MARTIN	From Embarkation to 13th July 1944	Wounded
Lieutenant P. MERCIER	From Embarkation to 3rd July 1944	Wounded
Captain J. L. J. MEREDITH	From 20th February 1945 onwards	
Lieutenant J. MICKLEWRIGHT	From Embarkation to 10th July 1944	Wounded
Captain W. B. MOTTROM	From 29th August 1944 to 12th Febr 1945	Posted Wilts R
2nd/Lieutenant E. A. MURCOTT	From 23rd July to 9th August 1944	Wounded
Captain J. R. NEWMARK	From Embarkation to 27th August 1944	Prisoner of War
Lieutenant-Colonel J. W. NICOL, DSO	From 13th July to 8th September 1944	Posted
Lieutenant R. M. NIXON	From 23rd March 1944 onwards	

Captain H. P. NORGATE	From Embarkation to 17th July 1944 and 23rd July 1944 onwards	Wounded
Lieutenant L. O. O'BRIEN	From 19th August to 27th August 1944	Died of Wounds
Lieutenant J. F. PARRACK	From 26th Novbr 1944 to 27th March 1945	Died of Wounds
Captain B. PEARSE	From 17th July to 12th August 1944	Killed in Action
Captain F. J. PINN	From 17th July to 9th August 1944	Wounded
Lieutenant H. F. PIZZEY	From Embarkation to 9th August 1944	Wounded
Lieutenant H. PROCTER	From 21st July 1944 onwards	
Lieutenant P. C. RAYNER	From Embarkation to 11th August 1944	Wounded
Lieut.-Colonel I. L. REEVES, DSO & Bar, MC	From 23rd January to 27th March 1945	Wounded
Reverend I. J. RICHARDS (CHAPLAIN)	From Embarkation to 26th December 1944	Posted
Major L. ROBERTS, MC	From 29th August 1944 onwards less 19-26th November 1944 wounded and returned	
Captain A. F. SCANNALL	From Embarkation to 10th July 1944	Wounded
Lieutenant G. SHEARMAN	From 6th February 1945 onwards	
Captain R. W. SMALL	From Embarkation to 13th July 1944	Wounded
Lieutenant A. T. SMITH	From 21st August 1944 onwards	
Lieutenant L. SOUTHWELL	From 22nd August to 28th September 1944	Hospital
Captain J. S. TOWNSHEND	From Embarkation to 13th July 1944	Wounded
Captain R. P. TOWNSHEND	From Embarkation onwards	
Captain J. M. TAYLOR, MC	From 13th December 1944 onwards	
Lieutenant W. THARP	From Embarkation to 22nd September 1944 and 20th March 1945 onwards	Wounded
Captain E. A. A. WARNER	From Embarkation onwards	
Lieutenant W. J. WEST	From 7th November 1944 to 12th April 1945	Posted
2nd/Lieutenant F. K. C. M. WHEELER, MM	Embarkation with unit—commissioned direct from ranks From 11th February to 15th April 1945	Hospital
Lieutenant A. C. A. WHITE	From Embarkation to 7th July 1944	Killed in Action
Major K. J. WHITEHEAD, MC	From Embarkation to 7th August 1944 and 7th March 1945 onwards	Wounded
Lieutenant D. J. WILLIAMS	From Embarkation to 1st July 1944	Wounded
Lieutenant D. G. WILSON	From 21st March to 24th April 1945	Wounded
Reverend J. H. F. WILSON (CHAPLAIN)	From 26th December 1944 onwards	
Lieutenant R. A. WOLLHEIM	From 29th April 1945 onwards	
Major J. S. WOOD	From 2nd March 1945 onwards	
Captain G. WREFORD	From 21st July to 15th August 1944 and 7th December 1944 to 17th February 1945	Wounded Wounded
Lieutenant J. R. A. WRIGHT	From 1st October 1944 to 14th March 1945	Posted
Major S. C. W. YOUNG, MC	From Embarkation to 22nd September 1944	Died of Wounds

WARRANT OFFICERS

RSM. P. DURMAN	From Embarkation to December 1944	Posted
RSM. H. E. KNIGHT	From February 1945 onwards	
RQMS. S. J. CLARKE	From Embarkation onwards	

"HQ" COY

CSM. F. HILLIER	From Embarkation to August 1944	Posted
CSM. S. J. CLATWORTHY	From August 1944 to March 1945	Posted OCTU
CSM. H. WOOD	From April 1945 onwards	

"S" COY

| CSM. H. E. FORD | From Embarkation onwards | |

"A" COY

CSM. A. FOOTE	From Embarkation to August 1944	Wounded
CSM. R. MORLAND	August 1944	Prisoner of War
CSM. W. CARR	From August to September 1944	Wounded
CSM. A. GOODE	From September 1944 onwards	

"B" COY

| CSM. T. TRINDER | From Embarkation to September 1944 | Killed in Action |
| CSM. D. CLARKE, MM | From September 1944 onwards | |

"C" COY

| CSM. A. J. LONGNEY | From Embarkation to July 1944 | Wounded |
| CSM. L. EVANS, MM | From July 1944 onwards | |

"D" COY

CSM. T. RICHARDSON	From Embarkation to July 1944	Prisoner of War
CSM. A. W. COGGINS	From July 1944 to February 1945	Wounded
CSM. W. SCOTT	From March 1945 onwards	

COLOUR SERGEANTS

"HQ" COY

| C/Sgt. A. MULLEN | From Embarkation onwards | |

"S" COY

| C/Sgt. S. J. CLATWORTHY | From Embarkation to August 1944 | Promoted CSM |
| C/Sgt. J. TYLER | From August 1944 onwards | From "A" Coy |

"A" COY

| C/Sgt. J. TYLER | From Embarkation to August 1944 | To "S" Coy |
| C/Sgt. H. MILLARD | From August 1944 onwards | |

"B" COY

| C/Sgt. S. I. LAWRENCE | From Embarkation onwards | |

"C" COY

| C/Sgt. L. EVANS, MM | From Embarkation to July 1944 | Promoted CSM |
| C/Sgt. H. SULLY | From July 1944 onwards | |

"D" COY

| C/Sgt. C. W. COOK | From Embarkation onwards | |

ORDERLY ROOM

WO II. D. C. W. MILTON	At GHQ 2nd Echelon throughout Campaign	
C/Sgt. C. F. CLARKE	From Embarkation to July 1944	Evacuated
C/Sgt. J. W. HOARE	From July 1944 onwards	

*　　*　　*

DECORATIONS AND AWARDS WON · 1944-1945

for service with the Seventh Battalion · The Somerset Light Infantry
(with extracts from Citations)

DISTINGUISHED SERVICE ORDER · Lieutenant-Colonel J. W Nicol · August 1944

> *"For outstanding courage and leadership in the attack carried out by his battalion East of Le Plessis Grimault on 9th August. His task was to advance with his battalion about two thousand yards in order to secure the right flank of the 50th (Northumbrian) Division which was advancing on Conde-sur-Noireau at the same time. On arrival of his battalion on the start line, he found that about fifty of the enemy with three machine guns were still in the area. He quickly took charge of the situation and having eliminated this opposition, proceeded with his task. As a result the flank of the 50th Division was made secure: all objectives were taken, considerable numbers of enemy were killed, and over two hundred and fifty prisoners taken. Throughout the operation he showed outstanding personal courage and capacity to command in the face of heavy resistance."*

BAR TO DISTINGUISHED SERVICE ORDER · Lieutenant-Colonel I. L. Reeves, D.S.O., M.C. February 1945 at Hau and Goch

> *"For outstanding personal courage, professional skill and success..."*
> *(Quoted in full in Chapter XVI. The Goch Escarpment.)*

MILITARY CROSS · Lieutenant P. A. Eves · 2nd July 1944, Verson

> *For leadership of his platoon in the Verson-Jumeaux patrol related in Chapter II. "Lieutenant Eves withdrew his platoon—section by section—remaining himself to the last. He exposed himself from time to time to draw the enemy fire, and throughout showed extreme coolness..."*

MILITARY CROSS · Major S. C. W. YOUNG · 2nd July 1944, Verson

> *Verson-Jumeaux Company patrol (see Chapter II). "Throughout the operation he showed great initiative and skill in handling the force under his command and penetrating three miles into enemy territory ... his confidence and personal bravery inspired his men in accomplishing a bold venture with marked success."*

MILITARY CROSS · Captain W. H. Goudie · 13/14th July, Chateau de Fontaine

> *Story told in Chapter III. "Very largely through Captain Goudie's coolness and efficiency, the relief was carried out according to plan. He was Acting Adjutant, and when wireless and line communications failed he went, with complete disregard for his own safety, time and again through heavy mortar fire to issue orders to his Companies and to the Mortar platoon."*

MILITARY CROSS · Major K. J. Whitehead · 1st August 1944, St. Pierre du Fresne

> *(See Chapter IV.) "Through skilful leadership and personal example Major Whitehead secured his objective..." here follows an account of the "B" Company morning battle... "Major Whitehead appeared wherever the battle was most critical, and was largely responsible for securing and holding a position which was of great importance to the operation in progress at that time."*

MILITARY CROSS · Lieutenant D. F. Bean · 12th August 1944, Mont Gaultier

> *"Lieutenant Bean, in command of the Pioneer platoon, was ordered to move behind the leading Company to clear the roads for transport. He swept the road with a Polish mine detector while it was under heavy mortar fire ... Having completed his task he went forward himself to assist in any way he could as an infantry officer. With a Bren gun he and his men repelled a counter-attack by tanks and infantry, and chased the enemy when they started to run ... Later he was attending to a wounded man in a ditch when he came under heavy mortar fire. Regardless of his own safety he made no attempt to take cover but shielded the wounded man with his own body. In consequence he was himself seriously wounded."*
> *(Chapter VI. Les Hameaux. Lieutenant Bean died of wounds nearly three months later.)*

CROIX de GUERRE (Gilt Star) · Major W. J. Chalmers · July 1944, Chateau de Fontaine

> *"On the evening of 13th July at Chateau de Fontaine, whilst the Seventh Somersets were being relieved by the Seventh Hampshires, a direct hit on Battalion Headquarters killed the Commanding Officer, caused several casualties amongst key personnel and killed the Commanding Officer and Second-in-Command of the Seventh Hampshires. The Acting Adjutant, Captain Goudie, sent for Major Chalmers, then serving as Company Commander in the Seventh Somersets, to assume command. With the Commanding Officer killed and heavy enemy mortaring of the area, conduct of the relief became a difficult operation. Major Chalmers took complete command of the situation, issued clear orders and proceeded calmly to carry out the relief, taking every possible precaution to avoid casualties, whilst showing a complete disregard for his own safety. He was the last to leave the position under heavy mortar fire. Throughout, his coolness and courage were an inspiration to all ranks."*

CROIX de GUERRE (Gilt Star) · Major D. B. M. Durie · 16th August 1944, The Noireau

> *"...Major Durie immediately sought and obtained permission to attack the village of Le Canet ... Thanks largely to Major Durie's splendid example of bravery in exposing himself to enemy fire and encouraging his men, his Company captured the village after heavy fighting. This action was of considerable assistance to the advance of another brigade next day..."*
> *(Account in full — Chapter VII.)*

MILITARY CROSS · Major D. B. M. Durie · February 1945, Hau and Goch

> *"In contact with the enemy from the Start Point this officer commanded his Company throughout a four thousand yard advance with the greatest gallantry, coolness, and determination, whilst continuously under fire. He showed marked resourcefulness in dealing with a well organised enemy which endeavoured to bar his way from every one of a line of houses, barns and farm buildings bordering the road . . ." Again, on the Goch escarpment—"Organising the support of tanks and artillery fire this Company Commander worked himself to a state bordering on exhaustion, whilst continually exposing himself to fire in assault after assault."*
> *(Story—Chapters XV, Hau, and XVI. The Goch Escarpment.)*

MILITARY CROSS · Major L. Roberts · 16th February 1945, The Goch Escarpment

> *"This officer calmly overcame the difficulties (on the start line), and led his Company to the correct position. During two hours of continuous fighting this Company advanced along a road lined throughout with buildings, the majority of which had been turned into strong points and were defended with considerable vigour. Major Roberts' skill and calmness, whilst under fire, in dealing with the opposition was most remarkable—an atmosphere which was noticeable throughout the Company to whom he set this example . . . Again (17th February) this Company reached its objective on the Goch Escarpment at least an hour before the other Companies. It was entirely due to the high degree of determination and aggressive manner shown by Major Roberts in organising the fire power of all arms under his command."*
> *(See Chapter XVI. The Goch Escarpment.)*

MILITARY CROSS · Captain J. M. Taylor · 24/25th April 1945, The Bremen Autobahn
(Story told in Chapter XXIV. Bremen.)

> *". . . the attacks were put in with terrific speed and spirit thanks to Captain Taylor's superb leadership, and the objectives were captured at the double . . . it was very largely due to his enormous enthusiasm that tired and hungry troops were able to carry out the attacks with so much dash."*

DISTINGUISHED CONDUCT MEDAL · Corporal A. Comm · March 27th 1945, The Vehlingen Autobahn

> *". . . he at once brought accurate fire to bear on the enemy, himself got the wounded back, continued to neutralize the opposition, and indicated the enemy to the supporting tanks. Under the tanks fire this N.C.O. then led his section forward under a hail of criss-crossing enemy bullets, and got to close quarters. This brave and skilful advance under exceptionally heavy fire at once enabled the flanking platoons to advance and close with the enemy . . ."*
> *(Chapter XX. The Rhine break-out.)*

CROIX de GUERRE (Bronze Star) · Corporal D. Yorke · 9th August 1944, Le Saussay

"On 9th August 1944 whilst attacking Le Saussay, the part of 'B' Company with which this N.C.O. was operating was held up at very close range by heavy and accurate Machine Gun fire. Four men of the leading section were killed whilst returning fire, and there was danger that the momentum of the attack would be lost against an enemy who were very superior in numbers.

Without regard to his personal safety and with great dash and initiative this N.C.O. manoeuvred his Bren gun into position and silenced the machine gun. He then led his section across very open ground, and although grenades were thrown at them he succeeded in making good a farmhouse which contained a large number of enemy."

MILITARY MEDAL · Private J. E. Gant · 2nd July 1944, Verson—Jumeaux

(See Chapter II. "D" Company-group patrol.) "... Private Gant was Bren gunner of his section and was ordered to cover their withdrawal. Being unable to do this from the ground owing to the height of the corn he stood up and fired from the hip. In so doing he exposed himself to the view of the enemy, drawing the fire of their many automatic weapons. This allowed his section to withdraw without casualties."

MILITARY MEDAL · Private L. Carpenter · 2nd July 1944, Verson—Jumeaux

(See Chapter II.) "...as Bren gunner to his section he got his gun into action and gave excellent covering fire whilst himself exposed to enemy machine guns. He was wounded in the shoulder but still continued to fight, and covered the section out. By this act of bravery Private Carpenter prevented many casualties in his patrol, and enabled them to withdraw with extremely valuable information."

MILITARY MEDAL · Private R. W. Homer · 6/7th July 1944, Verson

For gallantry in the patrol to Fontaine Etoupefour in which Lieutenant White was killed. (Told in full in Chapter II.)

MILITARY MEDAL · Private G. Barrell · 13/14th July 1944, Chateau de Fontaine

As Company runner of "C" Company. "When other communications failed he carried several important messages to and from Battalion Headquarters under heavy enemy mortar fire. When, under cover of heavy mortar concentrations, the enemy appeared to be starting an attack, and when our own three-inch mortars started dropping bombs dangerously close to our own troops, Private Barrell was sent to our Mortar platoon to give them the necessary range corrections. He passed through a hail of mortar fire and successfully delivered this important message. Private Barrell showed a steadfast devotion to duty, and coolness and courage of the highest order."

MILITARY MEDAL · Corporal R. W. T. Love (later a Commissioned Officer of the Battalion)
9th August 1944, Les Hameaux

"On 9th August 1944, in the attack on Hameau au Roi, Corporal Love's section was leading his platoon, when the Company came under heavy machine gun fire. The Platoon Commander was wounded. Corporal Love attended to his wounds, arranged for fire support from a tank, and then led his section up a hedgerow in which the enemy were located. Throughout he showed marked coolness and daring and contributed in no small way to the elimination of the enemy."

MILITARY MEDAL · Corporal J. N. McClernon · 1st August 1944, St. Pierre du Fresne

For outstanding and resolute leadership of his section in the "B" Company battle described in Chapter IV.

MILITARY MEDAL · Lance-corporal A. L. Cockayne · 23rd September 1944, Oosterhout

"During the attack by 'A' Company Lance-corporal Cockayne commanded a section with the task of screening Company Headquarters.

Although small arms fire came from unexpected places and from all sides and the enemy DF mortar fire was very heavy, Cockayne led his section fearlessly forward, and carried out his orders so well that the killing and destruction of many enemy resulted.

Throughout the attack Cockayne exposed himself to draw enemy fire, and then with speed and ruthlessness personally led his assault group to eliminate the enemy. When the objective was taken he was sent with his section to patrol and clear-up a road. He returned with over twenty prisoners, and valuable information regarding flank troops."

MILITARY MEDAL · Sergeant F. Wheeler (later a Commissioned Officer of the Battalion)
22nd November 1944, Hocheid Woods

As told in Chapter XII. "...Throughout the whole of this action which started with the assault on Niederheide on the 18th November, Sergeant Wheeler's fine example and his complete disregard for his own safety were an inspiration to his men. During the period of heavy shelling on the wood north of Hocheid on 20/22nd November, he was constantly round his platoon encouraging his men and ensuring that all was well."

MILITARY MEDAL · Lance-Corporal S. Shepperd · 22nd November 1944, Hocheid Woods

Story told in Chapter XII. "...Throughout the attack and during the days of heavy shell fire which followed, Lance-corporal Shepperd's example and complete disregard of personal danger was an inspiration to his section and to his platoon."

MILITARY MEDAL · Sergeant J. Chinnock · 16th February 1945, Forst Cleve

"Throughout this operation Sergeant Chinnock was a source of inspiration to his men. His initiative, courage, and disregard for his own safety assisted the Company to reach its objective successfully and with speed."

Action told in detail Chapter XVI. The Goch Escarpment.

MILITARY MEDAL · Company Sergeant-Major L. Evans · 12th February 1945, Hau

> *"...On the night of 11/12th February, on the advance from Materborn to Hau C.S.M. Evans
> took part in the house clearing operations which confronted his Company... Unperturbed
> throughout a 4000 yard advance and continuous fighting for ten hours on end, he set a very
> great example of cheerfulness and courage..." (Story of "C" Company, Hau and the Goch
> Escarpment, Chapters XV and XVI.)*

MILITARY MEDAL · Private William Bond · 11/12th February 1945, Hau

> *A Bren Gunner of "C" Company during the advance on Hau and again on the Goch Escarp-
> ment. "...In the house clearing operations he was always to the fore firing his Bren gun
> from the hip. His disregard for his personal safety when giving covering fire to his section
> enabled them to get forward on many occasions.*
> *Whenever it was possible he insisted on being allowed to be the first to enter a house occupied
> by the enemy. Such aggressive and offensive spirit was an inspiration to his platoon and
> enabled strongpoint after strongpoint to be successfully assaulted in the shortest possible
> time, in spite of the appalling conditions of cold, darkness, snow and rain."*

MILITARY MEDAL · Company Sergeant-Major D. Clarke · 17th April 1945, Forst Cloppenburg

> *Told in Chapter XXIII. Patrols from the Forest of Cloppenburg.*

MILITARY MEDAL · Sergeant B. Hinnells · 17/18th April 1945, Forst Cloppenburg

> *For patrols from the Forest of Cloppenburg to the village of Sage. Related in detail in
> Chapter XXIII.*

MENTIONED IN DESPATCHES

PRIVATE T. EVERS · 5th July 1944, Patrol into Verson; see Chapter II

LIEUTENANT P. MERCIER (Canadian Army) · 5th July 1944, Verson patrol

LIEUTENANT L. T. MARTIN · 8th July 1944, Verson

MAJOR W. J. CHALMERS · July 1944, Chateau de Fontaine and Hill 112

MAJOR E. J. BRUFORD TD · June and July 1944 · During which time he twice assumed Command of the Battalion
when Commanding Officers became casualties

PRIVATE J. D. JOHNSON · 1st August 1944, St. Pierre du Fresne

REVEREND I. J. RICHARDS (Chaplain to the Forces) · July and August 1944, Normandy

SERGEANT T. RICHARDSON · September 1944, The Island

CAPTAIN H. P. NORGATE · September 1944, The Island, and April 1945, The Bremen autobahn

Printed in Dunstable, United Kingdom